# A Primer on America's Schools

*The Hoover Institution gratefully acknowledges the following individuals and foundations for their significant support of the*

## Initiative
## on
## *American Public Education*

KORET FOUNDATION
TAD AND DIANNE TAUBE
LYNDE AND HARRY BRADLEY FOUNDATION
BOYD AND JILL SMITH
JACK AND MARY LOIS WHEATLEY
FRANKLIN AND CATHERINE JOHNSON
JERRY AND PATTI HUME
DORIS AND DONALD FISHER

---

*The Hoover Institution gratefully acknowledges generous support from*

TAD AND DIANNE TAUBE
TAUBE FAMILY FOUNDATION
KORET FOUNDATION

*Founders of the program on American Institutions and Economic Performance*

*and Cornerstone gifts from*

SARAH SCAIFE FOUNDATION

# A Primer on
# America's Schools

*Edited by*
*Terry M. Moe*

HOOVER INSTITUTION PRESS
STANFORD UNIVERSITY
STANFORD, CALIFORNIA

The Hoover Institution on War, Revolution and Peace, founded at Stanford University in 1919 by Herbert Hoover, who went on to become the thirty-first president of the United States, is an interdisciplinary research center for advanced study on domestic and international affairs. The views expressed in its publications are entirely those of the authors and do not necessarily reflect the views of the staff, officers, or Board of Overseers of the Hoover Institution.

www.hoover.org

Hoover Institution Press Publication No. 486

First printing 2001

Manufactured in the United States of America

07   06   05   04   03   02   01     9   8   7   6   5   4   3

The paper used in this publication meets the minimum requirements of American National Standard for Information Sciences—Permanence of Paper for Printed Library Materials, ANSI Z39.48-1984. ♾

Library of Congress Cataloging-in-Publication Data

A primer on America's schools / edited by Terry M. Moe.
    p.   cm. — (Hoover Institution Press publication ; no. 486)
"An assessment by the Koret Task Force on K–12 education"—Cover.
Includes bibliographical references and index.
ISBN 0-8179-9941-8 (alk. paper) — ISBN 0-8179-9942-6 (alk. paper)
1. Education—United States.   2. Educational change—United States.
I. Moe, Terry M.   II. Koret Task Force on K–12 Education.
III. Hoover Institution Press publication ; 486.
LA210 .P677   2001
370′.973—dc21                              2001024650

# Contents

# Foreword

## John Raisian

In 1998, Tad Taube and I met on several occasions to discuss the quality of schooling provided to America's children, particularly those in low-income situations. Tad, who is President of the Koret Foundation—a philanthropic organization that had recently committed to focus on issues of education in the United States—is also a member of Hoover's Board of Overseers, a member of the Executive Committee of the Board, and former Chairman of the Board's Communications Committee. We both felt strongly that the Hoover Institution could contribute significantly to a productive dialogue on improving American public education.

Thus, the Institution embarked on *The Initiative on American Public Education*, with the overall goal of presenting pertinent facts surrounding the current debate, contributing to the debate as a constructive commentator, and generating new ideas relating to education reform. This is a five-year commitment to the production of research and writing on education reform that citizens of the United States should be considering as a matter of public policy. It is an effort to identify and convey factual information about the state of American education, as well as to generate ideas for change that would enhance the opportunity for our children to gain more knowledge and assemble better skills. It also focuses on the underprivileged, for if we are committed to equal opportunity in this country, we must begin with equal educational opportunity.

The centerpiece of this initiative was recruiting a task force of educational experts who think about bold reforms yet are well regarded within the education community. The Board of Directors of the Koret Foundation were interested in supporting this effort to the extent of serving as partners toward the advancement of ideas that might move our educational methodology forward. Therefore, they made a founding financial commitment to this *Initiative*, with special interest in the formation of the task force, now known as the Koret Task Force on K–12 Education.

As Terry Moe describes in the introduction that follows, the Koret Task Force consists of eleven exceptional people who are committed to working together to address education policy in the United States. Each of these people has an aggressive individual agenda for the national dialogue on education issues. The proposition is that, if the Hoover Institution could convene the group, facilitate their working together with common goals and objectives, and disseminate their findings and recommendations, we could all benefit from the outcome.

The Koret Task Force was formally convened in 1999, and an investment in agendas, research, and writings began forthwith. The release of *A Primer on America's Schools*, edited by Koret Task Force member Terry Moe, represents the first of many joint publications in an aggressive multiyear agenda of tasks defined by the group. This volume describes the landscape we face in America concerning American education. Follow-on volumes will delve deeper into ideas for reform.

Many individuals have stepped forward to support this *Initiative*, many of whom are mentioned on the acknowledgement page. We could not have launched this ambitious effort without this significant support. I wish to thank Tad Taube for his help in crafting the design and intellectual foundation for the *Initiative*. And I would like to thank the Koret Foundation for their significant support allowing us to launch the *Initiative* and thus to demonstrate to others what can be achieved. We have strived to attract investors

to the project and continue to recruit support that is crucial to
the effort. The Koret Foundation provided the venture capital that
allowed us the opportunity to demonstrate the founding concept.
Let the returns to this concept commence!

John Raisian
*Director*
*Hoover Institution*

# Contributors

JOHN E. CHUBB is chief education officer and one of the founders of Edison Schools, a private manager of public schools, including many charter schools. Edison Schools today operates 113 schools in 21 states, with approximately 57,000 students attending. He is the co-author (with task force member Terry Moe) of *Politics, Markets, and America's Schools*, a seminal work that argues for the introduction of free market principles within the American education system.

WILLIAMSON M. EVERS, research fellow at the Hoover Institution, served as a commissioner of the California State Commission for the Establishment of Academic Content and Performance Standards and is a member of the panels that write mathematics and history questions for California's statewide testing system. He is the editor of and a contributor to the book, *What's Gone Wrong in America's Classrooms* (Hoover Institution Press).

CHESTER E. FINN JR. is president of the Thomas B. Fordham Foundation and the John M. Olin Fellow at the Manhattan Institute. A professor of education and public policy at Vanderbilt University (on leave), he also served as assistant secretary for research and improvement and counselor to the secretary of the U.S. Department of Education. With William J. Bennett and John Cribb, he recently authored *The Educated Child: A Parent's Guide From Preschool Through 8ᵗʰ Grade* and he currently serves as the senior editor for *Education Next.*

ERIC A. HANUSHEK is the Paul and Jean Hanna Senior Fellow at the Hoover Institution. His works on education policy include *Improving America's Schools: The Role of Incentives; Making Schools Work: Improving Performance and Controlling Costs;* and *Educational Performance of the Poor: Lessons from Rural Northeast Brazil.* His current research involves understanding the role of teachers, programs, and funding in determining student achievement.

PAUL T. HILL is a research professor in the Daniel J. Evans School of Public Affairs and director of the Center on Reinventing Public Education, both at the University of Washington. The center develops and helps communities adopt alternative governance systems for public K–12 education. His most recent publication is *Fixing Urban Schools.* He also contributed a chapter to *Private Vouchers,* a groundbreaking study edited by Terry Moe.

E.D. HIRSCH JR. is a professor of education and humanities at the University of Virginia. He is the author of several books on education issues, including *The Schools We Need and Why We Don't Have Them,* and a series beginning with *What Your Kindergartner Needs to Know* that continues through each grade and concludes with *What Your Sixth Grader Needs to Know.*

CAROLINE M. HOXBY is a professor of economics at Harvard University. She is the editor of a forthcoming book, *The Economics of School Choice,* and the author of several influential papers on education policy, including "Does Competition Among Public Schools Benefit Students and Taxpayers," "The Effects of Class Size and Composition on Student Achievement: New Evidence from Natural Population Variation," and "Not All School Finance Equalizations Are Created Equal."

TERRY M. MOE, senior fellow at the Hoover Institution and professor of political science at Stanford University, is the author of

*Schools, Vouchers, and the American Public,* and the co-author (with Task Force member John Chubb) of *Politics, Markets, and America's Schools.* He also edited *Private Vouchers* (Hoover Institution Press), the first book to chronicle the growing support for school vouchers for low-income children.

PAUL E. PETERSON is a senior fellow at the Hoover Institution and the Henry Lee Shattuck Professor of Government and Director of the Program on Education Policy and Governance at Harvard University. He is the editor-in-chief of *Education Next* and the author of several important works on U.S. education, including *Earning and Learning: How Schools Matter; Learning from School Choice; The Politics of School Reform: 1870–1940;* and *School Politics Chicago Style.*

DIANE RAVITCH, research professor at New York University, holds the Brown Chair in Education Policy at the Brookings Institution. She is a member of the National Assessment Governing Board, to which she was appointed by Secretary of Education Richard Riley. From 1991 to 1993, she served as assistant secretary of education and counselor to Secretary of Education Lamar Alexander. A historian of American education, she is the author of many books, including *The Great School Wars, The Troubled Crusade,* and *Left Back: A Century of Failed School Reforms.*

HERBERT J. WALBERG, formerly research professor of education and psychology and now University Scholar at the University of Illinois at Chicago, has edited more than sixty books and written approximately 350 articles on educational productivity and human accomplishment. He is one of ten U.S. members of the International Academy of Education and a fellow of several scholarly associations in the United States and abroad.

# Introduction

## *Terry M. Moe*

Education is at the top of the nation's policy agenda, and has been for many years. The sheer tenacity of the issue is an interesting phenomenon in itself. During the normal course of events, political issues rise and fall in salience, and few capture the attention of policymakers or the broader public over an extended period of time. One year it's health care. The next it's welfare or social security. But since *A Nation at Risk* first warned (in 1983) of a "rising tide of mediocrity" in the schools, education reform has consistently commanded the nation's attention and occupied its political leaders.[1] Every president vows to become the education president, every governor the education governor.

In some parts of the country, mediocrity only begins to suggest the true depth of the problems that plague public education. The evidence is plain that many urban school districts are in crisis, often failing to graduate even half of their students, and turning out graduates who in many cases can barely read, write, or do basic arithmetic. This is a crisis of quality. But it is also a crisis of social equity: the children who most desperately need educational opportunity—children who are mainly poor and minority—are

1. National Commission on Excellence in Education, *A Nation at Risk* (Washington, D.C., 1983).

the ones trapped in our nation's worst schools. They are without hope in the absence of major reform.

In much of the rest of the country, the schools are not in crisis. But neither are they doing an effective job of educating the nation's children (although there are obvious exceptions, usually in the suburbs).[2] There is widespread recognition that, in a fast-paced world of international competition, the nation's well-being turns on a trained, flexible, well-educated workforce—which the schools are failing to provide. In critical fields such as math and science, American twelfth-graders routinely score well below comparable students in most other industrialized countries.[3] Our public schools are simply not preparing them for the rigors of the twenty-first century. In fact, evidence from the National Assessment of Educational Progress shows that American children are not learning any more than comparable kids in this country learned *thirty years ago*.[4]

Policymakers have been trying to do something about this. Since the early 1980s, the nation has been caught up in a whirlwind of education reform that has left no state untouched, bringing change upon change to the laws, programs, structures, and curricula that govern their public education systems, as well as more money to see that these changes are carried out.[5] In an important sense, all

2. For an overview of relevant data and studies, see Herbert J. Walberg, "Achievement in American Schools," this volume, and Andrew J. Coulson, *Market Education: The Unknown History* (New Brunswick: Transaction Publishers, 1999), especially chapter 6.

3. See, for example, the Third International Mathematics and Science Study (TIMMS), which is discussed in a number of reports available online at *www.timss.bc.edu* (as of March 15, 2001).

4. See, for example, Jay R. Campbell, Clyde M. Reese, Christine O'Sullivan, and John A. Dossey, *NAEP 1994 Trends in Academic Progress* (Washington, D.C.: National Center for Education Statistics, 1996), and Jay R. Campbell, Kristin E. Voelkl, and Patricia Donahue, *NAEP 1996 Trends in Academic Progress* (Washington, D.C.: National Center for Education Statistics, 1997).

5. See, for example, Frederick M. Hess, *Spinning Wheels: The Politics of Urban School Reform* (Washington, D.C.: Brookings Institution, 1999); and Richard F. Elmore, "The Paradox of Innovation in Education: Cycles of Reform and the Resilience of Teaching," in Alan A. Altshuler and Robert D. Behn, eds.,

this effort is a very good sign: for a democracy is functioning well when it recognizes social problems and dedicates itself to solving them. The nation deserves to be proud of its track record of tackling education problems with such persistence.

But there is a dark side to its persistence as well. The dark side is that the countless reforms of the last two decades, pursued with much fanfare and sky-high expectations, have not worked very well.[6] The nation is constantly busy with education reforms not simply because it is responsibly taking action to address important problems, but because it is never very successful at solving them, and the problems never go away. The modern history of American education reform is a history of dashed hopes—and continuing demands, as a result, for "real" reforms that will bring significant improvements. This is what keeps the process going and the issue salient: not democracy, not responsibility, but failure.

How can America get off the treadmill of perpetual reform and succeed in improving its schools? There is no easy answer. But one requirement is surely fundamental: policymakers must know what to do. They must have good ideas that are well supported by theory and evidence, and they must know how to put these ideas into action.

As things now stand, this requirement has not been met. In the practice of school reform, the ideas that find their way into policy—about lowering class size, for instance, or putting teachers through a more rigorous credentialing process, or spending more money—are popular for reasons that have nothing to do with their true efficacy. Typically, there is no solid evidence that they will actually work. Indeed, to the extent there is a body of serious research on popular reform idea, it often suggests that they will not work, or that any improvements will be so modest—and so

---

*Innovation in American Government* (Washington, D.C.: Brookings Institution, 1997).

6. See the sources in note 5. See also Eric A. Hanushek, *Making Schools Work: Improving Performance and Controlling Costs* (Washington, D.C.: Brookings Institution, 1994); Coulson, *Market Education*; and Walberg, "Achievement in American Education."

costly for the little gain they bring—that they are destined to disappoint.[7]

The only "justification" for most reforms, truth be told, is that they have a certain commonsense appeal, both to policymakers and the broader public, and that they are politically acceptable to the established education groups—particularly the teachers unions—that find real change to be threatening. Such criteria, needless to say, can hardly be reliable guides for effective reform. They drastically restrict the range of possible action, and they channel reforms down familiar, well-worn paths that have long been unproductive. What they give us is more of the same, when what we need is something different. Something that works.

This, then, is the fundamental challenge of American education reform. The nation must demand genuine knowledge and productive ideas about how to improve its schools—and be courageous enough, both intellectually and politically, to make a break from the past.

## THE KORET TASK FORCE

It was this challenge that prompted John Raisian, director of the Hoover Institution, to propose the creation of a new task force for the study and reform of American education. His approach was novel: to bring together a select set of experts who are respected for their knowledge of America's schools and actively engaged in education research, but who are not wedded to the existing system and are recognized for thinking outside the box about problems and solutions. Once these experts were recruited, they would become a continuously functioning group, meeting regularly to determine their own projects and goals, and directing their collective

7. See, for example, Eric A. Hanushek, "The Economics of Schooling: Production and Efficiency in the Public Schools," *Journal of Economic Literature* 24 no. 3 (1986): pp. 1141–77; Eric A. Hanushek, "The Evidence on Class Size," in Susan E. Mayer and Paul E. Peterson, eds., *Earnings and Learning: How Schools Matter* (Washington, D.C.: Brookings Institution, 1999); Dale Ballou and Michael Podgursky, "Teacher Training and Licensure: A Layman's Guide," in Marci Kanstoroom and Chester E. Finn, eds., *Better Teachers, Better Schools* (Washington, D.C.: Thomas B. Fordham Foundation, 1999).

efforts—now coordinated, rather than separate—toward the kinds of knowledge and ideas that promise major improvements.

With financial support from the Koret Foundation, as well as other contributors, Raisian's proposal came to fruition. The Koret Task Force on K–12 Education was assembled in early 1999, and had its inaugural meeting in September of that year. Here is a list of its members:

—John Chubb, founding partner of Edison Schools, formerly a senior fellow at the Brookings Institution and professor of political science at Stanford University.

—Williamson Evers, research fellow at the Hoover Institution, formerly a commissioner of the California State Commision for the Establishment of Academic Content and Performance Standards.

—Chester Finn, president of the Thomas B. Fordham Foundation and a fellow at the Manhattan Institute, formerly professor of education and public policy at Vanderbilt University and Assistant Secretary of Education.

—Eric Hanushek, senior fellow at the Hoover Institution, formerly professor of economics at the University of Rochester.

—Paul Hill, research professor in the Daniel J. Evans School of Public Affairs and director of the Center on Reinventing Public Education, both at the University of Washington, formerly a researcher at the Rand Corporation.

—E. D. Hirsch, professor of English at the University of Virginia.

—Caroline Hoxby, professor of economics at Harvard University.

—Terry Moe, professor of political science at Stanford University and senior fellow at the Hoover Institution.

—Paul Peterson, professor of government and director of the Program on Education Policy and Governance at Harvard University, both at Harvard University, and senior fellow at the Hoover Institution.

—Diane Ravitch, research professor at New York University and senior fellow at the Brookings Institution, formerly Assistant Secretary of Education.

—Herbert Walberg, formerly research professor of education and psychology and now university scholar at the University of Illinois at Chicago.

A core purpose of the Koret Task Force is to encourage a stronger connection between policymaking and good social science. As things now stand, the connection is weak indeed. This is partly because the research and expertise available to policymakers is often simply inadequate, and incapable of giving good guidance. But it is also because policymakers themselves do not always care what social science has to offer, and are far more motivated by considerations of popularity, special interest, and political power. A key job of the task force is to identify inadequate social science for what it is, to spotlight and help produce the kind of social science that policymakers can rightly have confidence in—and to promote reform ideas that, with the weight of science behind them, can attract important political groups to their side. The reality is that good ideas can generate political power. And when they do, policymakers will listen.

Another core purpose of the task force has to do with *which* experts the policymakers are going to listen to. The nation's community of education experts has long been remarkably homogeneous in its approach to reform, at least on fundamental issues related to the structure of the system itself. Most experts are professors at education schools: where teachers and administrators are trained, and where programs, funding, and personnel are heavily dependent on the existing public school system. It is fair to say that virtually all research coming out of the education schools, and more generally, virtually all their ideas about schools and school reform, take the traditional structure of the existing system as a given. Ideas that argue for fundamentally different approaches—for example, through greater choice and competition—tend to be denigrated and opposed. Aspects of public education that are clearly relevant to school performance, but that touch on powerful established interests—notably, the effects of teachers unions on school organization and student achievement—are assiduously avoided as topics of research, and conspicuously absent from expert discussions of problems and solutions.

When America's policymakers pay attention to experts at all, then, it is to the education schools that they typically turn for research, knowledge, and ideas; and what they get is a highly constrained, mainstream set of responses that are very much inside the box. The Koret Task Force is an explicit attempt to offer the nation an *alternative* source of expertise, built around scholars who are not part of the nexus that binds education schools to the status quo—and who are quite willing, when social science justifies it, to say that the system is flawed in fundamental ways, that traditional approaches and solutions haven't worked, and that something different needs to be done.

## A Primer on America's Schools

Any effort to think seriously about school reform must begin at the beginning, by simply describing and assessing the current state of American education. That is the purpose of this book, which is the first project of the Koret Task Force, and the logical first step in what we hope will be a long and productive process of collaboration.

Our aim here, more specifically, is to provide a broad overview of the American education system—by pulling together basic facts and research findings about its most essential features (and thus summarizing, as best we can, what is currently known), identifying central problems that stand in the way of better performance, and explaining why these problems seem to exist. In some of the chapters, the analysis naturally leads to discussions of reform and specific proposals for improvement. But reform is not the focus. This is mainly an effort to set out the facts of American education in a clear, simple, straightforward way, and to offer insight and perspective on what they mean.

That is why we call the book a primer. Our hope is that anyone who wants to know about American education—whether policymaker or academic, political activist or ordinary citizen—can turn to this volume for basic information and find a discussion that is useful and enlightening. It is impossible to be truly comprehensive in surveying a system as complex as this one, and we have no pretensions in this regard. But we have tried to cover a broad range of topics that are important in their own right and, when considered together, convey a strong sense of the bigger picture of American education.

Each chapter is written by a task force member who is an expert on that subject. The chapter on the traditions and ideals of public education, for example, is written by Diane Ravitch, who is one of this country's leading educational historians. The chapter on educational costs is written by Eric Hanushek, who is one of the nation's best-known experts on the economics of schooling. The chapter on curriculum is written by E. D. Hirsch, who is celebrated for his work on what children should know and how they should be taught. And so on. In each case, task force members have been asked to take responsibility for subjects they have been studying for many years, to cut through all the complexities (and often, the unwarranted assumptions and unfounded assertions), and to convey—in simple language devoid of the usual academic jargon—the basic facts that people need to know about these aspects of American education.

They also do more, of course, than just report the facts. All experts do. Indeed, it is in going beyond the facts that experts have the most to contribute. For the challenge they face is not simply to collect a mass of evidence, but to make sense of it by offering coherent, supportable interpretations of its meaning and consequences. Without such interpretations, true knowledge is inherently limited, and there can be little foundation for understanding *why* the facts are as they are, or what needs to be done (via specific reforms) to solve problems and improve the schools. In each chapter, then, task force members lay out the facts of their respective subjects, but they also offer their own perspectives on what those facts mean and what their consequences are. In the grander scheme of things, this is the greater measure of their contributions—and the source of valuable ideas, persuasive arguments, and proposals for change.

These perspectives, I should emphasize, reflect their judgments as individual scholars. There is no party line at work here. The fact is, we come from different academic disciplines (political science, economics, history, psychology). We have different backgrounds in theory and methodology. We have different career experiences. And if we were asked to come up with a single vision of how education reform should be pursued, it is doubtful that we could achieve total agreement. This said, what we have in common far outweighs our differences; and the differences, we find, are a source of healthy debate that help us challenge our unstated assumptions, avoid group-think, and respect and learn from alternative views.

We offer this primer, then, not as a unified statement of the Koret Task Force, but as a collection of separate statements by separate scholars who see themselves as part of the same team—a team critical of the existing system, willing to look at fundamental ways of transforming it, and dedicated to the kinds of clear-eyed, factual assessments that can help identify what works. Our goal is to get this nation off the treadmill of failed reforms, and to provide ideas and analysis that can promote the cause of progress. Real progress. This primer is our first attempt, as a group, to construct a useful basis for moving ahead. There will be more to come.

# CHAPTER I

# American Traditions of Education

## *Diane Ravitch*

Attached to the cornerstone of a large New York University building at the intersection of Waverley Place and University Place is a
plaque, erected in 1909, that reads as follows:

> In honor of the seven public-school teachers who taught under Dutch
> rule on Manhattan Island:
> Adam Roelandsen
> Jan Cornelissen
> Jan Stevenson
> William Vestens
> Jan de la Montagne
> Harmanus Van Hoboken
> Evert Pietersen

This is a touching tribute, but there is one problem with it: the
men it honors actually taught in the parochial schools of the Re-
formed Dutch Church of New Amsterdam, as New York was
called before the English took control in 1664. There were no public schools in the Dutch colony of New Netherland. The teachers
in the Dutch parochial schools were licensed to teach by Dutch
church authorities; their pupils, except for children of the poor,
paid fees to the schoolmaster. The teachers taught children to read
and write Dutch and to recite their catechism and prayers.

The university's error is understandable, however, because the history of American education is so little known or understood. Few, aside from historians, seem to know that there are many different traditions of education in the United States. Few seem to realize that the line between public and private schools was not especially sharp until the latter decades of the nineteenth century.

In public debates, it is clear that many people think that the public school, as we know it today, represents the one and only American tradition. That this view is so widespread can be credited not only to the unquestioned success of the common school movement of the mid–nineteenth century, which made the idea of state control of education appear to be synonymous with patriotism, nationalism, and progress, but also to a well-established tradition of boosterism in the field of educational history.

Historians of schooling, writing in the early decades of the twentieth century, chronicled the triumph of the common school movement over its benighted competitors. This narrative was earnestly disseminated to generations of administrators and teachers. The historians, located in newly created schools of education, saw American education history as a morality tale that went like this: in the colonial era and for about half a century into its young nationhood, America had diverse forms of education, some of them organized by churches, others by local groups of parents. Then, in the mid–nineteenth century, selfless and public-spirited reformers realized that the only democratic form of education was one that was entirely controlled by the state. These reformers fought valiant campaigns against special interests and selfish, narrow-minded people in state after state. Eventually, when the public agreed with them, every state created a public school system to advance the public interest. And, on this rock of state control of public education, our democracy rests.

As Harvard historian Bernard Bailyn showed in his seminal work *Education in the Forming of American Society*, this morality tale appealed to the education profession's amour propre. Leading educators in the 1890s enjoyed debating whether the earliest public school could be traced to the Puritans in Massachusetts or to the Dutch in New York. Both sides, Bailyn pointed out, were wrong: public education "had not grown from seventeenth-century seeds; it was a new and unexpected genus whose ultimate character could not have been predicted and whose emergence had troubled well-disposed, high-minded people." The school historians of the late nineteenth century and early twentieth century, said Bailyn, were professional educators who wanted to give the student of education "an everlasting faith in his profession." These "educational missionaries" believed passionately in their profession, and they "drew up what became the patristic literature of a powerful academic ecclesia."[1]

The most prominent of the early twentieth-century school historians was Ellwood P. Cubberley. Before he taught at Stanford (and became dean of its school of education), he had been superintendent of schools in San Francisco. His history of American education and his history of Western education asserted confidently that a nation's educational progress could be measured by whether control of education passed from church to state, from private to public, and from laypeople to professionals. The highest form of educational development, he proposed, was "state control of the whole range of education, to enable the State to promote intellectual and moral and social progress along lines useful to the State." Cubberley divided supporters and opponents of state control of schooling into two camps. Supporting state control were "Citizens of the Republic," philanthropists and humanitarians, "public men of large vision," city residents, urban workingmen, nontaxpayers, Calvinists, and "New England men." On the other side, the opponents of state control included aristocrats; conservatives; "politicians of small vision"; rural residents; "the ignorant, narrow-minded, and penurious"; taxpayers; Lutherans, Reformed-Church, Mennonites, and Quakers; Southerners; private school proprietors; and "the non-English-speaking classes."[2]

In Cubberley's view, a democratic school system was one in which the state exercised complete control; everything else— including schools operated by private individuals, churches, school

1. Bernard Bailyn, *Education in the Forming of American Society* (Chapel Hill: University of North Carolina Press, 1960), p. 8–11.

2. Ellwood P. Cubberley, *The History of Education* (Boston: Houghton Mifflin, 1920), pp. 578, 673; also, Ellwood P. Cubberley, *Public Education in the United States* (Boston: Houghton Mifflin, 1919), pp. 120–21.

societies, academies relying on private initiative, or even the district system of local school boards—were no more than way stations preceding the "rising" of a "democratic consciousness." He saw the nineteenth century as a series of battles against "apathy, religious jealousies, and private interests," culminating in the creation of "the American State School, free and equally open to all . . . the most important institution in our national life working for the perpetuation of our free democracy and the advancement of the public welfare."[3]

The "good guys" in his telling were "the New England men," who struggled first to provide some form of state aid or taxation to benefit schools, then to use that leverage to impose state supervision and control of local school systems. Opposition to state control, he acknowledged, came not only from private and sectarian interests but from local school districts as well, which were not eager to submit to state authority. In 1812, New York became the first state to create a superintendent of schools; however, the position was abolished by the legislature in 1821, not to be created again until 1854. Maryland created the post in 1826, only to abolish it in 1828 and reestablish it in 1864. By 1850, there were regular state school officers in only seven of the thirty-one states, and by 1861, there were nineteen in thirty-four states.[4] The primary goal of these officials, which Cubberley lauded, was imposing state control over local school districts.

Cubberley described the expansion of state power as the foundation of democratic education. Similarly, the secularization of education, and the withdrawal of state aid from sectarian schools, he said, was "an unavoidable incident connected with the coming to self-consciousness and self-government of a great people."[5] The evolution of democratic institutions of schooling inevitably led to state control of schooling, he maintained. He presented resistance to this idea as backsliding or reaction. He noted, for example, that the city of Lowell, Massachusetts, had treated two parochial schools as public schools in 1835 but that the experiment was

3. Cubberley, *Public Education in the United States*, pp. 78, 123.
4. Ibid., pp. 157–59.
5. Ibid., p. 173.

soon abandoned, thus allowing the continuing growth of the democratic idea.

Using history as his vehicle, Cubberley campaigned for professional supervision and control of schools, as far removed as possible from parents and other private and allegedly selfish interests. In the best of all possible worlds, he suggested, local districts would submit to state-level administrators; those administrators would cede their powers to the national government; and expert professionals would run the schools, free of political interference by elected officials. Thus would the schools be securely lodged "in the hands of those whose business it is to guard the rights and advance the educational welfare of our children."[6]

Cubberley's version of the rise and triumph of public education was, as Bailyn showed, anachronistic and just plain wrong. The story of American educational development was far more complex and interesting than Cubberley and the other boosters of his era ever suggested.

## SCHOOLING IN EARLY AMERICA

The Founding Fathers prized education but the words "education" and "schooling" do not appear in the Constitution. In colonial days and in the first half-century of the new nation's existence, there were many different kinds of schooling available (except for enslaved African Americans in the South). The only accurate way to describe American schooling in the years before 1850 would be in terms of variety and pluralism, for there was no single pattern of schooling in the nation's rural areas, towns, and cities.

In towns and cities, parents had many choices about how and where to educate their children; most took advantage of them. In addition to whatever instruction they were able to provide at home, they could choose among dame schools (that is, instruction offered by individual female teachers, usually in their homes), schools managed by private benevolent associations, private-ven-

6. Ibid., pp. 480–82. See also Lawrence A. Cremin, *The Wonderful World of Ellwood Patterson Cubberley* (New York: Teachers College Press, 1965).

ture schools, Latin grammar schools, religious schools, boarding schools, and private academies. Some of these received public funding, others did not. The Latin grammar schools, usually found in New England, were town schools, governed by an elected board and funded by local and often state aid. Churches sponsored schools for their members' children and charity schools for the children of the urban poor. Itinerant schoolmasters offered their services for a winter term or two and were paid by parents. Some towns set up schools for local children, funded by a combination of tuition and taxes. Sometimes schooling was left to families, who organized subscription schools or hired a schoolmaster. Entrepreneurial teachers established schools and advertised for students. In larger cities, philanthropic societies organized free schools for poor children.

Also broadly available were academies that provided secondary education and offered a broader curriculum than Latin grammar schools. Many private or quasi-public schools were often chartered by the state, the same as colleges. Controlled by an independent board of trustees, the academies relied on tuition but received significant public funding from their localities and states. In his historical essay on the academy, Theodore Sizer pointed out that the age of the academy extended from the Revolution to the Civil War. Henry Barnard reported more than six thousand academies in 1850, spread across the land, in every state and territory (Sizer believes that this figure was conservative); even Texas, still largely unsettled at that time, had ninety-seven academies. The academies provided secondary schooling before the creation of public high schools. Not only were they open to all children in the community, but most "implored all comers to enroll, bearing their life-giving tuition." Much like charter schools in the 1990s, academies were founded by "optimistic entrepreneurs" and were closely tied to their local communities. In some cases, groups of civic leaders pooled their resources, got a state charter, and obtained public funding; others, wrote Sizer, "set up a stock company, gathered small amounts of money for each share of stock, and permitted the shareholders to vote for the trustees." Academies were supported by tuition, state grants, contributions of student labor, endowments, state lotteries, and even goods bartered for schooling.[7]

Rural areas developed district schools with local boards composed mainly of parents. Until the mid-nineteenth century, it was common for parents to pay tuition, even for their local public school. In exchange, parents had a large voice in controlling the schools. As historian Carl Kaestle observed, the parents in rural communities controlled "what textbooks their children would use . . . what subjects would be taught, who the teacher would be, and how long school would be in session."[8] In these areas, where most Americans lived, teachers usually "boarded around," taking food and lodging from parents in the area, which gave parents ample opportunity to monitor the teachers' personal lives and put in their two cents about how the school should be run.

Family, church, and workplace were important elements in education in this era. With few exceptions, there were no state departments of education, and those few had no power over local school boards. In many cities, public schools would not accept children unless they already knew how to read and assumed that they learned to do so either at home or a dame school. Churches played a large role in education; in some states, religious schools received a pro rata share of public funds for education. In communities with public schools, ministers usually were members of the local school committee and interviewed teachers before they were hired, making sure that their ideas, their religious views, and their morals were sound. Youngsters who became apprentices learned a trade and often literacy as well from their masters.

In his history of the common schools, Carl Kaestle made two important observations about the origins of American public education. First, in the early nineteenth century, the only free schools in the cities of New England, the Middle Atlantic states, and the South were charity schools for poor children or public schools attended generally by children from low-income families and

7. Theodore R. Sizer, *The Age of the Academies* (New York: Teachers College Press, 1964), pp. 1–22.
8. Carl Kaestle, *Pillars of the Republic: Common Schools and American Society, 1780–1860* (New York: Hill & Wang, 1983), p. 22.

shunned by the affluent; these schools began to monopolize public funds in the 1820s and eventually became the foundation for the public school system in those cities. As he described it, "In many cities, the charity schools literally became the public common schools." Unlike district schools or pay schools, where parents had a large role, the charity schools had never been accountable to parents but tended instead to see them as a problem. Second, he observed that the expansion of charity schooling into public schools did not increase the percentage of urban children who went to school. Kaestle emphasized "the stability of combined public and private enrollment rates over the first half of the nineteenth century." The growth of public school enrollments, he suggested, reflected a shift of children from private schools to free schools rather than increased participation by unschooled children.[9]

## THE COMMON SCHOOL MOVEMENT

In the 1830s and 1840s, the growth of the economy—fueled by the expansion of manufacturing and transportation and increased immigration from Europe, especially from Ireland and Germany—brought many changes to the nation, especially in the Northeast. The population of cities increased, as did the proportion of immigrants who were neither English nor Protestant. Along with these changes went a rise in social tensions as cities began to experience poverty, slums, crime, intemperance, and related ills. Prominent citizens in big cities such as New York, Philadelphia, and Baltimore worried about the morals of poor children and especially about the likelihood that they were influenced by the vices of their parents. Protestant ministers, who played a large role in social reform movements of the nineteenth century, looked askance at the growth of the Catholic population. Reformers expressed concern about the nation's social fabric and about its future unity. They looked to the schools to teach the rising generation the values, morals, and outlook that seemed necessary for the future well-being of the nation.

9. Ibid., pp. 57, 60–61.

The schools appeared to offer a perfect mechanism with which to address these concerns. In the case of the urban poor, reformers expected the schools to combat the bad examples of parents. As they contemplated the possibility of using the schools to uplift the poor and spread republican values, reformers agreed on the necessity of centralizing the control of public schools under state authorities; this assured that state authorities, not immigrant parents, would make important decisions about the nature of schooling. These reformers launched a campaign known as the common school movement from about 1830 to 1860. Its leaders were mainly allied with the Whig Party and with organized Protestant religions. Neither Catholics nor Jacksonian Democrats liked the centralizing aspects of this movement.

The leading figure in this campaign was Horace Mann, a Massachusetts state legislator who led the battle to create a state board of education, then resigned his political office to become secretary of the new board in 1839. In this position, he became the most eloquent spokesman for public education in the nation. The goal of this movement was to promote the development of tax-supported public schools, to train teachers, and to establish state support and direction of these activities. The Founding Fathers had written often about the importance of an educated electorate; the leaders of the common school movement sought universal education not only for this reason but to teach common values and to secure social stability.

But there was more to the common school movement than just a love of education and a desire for a harmonious, moral, prosperous society. The common school movement was one of a variety of social and moral reform movements inspired by the "Second Great Awakening," a religious revival of evangelical Protestantism that swept the northern United States in the late 1820s and 1830s. The common school movement shared the rhetoric and fervor of evangelical Protestantism; many of its leaders were ordained Protestant ministers who saw themselves as men with a mission. According to historian Lloyd P. Jorgensen, the most fundamental assumption of the common school movement was that the public school would be "an agent of moral and social redemption" and that this redemption would be the result of "non-sectarian" religious instruction.[10]

The common school movement is customarily described without qualification as a heroic crusade, but Jorgenson noted that its "dark underside" was the "spirit of nativism."[11] Even Cubberley observed, without disapproval, that the arrival of large numbers of Irish Catholics and German Lutherans in the 1840s was followed by intense controversy, including anti-Catholic riots in several cities, the formation of the anti-Catholic Native American Party, and the rise of the Know-Nothing Party. Nativists in these political parties believed that foreigners and especially Catholics in the United States were a threat to the American tradition of liberty. They were especially eager to prevent Catholics from obtaining any public funding for their schools and to require the use of the Protestant Bible in the public schools. In the 1850s, the Know-Nothing Party elected six governors and took control of several state legislatures, including those in Massachusetts, New Hampshire, Connecticut, Rhode Island, Maryland, and Kentucky.

In his important study *The State and the Non-Public School*, Jorgensen has shown that many of the common school leaders were "among the most vitriolic anti-Romanists of their time." The leadership of the common school movement included a large number of Protestant ministers, including the state superintendents in Ohio, Indiana, North Carolina, Virginia, and Kentucky. They were "educational evangelists," seeking to advance the cause of public education and to make sure that Catholic schools and other private schools were excluded from any public funding. From 1838 to 1879, all but one of Kentucky's eleven state superintendents were clergymen. One of them, Robert J. Breckinridge, was known as the "father of public education in Kentucky" because of his work as state superintendent from 1847 to 1852; Breckinridge was also well known as a zealous anti-Catholic who published diatribes against "papism" and inspired anti-Catholic riots when he was a minister in Baltimore from 1832 to 1845.[12]

10. Lloyd P. Jorgensen, *The State and the Non-Public School, 1825–1925* (Columbia, Missouri: University of Missouri Press, 1987), p. 23.

11. Ibid., pp. 28–29.

12. Ibid., pp. 31–54.

According to Jorgenson, "the long tradition of voluntary/public cooperation in education came to a dramatic end in the 1850s" because evangelical Protestants prevailed in their efforts to exclude Catholic schools from any participation in public funding. "In state after state during the fifties," he writes, "with Know-Nothing leaders in the forefront of the battles, state school officers and Protestant denominational bodies were able to obtain legislation denying public funds to nonpublic schools and requiring Bible reading in the public schools. There was no mistaking the motivation behind these campaigns; the leaders openly and boastfully made anti-Catholicism the dominant theme of their attacks." By the late 1850s, the principle of limiting public aid to public schools was well established in the states. "Much later," Jorgenson comments, "the disinheritance of the church-related schools, a doctrine largely born of bigotry at the state level, was transmuted by the U.S. Supreme Court into high constitutional principle."[13]

The common school movement was successful in its crusade; it established free, tax-supported public schools in every state and persuaded sympathetic state legislatures to pass laws barring any public funding of sectarian schools. The catch in this formulation, however, was that the common schools were nonsectarian but not necessarily nonreligious. Throughout the nineteenth century and in the first six decades of the twentieth century (and in rural districts, even longer), the public schools regularly engaged in practices that were nonsectarian but pan-Protestant: Bible reading, hymn singing, prayers, and recitation of the Lord's Prayer. Many parents, educators, and legislators believed that the schools were responsible for children's moral development and could not separate faith-based practices from moral aims. The matter was resolved, however, in 1963, when the U.S. Supreme Court struck down the laws in thirty-seven states that required or permitted school prayers or Bible reading in the public schools. Henceforth, the public schools would be nonreligious as well as nonsectarian.

13. Ibid., p. 69. A useful summary of state laws, constitutional amendments, and court decisions is contained in Samuel Windsor Brown, *The Secularization of American Education* (New York: Teachers College, 1912).

In the early decades of the twentieth century, several campaigns were launched to outlaw nonpublic schools altogether (in Washington, Ohio, California, Wisconsin, Indiana, and Michigan).[14] The most notable example of this activity occurred in 1922 in Oregon, where voters approved an initiative that required all children between eight and sixteen (with minor exceptions) to attend public schools. The measure was supported by Masons, the Ku Klux Klan, and patriotic societies and vociferously opposed by Roman Catholic groups, Lutherans, and Seventh-Day Adventists, as well as much of the state's press. The purpose of the measure was to destroy nonpublic schools, which enrolled only 7 percent of the children in the state. The law was challenged by a Roman Catholic order that ran several schools and by a private military academy; the U.S. Supreme Court held it unconstitutional in 1925. In *Pierce v. Society of Sisters of Holy Names of Jesus and Mary*, the Court held that the state had the power "reasonably to regulate all schools, to inspect, supervise, and examine their teachers and pupils; to require that all children of proper age attend some school, that teachers shall be of good moral character and patriotic disposition, that certain studies plainly essential to good citizenship must be taught, and that nothing be taught which is manifestly inimical to the public welfare." But the Court recognized that the state's law intended not to regulate the nonpublic schools but to destroy them. The Court declared that "the fundamental theory of liberty upon which all governments in this Union repose excludes any general power of the state to standardize its children by forcing them to accept instruction from public teachers only. The child is not the mere creature of the state; those who nurture him and direct his destiny have the right coupled with the high duty to recognize and prepare him for higher obligations."[15] The Pierce decision was critically important in preserving the right of nonpublic schools to exist, as well as the freedom of parents to send their children to such schools.

14. Jorgensen, *The State and the Non-Public School*, p. 206.
15. *Pierce v. Society of Sisters of Holy Names of Jesus and Mary*, 268 U.S. 510 (1925). For further discussion, see Jorgensen, *The State and the Non-Public School*, pp. 205–15.

## AMERICAN TRADITIONS OF SCHOOLING

As this brief overview of the history of schooling suggests, there are many traditions of schooling in the United States.

The first and most important tradition is that the family is primarily responsible for its children's education. In the colonial era as well as in most of the nineteenth century, families played a large role in teaching their children to read, reading poetry from the schoolbooks at the dinner table or at the fireside, and deciding where to send their children to school.

The second important tradition is pluralism. Until well into the nineteenth century, there was no single pattern of schooling. Children and adults learned in a variety of settings, including dame schools, public schools, academies, private schools, church schools, Sunday schools, libraries, and lyceums.

The third important tradition is the American common school, or public school. Since the mid–nineteenth century, public schools have been broadly available to American children in almost every community; by 1900, elementary school enrollment was nearly universal, thanks to the widespread availability of free public schooling. Secondary enrollments grew far more slowly, in large part because young people did not need a high school education to get a good job. In 1900, only about 10 percent of teenagers were enrolled in high school; this figure did not reach 70 percent until 1940 and now is about 95 percent. About 90 percent of American students are enrolled in public schools.

The fourth important tradition is one of cooperation between public and private sectors to achieve valuable social goals. Public schools often find it necessary and useful to reach out to the private sector for assistance. Nonpublic organizations run preschool centers, Head Start centers, after-school programs, tutoring programs, and many other educational services. Since the early 1990s, the public/private nexus has produced a hybrid agency called charter schools. These may be the lineal descendant of the nineteenth-century academy (although the original academy was a secondary school, and today's charter schools may offer any grade configuration). The modern charter school, like the academy, has an independent board of trustees, survives only because its students choose to enroll, and receives public funding on a per-pupil basis (unlike charter schools, academies were partially subsidized by tuition).

It is not altogether clear how Americans in the twenty-first century will draw on these historic traditions. What does seem likely is that the public will not indefinitely support schools in which children do not learn the skills and knowledge that they require for participation in our society. What has changed, and changed dramatically over the past two hundred years, is the importance of education. Globalization has changed our economy and made education a civic, social, and economic imperative. Young people who do not acquire the skills of literacy and numeracy and a solid education will find themselves locked out of all sorts of future opportunities. This is not tolerable for our society, and our pragmatic bent will prod us toward finding additional ways to spread the promise of education throughout the population.

# CHAPTER 2

# The System

## *John E. Chubb*

The institutions that make up the American education system are
such familiar elements of this country's public landscape that most
people take them for granted. Indeed, even as education has become the American public's number one concern, the public debate about improving education has focused largely on the schools
within the system and not on the system itself.[1] School reform is a
concept with which most people are familiar. Systemic reform is a
concept near and dear mostly to policy "wonks." Although there
is no shortage of ideas for changing America's schools, there is
considerably less thought about how to improve the institutions
that run the schools—local school districts, boards of education,
school superintendents, and district offices.

Thinking, however, has begun to shift. During the 1980s a small
number of reformers began to ask whether the system might be
part of the schools' problem. The system, they suggested, tended
to get bogged down in highly politicized issues such as sex education and busing and make little headway on more fundamental
issues such as raising student achievement. School politics, they

1. According to a Gallup Poll of 1,004 adults interviewed April 3–9, 2000,
89 percent view education as "extremely" or "very important," the highest-rank-
ing issue in the poll. Wendy Koch, "Senate Debates Sweeping Education
Changes," *USA Today,* May 2, 2000, p. 10A.

observed, were often dominated by well-organized groups, such as teachers unions, able to block systemic reforms that the general public strongly endorsed—for example, competency tests and merit pay for teachers. The system also tended to be bound by an inordinate number of rules and regulations—call it bureaucracy— which teachers and principals complained made it difficult to provide quality education. Finally, the 1980s had seen a great deal of conventional school reform, such as more funding, smaller class sizes, and tougher graduation requirements, without dramatic effects on student achievement.[2]

During the 1990s criticism of the system began to produce changes. States, in particular, began to apply serious pressure to local school systems. These pressures came in two forms. First, states began to adopt academic standards and administer tests to hold schools and school districts accountable for student performance.[3] Second, states began to provide families with ways out of the schools offered by local systems and with new sources of public education. Many states approved the operation of charter schools, which are free, open-admission public schools not controlled by local boards of education.[4] A few states authorized

2. The leading reformers from this period include two Republican U.S. secretaries of education, William Bennett and Lamar Alexander, a number of governors from both political parties, a few maverick urban legislators such as Democratic state representative Polly Williams of Milwaukee, Wisconsin, and a number of scholars. The most critical reform literature of the 1980s and early 1990s includes Chester E. Finn Jr., *We Must Take Charge* (New York: Free Press, 1991); John E. Chubb and Terry M. Moe, *Politics, Markets and America's Schools* (Washington, D.C.: Brookings, 1990); Diane Ravitch, *The Troubled Crusade, American Education, 1945–1980* (New York: Basic Books, 1983); National Commission on Excellence in Education (NCEE), *A Nation at Risk* (Washington, D.C.: NCEE, 1983); and Denis P. Doyle and David T. Kearns, *Winning the Brain Race* (San Francisco: Institute for Contemporary Studies, 1988). Critics of this reform literature include Jonathan Kozol, *Savage Inequalities: Children in America's Schools* (Crown Publishers, 1991) and Edith Rasell and Richard Rothstein, eds., *School Choice* (Washington, D.C.: Economic Policy Institute, 1993).

3. On the standards movement, see especially Diane Ravitch, *National Standards in American Education* (Washington, D.C.: Brookings, 1995); and Grant P. Wiggins, *Assessing Student Performance* (San Francisco: Jossey-Bass, 1993).

4. See Chester E. Finn Jr., Bruno V. Manno, and Gregg Vanourek, *Charter Schools in Action* (Princeton: Princeton University Press, 2000); and Nina Shok-

vouchers to enable disadvantaged families or families in failing schools to attend any public or *private* school of their choosing.[5] A number of communities, with the encouragement or blessing of states, contracted with for-profit firms to provide alternative schools.[6] These schools-of-choice initiatives represent a more fundamental challenge to the traditional educational system than the imposition of standards and testing, even though both types of challenges are important. The choice programs look to the forces of the market place—the demand for schools from parents and the supply of schools from a potentially wide range of sources: universities, teachers, community groups, churches, businesses—instead of the traditional forces of politics, to provide the country better schools.

The importance of considering market forces, as the country looks to improve education markedly, cannot be overestimated. The United States has relied on essentially the same system for providing public education since the mid-1800s. For all the variation that this system may seem to exhibit—over time, from one community to the next, and across fifty different states—the system works in predictably regular ways. The system is governed by politics and all that politics implies—good, bad, and indifferent. Markets work in predictable ways also. They do an unmatched job of producing goods and services that are well suited to a market economy, what economists call private goods, and they are unrivaled in raising standards of living. Markets also have limitations; if they are left strictly in private hands, they do not do a good job of producing public goods—for example, clean air or

rai Rees, *School Choice 2000: What's Happening in the States* (Washington, D.C.: Heritage Foundation, 2000), pp. xvi–xvii.

5. For highlights of the controversy surrounding the effects of private voucher programs, see Jay P. Greene, Paul E. Peterson, and Jiangtao Du, "School Choice in Milwaukee: A Randomized Experiment," in Paul E. Peterson and Bryan Hassel, eds., *Learning from School Choice* (Washington, D.C.: Brookings, 1998); and Cecilia E. Rouse, "Private School Vouchers and Student Achievement: An Evaluation of the Milwaukee Parental Choice Program," Department of Economics, Princeton University, 1996.

6. On for-profit schools, see John E. Chubb, "Lessons in School Reform from the Edison Project," in Diane Ravitch and Joseph P. Viteritti, eds. *New Schools for a New Century* (New Haven: Yale University Press, 1997), ch. 4.

ample highways—or of ensuring much equality in social outcomes.[7] Education has certain of the features of an economist's
public good: in particular, the public has an interest in the education of all children; the private interest of the family should not be
the sole determinant of how American children are educated. But
education could be restructured to take advantage of market
forces while remaining ultimately public. This is what initiatives
such as charter schools, vouchers, and for-profit schools aim to
do. They aim to improve public schools by changing the basic
ways the system that produces the schools operates.

Whether the United States looks more to market forces to promote better schools, or seeks improvement within the existing system, the system must be well understood. Efforts to improve
schools within the system must work through the institutions that
govern and control the schools and negotiate the politics and bureaucracy that make change anything but straightforward. Similarly, efforts to inject competition into the system must succeed
within a marketplace created by the democratic process and
geared to accomplish public goals—not within a classic private
market. Let us consider, then, the workings of the venerable system, first on the system's own terms and then subject to the pressures that market-oriented reforms might create.

## IGNORANCE IS BLISS

Education, we are reminded time and again, must get stronger.
Children today must be prepared to compete in a rapidly changing
world of international commerce and technological innovation.
Education that may have been good enough in the twentieth century will never do in the twenty-first—and many schools in the
twentieth century, particularly urban schools, were not nearly
good enough even then.[8] Whatever the merits of these reminders,

7. On the costs and benefits of the market, see the classic monograph, Arthur
Okun, *Equality and Efficiency: The Big Tradeoff* (Washington, D.C.: Brookings,
1977).

8. A thorough annual summary of student achievement and school reform,
state by state, is *Quality Counts*, prepared by *Education Week*. See most recently
"Quality Counts 2000," *Education Week*, 19, no. 18 (January 13, 2000).

the American public clearly believes them. Throughout the 2000 presidential election campaign George W. Bush and Al Gore spent more time pitching their educational plans to the American public than addressing any other issue.

The presidential candidates are but two of the many voices calling loudly for reform. From the Congress to the state houses to far-flung boards of education, leaders are demanding improvement. Some of these demands, to be sure, come with proposals for charter schools or vouchers or other market-oriented reforms. But by and large, the demands recommend a different approach, best described as "tough love." Give public schools more resources and hold them responsible for producing better results—or else. Reduce class sizes, hire lots of new teachers, replace dilapidated facilities, and increase access to technology. Then, set high academic standards, administer standardized tests, and insist that schools show progress against them. The public generally applauds these measures, and politicians are only too happy to offer them up.

There are some problems with these measures, however. A big one is cost. For example, if schools reduce their class sizes by just 20 percent—from, say, twenty-five students in a class to twenty—schools will require 25 percent more teachers to serve the same number of students. Teacher compensation consumes about half of the public education budget, so 25 percent more teachers could mean a 12.5 percent increase in education spending. The United States spent $351 billion on K–12 education during the 1999–2000 school year; 12.5 percent of that could amount to nearly $45 billion a year in new education costs.[9] And this calculation says nothing of the cost of new facilities and additional classrooms that smaller classes necessitate. There may be a more fundamental problem, though, with the various proposals for more resources. There is little evidence that they will raise student achievement at all, let alone promote the dramatic gains that the nation seems to want. Class-size reduction is the only proposed use of new resources for which there is any empirical support.

9. National Center for Education Statistics, *Digest of Education Statistics*, (Washington, D.C.: U.S. Department of Education), table 31, p. 34.

The effects of tougher standards and assessments largely remain to be seen.[10]

These reforms have an important virtue, however. They fit nicely within the established education system. They promise improvement through means that are familiar and that seemingly make sense. They do not challenge any deeply held assumptions about how schools should work. They avoid tough and fractious questions about why the schools may not be measuring up. They gloss over the enormous challenges that remain. They conveniently assume that schools will hire excellent new teachers and train them to high levels of proficiency; take advantage of smaller classes to change instruction and produce better results; integrate technology into the core curriculum; and help students meet high academic standards—all things that schools have not done consistently well in the past.

In point of fact, these challenges are simply handed off to the system to meet. Schools are not left to their own devices. Congress hands off to the U.S. Department of Education and other federal agencies. State legislatures delegate implementation to their own education departments. Local boards of education rely on superintendents and district offices. From Washington to state capitals to cities and towns, the American education system supports the schools in carrying out the policies that are ultimately supposed to improve how students learn. The system, it is widely assumed, will put new resources to good use and deliver the ambitious results asked of it.

This is surely the most comfortable assumption to make. Any other assumption calls into question the venerable system itself. Politicians who ask whether the system is up to the new challenges before it risk the wrath not only of the millions of teachers and administrators with vested interests in the system but of the general public, most of whom were educated by the system and often

10. On the effects of school resources on school performance and student achievement, see Allan Odden and Carolyn Busch, *Financing Schools for High Performance* (San Francisco: Jossey-Bass, 1998); and Gary Burtless, ed., *Does Money Matter? The Effect of School Resources on Student Achievement and Adult Success* (Washington, D.C.: Brookings, 1996).

have warm feelings toward it and its most powerful symbols. Politicians who dare suggest that the system may need fundamental reform—particularly reform that would subject the system to competitive pressures from charter schools, private schools, or for-profit schools—are tarred with the brush of "destroying our public schools." The institution of public education, the system itself, is viewed by much of the public as just as important as the results it achieves. Why the system is so revered has much to do with the hallowed principles on which it is supposed to rest.

## Fundamental Principles

The American education system is a thoroughly public system and has been largely so for 150 years. Education is provided free of charge, at taxpayer expense, to all children and families who want it. All children must attend school (though it may also be a private school) until some time in their midteens. All public schools are run directly by government authorities of some kind. The government provides little financial support to private schools, and most of that is indirect, such as the tax relief provided to all not-for-profit entities. Direct government support for schools that the government does not run itself is still rare: scholarship programs and charter schools today enroll less than 1 percent of students nationwide.[11]

As a public system, education is shaped primarily by politics: electoral politics, legislative politics, executive and administrative politics, judicial politics. These periodic and ongoing contests for the right to exercise legitimate democratic authority over the schools are what have shaped the education system over time and continue to shape it, even as the system seeks desperately to improve. The politics of education could take the education system almost anywhere. The political process could decide tomorrow to "blow the whole system up," as New York mayor Rudy Giuliani suggested in 2000. The current system is not mandated by the U.S.

11. The Center for Education Reform, *Charter School Laws across the States 2000* (Washington, D.C.: Center for Education Reform, 2000); and Rees, *School Choice 2000*.

Constitution. The Constitution is silent on how children shall be educated, which means that the responsibility for education rests with the states. But this has not stopped the federal government from playing a large role in the current system or from contemplating an even larger one: note again how large a role education played in the 2000 presidential race. The Constitution is unclear on the acceptability of vouchers, but it would be no surprise if the Supreme Court some day were to endorse a voucher system that would change completely the way schools are funded and shake the current education system at its very foundation.[12]

Politics has enormous leeway to reshape the education system. But politics has historically respected certain fundamental principles about how education should be organized. These principles carry normative weight. They are part of America's democratic tradition. And they have served the interests of groups in positions to exert power in their name. Today, they are fundamental to understanding how the American education system is supposed to work—and why it is supposed to work well.

The first principle is *local control*. Public schools are governed and administered at the local level. Boards of education, elected or appointed through democratic processes, representing local communities, directly govern and administer virtually all public schools in America.[13] This organizing principle is supposed to put education decisions in the hands of the communities closest to the children and families being educated and in the best position to know what kind of education to provide.

The second principle is *federalism*. The Constitution stipulates a sharing of powers between the national government and the states, a stipulation that silently reserves education to the states. The states have by tradition delegated much of this responsibility

12. On the prospects of an endorsement of vouchers by the U.S. Supreme Court, see Joseph P. Viteritti, *Choosing Equality* (Washington, D.C.: Brookings, 1999).

13. The only major exceptions to this rule are schools in Hawaii, which are governed by one state education system (though there are intermediary authorities serving schools on each island), and schools organized by the U.S. Department of Defense to serve American families working for the armed forces overseas.

to local communities, which should only enhance the objectives on which federalism rests. Federalism was originally meant to discourage any single faction from imposing its will nationally; over time federalism has been valued for encouraging a diversity of approaches to the needs government must meet. With fifty states and thousands of communities providing public education, federalism offers an extensive laboratory for promoting and evaluating a diversity of innovations.

The third and final principle is *professionalism*. Education is too important to be subjected to the direct influence of politics. The victors in the last election should not appoint the teachers, principals, and key administrators that deliver education. Education should be delivered by professionals, individuals who have been certified as skillful and knowledgeable and who can be trusted to make decisions objectively, consistent with education policy and the best interests of children.

## PRINCIPLES IN PRACTICE

Although these principles took hold in American education as much for the particular interests they protected as for the greater good they advanced, they have been enshrined as fundamental reasons for valuing the system as it now stands. In practice, however, the system falls short of fulfilling the promise that these principles are supposed to offer.

### Local Control

Local control may be the most powerful myth in public education. Among the three principles on which the education system rests, local control is certainly the most venerated symbol of what the system is supposed to be. It is surely invoked more often than the other two in political debates. In recent years the cry for local control has played an important role in slowing the push for accountability. Efforts by the federal government to establish national education standards are regularly and effectively countered by claims that such standards threaten the tradition of local control. Efforts by state governments to institute mandatory tests are resisted by communities standing up for the near-sacred principle of local control. But just as myths can hold great symbolic value, they can also be untrue. Such is the case with local control. The virtues that defenders of local control seek to protect have been eroding for quite some time.

During the Progressive Era, some one hundred years ago, reformers sought to insulate local education systems from the vicissitudes, patronage, and other unwelcome (read: immigrant) influences of politics.[14] Among reforms the Progressives pursued were the separation of school governance from general local governance and the selection of school boards through nonpartisan elections, held at times other than the regular primaries or general elections. These reforms aimed to take the politics out of education. They hoped to protect schools from the political pressures of mayors, city councils, political parties, and the other institutions of local government. These reforms were widely implemented in public education during the first decades of the twentieth century.

The effects of these reforms have fallen quite short of what the Progressives sought. To be blunt, the Progressives did not end education politics at the local level but fostered politics of another, less desirable kind. Separated from the bulk of local government and the formal apparatus of political parties, school systems became political backwaters. School board elections became low-visibility affairs, typically losing the spotlight to elections of mayors and city or town councils, offices in charge of the gamut of local government services. Turnout in school board elections today is the lowest of any general election, averaging perhaps 10 percent of local voters.[15] School boards have difficulty even recruiting candidates to run for office, and incumbents frequently run uncon-

14. On the impact of the Progressives on education, see especially David B. Tyack, *The One Best System: A History of American Urban Education* (Cambridge: Harvard University Press, 1974); and Lawrence A. Cremin, *The Transformation of the School: Progressivism in American Education, 1876–1957* (New York: Knopf, 1961).

15. An egregious example of poor turnout is the 1997 board election in New York City, which saw a 3 percent turnout, *New York Daily News*, December 14, 2000.

tested. Stripped of political parties, school board elections become contests among individuals and often among personalities. Voters cannot base their votes on education policy or issues unless they can discern the positions of individual candidates on these important matters. Political parties tend to simplify issue voting for the average voter by providing candidates an easily recognized identity. For example, Republicans often favor school choice while Democrats often oppose it. Even if the voter knows nothing about the specific candidates, the voter can use party affiliation to infer which candidate is mostly likely to match the voter's position on school choice. In school board elections, candidates run without party labels and often without clear identities for voters to follow. Although the causes of abysmally low turnout in school board elections are not fully understood, turnout is certainly depressed when the visibility and meaning of an election are unclear.

Not everyone stays out of school board elections, however. Groups that care intensely about school matters do get involved. No one cares more intensely about the makeup of the school board than teachers. The board is "management," determining teacher pay and working conditions. To increase their leverage with management, teachers have, during the last fifty years, increasingly organized teacher unions. The overwhelming majority of U.S. teachers now belong to unions and are represented by unions in negotiating employment agreements with local school systems. Teacher unions are in an unusually powerful position as unions go. They are able to influence the makeup of the management team with which they will be bargaining. Unions frequently recruit and endorse candidates in school board elections and contribute to election campaigns. The precise influence of these practices is difficult to calibrate. Union influence is clearly greater in the Northeast and Midwest, where unions are nearly universal, than in the South, where unions are generally not able to engage in collective bargaining. Overall, it is fair to say that school board elections, being low participation affairs for candidates as well as voters, can be easily influenced by organizations with the vast resources that unions can marshal.

Unions are not the only groups that seek to influence board

elections. There is an important difference between unions and all
the others, however. Unions have a uniquely strong and enduring
incentive to be involved: the livelihoods of individual teachers are
constantly at stake. Others who become involved in board elections or politics have interests that are more episodic or diffuse.
Parents obviously care deeply about their children, but their interests in education policy rarely provide the same spur to political
action that teachers experience around their personal working
conditions. Parents tend to become involved in schools directly,
where they can address the needs of their own children. For example, 70 percent of elementary parents attend parent-teacher conferences to hear about their own children's progress.[16] But parents
rarely join interest groups to affect education policy, and their
turnout rates in board elections are low. Teacher unions, organized
to protect the personal welfare of teachers, are permanent organizations, funded by employee dues, with resources unrivaled by any
other organized interest in the country.

To be sure, boards have been taken over by or heavily influenced
by interests other than teachers. In recent years, notable victories
have been won by the so-called religious right, concerned with sex
and values education, and by groups advocating special education,
bilingual education, and gay rights, to cite only the most prominent. But these cases also underscore the more general shortcomings of school board politics. School boards have become
vulnerable to easy capture by interests with intense concerns and
the ability to muster resources around them. Board elections turn
on very few votes, and the general public often has little idea which
way to vote, if it votes at all. School board elections do not easily
reflect the broad sentiment of a community. They tend to reflect
instead the interests of those who have the determination to find
out what the issues are, get candidates in the race, and rustle up
the votes needed to win. Teacher unions do this routinely. Other
groups with intense interests do this occasionally. The general public and parents do this rarely.

The concept of local control has therefore become one that we

16. *Digest of Education Statistics*, table 25, p. 30.

honor mostly in the breach. The specter of losing local control still raises fear as political rhetoric. But the fact is, local control is not exercised effectively by parents or communities at large, the very groups that are supposed to benefit from governing America's schools at the local level. This has implications for improving America's schools. The changes that schools may need to make may not be ones that the system, as it is now influenced and controlled, is willing to make. Improving the schools may require changes in how they are governed and controlled, away from the current model of local control.

## Federalism

The American education system is composed of nearly fifteen thousand local school systems.[17] These systems operate nearly ninety thousand public schools.[18] The schools and the systems that run them are governed by the education policies of their respective states, which are ultimately responsible for public education under the Constitution. In a country as large as the United States, the principle of federalism would seem to provide a critical means to meet the educational needs of an increasingly diverse population. Federalism would also seem to offer a valuable chance to explore educational innovations.

In important respects, federalism has fulfilled its promise. In recent years, for example, something of a consensus has developed nationwide around the desirability of academic standards and testing. The public generally supports the idea that students and schools should be responsible for meeting high standards and passing tests to demonstrate competence. There is no national consensus, however, around exactly what these standards should be or how they should be tested. During the early 1990s the Bush administration and the nation's governors agreed that standards and testing should be established by each of the fifty states. The

17. At last count, in 1996–97, the number was 14,841. *Digest of Education Statistics,* table 90, p 97.
18. At last count, in the fall 1996, the number was 88,585. Ibid.

federal government would sponsor efforts to draft model national standards, but each state would decide for itself what standards it would follow, if any. Ten years later, every state but one has developed and implemented academic standards, and all but a handful have mandated standardized tests. If the federal government's effort is any indication, standards would not be a reality today had the responsibility not been delegated to the states. Efforts to reach consensus at the national level often became embroiled in controversy.[19] But at the state level, although the issues are often difficult, they are narrower in scope and more manageable.

Federalism has enabled the country to tailor other education policies to reflect local needs and values. Bilingual education is provided differently from state to state, as the views of nonnative and native English speakers vary widely. Special education and gifted and talented programs vary, too. States have long differed in the curriculum frameworks they provide and in the texts that they approve for instruction. States vary in the funding they provide their schools, depending on much more than the wealth of the state. Critics, from both the liberal and the conservative perspective, have often criticized this interstate variation. Liberals, for example, cannot abide the stingy and inequitable funding that they believe some states provide their schools. Conservatives despair the vague and undemanding standards that some states adopt in the name of accountability.[20] But, without federalism, it is easy to imagine education policy hopelessly deadlocked. Federalism allows each state to move forward at its own pace.

But federalism has provided less support for educational improvement than it might appear. The sheer number of districts and the high-profile differences among the states imply more diversity and innovation than is actually there. Indeed, as the full sweep of the federal system is taken in, the sameness of the system is what overwhelms. This impression is greatest when examining basic school operations.

19. Ravitch, *National Standards in American Education*.
20. Chester E. Finn Jr. and Michael J. Petrilli, eds., *The State of State Standards 2000* (Washington, D.C.: Thomas B. Fordham Foundation, 2000)

Across nearly fifteen thousand school districts there is essentially one way of doing business. The board of education hires a school superintendent to open and operate a system of public schools to serve the children within the board's jurisdiction. The superintendent, in turn, hires an administrative team—otherwise known as a district office—to administer the system of schools. The schools are set up around an age-graded structure through which students are expected to pass, meeting expectations in annual increments each year as they age. The district hires teachers once they have been awarded a teaching credential by the state. The credential certifies that teachers have met certain educational requirements and have served a brief apprenticeship. Once on the job, teachers are compensated based on their years of experience and the educational credentials they continue to acquire.

Principals, hired by districts to run schools, are generally given limited discretionary resources to do so. The number of teachers— often who those teachers are—and the curriculum and technology in the school are all determined by the board or the district administration. In a school spending $3 million dollars a year—typical of an elementary school—the principal might control $50,000. The principal also has limited control over the teachers he or she is supposed to manage. The ability of the principal to direct, observe, evaluate, and reward teachers is severely circumscribed by board policy or collective bargaining agreements. The schools are filled with students according to administrative convenience. Students are generally assigned to attend the school nearest their home; attendance boundaries are set and shifted by the district to maintain equal enrollments in the schools.

Not every school district operates precisely according to these rules. Districts may deviate from one or even a few of them. Some districts allow students to choose to attend schools out of their neighborhood. Other districts hire teachers without certification and permit them to be become certified on the job. But these are the exceptions that prove the rule. Across nearly fifteen thousand school districts, education has come to be organized around a consistent set of rules of public administration, emphasizing formal processes, such as moving students through annual grades; objective criteria, such as teacher certification and seniority; and administrative efficiencies, such as assigning students to schools to maintain equal enrollments—to name but a few of the common threads.

These practices exclude a host of plausible alternatives. Students could be allowed to choose their public school, a rule that might cause schools to become concerned with whether they would be chosen—and adjust their performance accordingly. Principals could be given the full resources of the school to allocate among teachers, curriculum, and technology—to maximize school performance. Teachers could be evaluated informally through ongoing observations by principals and compensated on the basis of their work in the classroom and the performance of their students—to improve the link between the quality of teaching and the rewards for it. These examples only scratch the surface of alternative ways of organizing a school system. But they underscore the fundamental sameness of school operations in America, despite nearly fifteen thousand opportunities for public school systems to do things differently.

Many reasons exist for the consistency of school administration across the nation. One is the model of "scientific management" on which school administration (and much public administration) rests. It is a Progressive legacy of efforts to rid the schools of the patronage and corruption that plagued them before formal rules were put into place. Another reason is the political influence of teacher unions, which value the impartiality of a rule-based system. The current system prevents one teacher from being easily judged better than another, protects all teachers from the potential arbitrariness of principals, and ensures that all schools have rights to students and resources regardless how they may be performing. Union strength stems from the ability to enroll as many teachers as possible, whether those teachers are excellent, solid, or mediocre. The rules of the current system protect all teachers without distinction and are therefore in the best interest of unions.

The consistency of district practice also reflects a steady nationalization of education. Since the 1930s and President Franklin Roosevelt's New Deal, the role of local government in the United

States has generally declined and the roles of the federal and state governments have grown.[21] This trend accelerated during the 1960s with the Great Society policies of President Lyndon Johnson, finally peaking during the 1980s with President Ronald Reagan's efforts to limit the growth of the federal government. Education has followed the same course as domestic policy more broadly. During the 1920s the federal government provided less than 1 percent of the funding for K–12 education; the states provided 16.9 percent, and local government provided the lion's share, 82.7 percent.[22] During the 1930s the states moved into education funding in a big way, upping their share of education spending to 30.3 percent while the local share fell to 68 percent. The federal share, though still small, quadrupled, to 1.8 percent. Over the next thirty years these trends continued and then picked up steam, dropping local government into second place as a source of education funds in the 1970s. By that point local government was providing only 43.4 percent of the funds for public schools, the states 46.8 percent, and the federal government 9.8 percent.

Although these trends have reached a plateau, and the federal role has scaled back to about 6.5 percent today, the impacts on American education are clear. As local government lost its dominant control over education spending, local government also lost exclusive say over how schools were run. Federal policies for vocational education, disadvantaged education, special education, bilingual education, and many other particular needs in education required school districts to build consistent administrative systems from state to state. State policies also began to impose order on the schools.

The greatest legacy of state influence is the massive consolidation of local school districts. During the 1930s the then forty-eight states included 117,108 school districts. Most of these districts were so small they included only a single school. Districts this tiny had no

21. On the general trend toward centralization in American government, see John E. Chubb, "Federalism and the Bias for Centralization," in John E. Chubb and Paul E. Peterson, eds., *The New Direction in American Politics* (Washington, D.C.: Brookings, 1985).

22. *Digest of Education Statistics*, table 39, p. 50.

capacity to account for external funds or manage intergovernmental programs. Developing the capacity would have been prohibitively expensive. From the 1930s through the 1960s the states aggressively encouraged or required districts to consolidate with one another. The number of school districts plunged to roughly 80,000 in 1950, 40,000 in 1960, and less than 20,000 in 1970. During the 1990s the number dropped below 15,000 where it stands today.[23] The consolidation process helped shape school districts around a consistent model of governance and administration.

This model includes the practices highlighted above, as well as significant others. In particular, consolidation reinforced an administrative preference for larger schools. Just as certain districts were deemed too small to be efficient, so too were many schools. In 1930 the average public school served 227 students.[24] In 1996, the most recent date for which data are available, the average public school served 515 students. From 1930 to 1996 enrollment in public schools nationally grew from 25.7 million students to 45.6 million, an increase of 78 percent. Over that same period the number of schools serving public school students *declined* by 22 percent. In 1930 the United States had nearly 113,000 public schools; in 1996 it had only 88,585. Whether public schools today are too large is difficult to say. Research suggests that schools can become too large to be successful.

But the interesting point is that the public system made the distinctive and consistent decision to close small schools and replace them with ones that are much larger. Contrast these trends with those in private education. From 1930 to 1996 enrollment in K–12 private schools increased from 2.7 million students to 5.8 million, an increase of 118 percent—or somewhat more in percentage terms than enrollment in public schools. To meet this new demand the number of private schools also increased, from 12,500 schools to 36,095 schools, an increase of 188 percent. The effect of the sharp increase in the number of private schools was to *decrease* the average size of private schools from 211 students to 160 students.

23. Ibid., table 90, p. 97.
24. Ibid., table 3, p. 12, and table 90, p. 97.

Comparing the public and private responses to increased demand is instructive. In 1930 the average size of public and private schools was nearly identical, 227 and 211 students, respectively. Over the ensuing half-century both sectors faced roughly a doubling of demand. The public system, responding to political and administrative pressures, consolidated schools, doubling them in size. The private system, responding to the pressures of parents and the marketplace, increased the number of schools, slightly reducing their average size. The point is not that either of these developments is superior educationally. The point is that the public system moved toward a model of schooling consistent with the pressures for central control and uniformity while the private system gave families something else.

It must be emphasized, before leaving the principle of federalism, that the nearly 15,000 school districts across America are not a completely consistent lot. The New York City public school system serves more than one million students, supports more than a thousand schools, covers a densely populated urban area, and spends roughly $8 billion a year. In contrast, a number of school systems around the country include only a single school but might serve a vast rural expanse. In between lie districts of many shapes and sizes. This immense variation, however, can be simplified.

American school districts are of three basic types: small, medium, and large.[25] The large districts enroll twenty-five thousand or more students. In 1996, 226 districts fell into this category. Although these districts represent only 1.5 percent of districts nationwide, they enroll nearly one-third of all U.S. students, 31.1 percent to be exact. Medium districts enroll 2,500–25,000 students. There are 3,662 medium districts, or about 25 percent of all districts. Medium districts enroll 50.1 percent of American students. Finally, more than ten thousand small school districts, nearly three-fourths of them all, enroll less than 2,500 students and serve about 19 percent of students nationwide.

These categories are useful for refining the picture of how the

25. The data below can be found in ibid., table 91, p. 97.

education system works. Although all public school systems tend to follow the same administrative model, districts vary in several notable ways. Problems of bureaucracy are undoubtedly linked to district size. The large school systems, only 1 percent of all districts but serving a third of kids nationwide, are the ones where bureaucracy and politics are most likely to interfere with school performance in significant ways. These are the districts where rules governing who can do what, where, when, and how most easily impede efforts to manage schools with judgment, discretion, cooperation, and a focus on results. In sharp contrast are the more than ten thousand small districts. These systems operate according to the same rules as other public school systems except they can barely afford the essential administrative operation that they need. Bureaucracy is not the problem in these systems; the problem is that the system struggles to provide schools meaningful support.

In between these extremes are the medium systems, trying to strike a balance between supporting the schools with valuable services such as professional development, assessment, and technology and not burdening the schools with bureaucracy. Although medium districts can be found throughout the country, they tend to predominate in suburban areas. If suburban districts appear to be where American schools are working, part of the reason is that suburbia is where school systems are most often of a size that is politically and administratively manageable. Large districts tend to be associated with major urban areas. These districts are therefore burdened not only with the enormous educational challenges of poverty and despair but by the tensions and rigidities of large bureaucracies. Finally, America's rural areas are places where school performance is generally not strong and where districts are often small and ill equipped to provide schools substantial support.

This variation should not obscure the fundamental shortcomings of federalism as a source of educational innovation and improvement. Although the system is hardly a monolith, its evolution has been in the direction of structural uniformity. The differences that do exist offer little in the way of fundamental change. The differences do little for the urban and rural schools that need improvement the most.

## Professionalism

The concept of professionalism, like the concepts of local control and federalism, is a powerful symbol in American education. Americans value the public education system because it is run and served by trusted and dedicated professionals. This appreciation begins with teachers. Teachers are among the most esteemed group of workers in America, ranked by the public well ahead of business people, politicians, and other civil servants.[26] During the 1996 presidential race, the Republican candidate, Senator Robert Dole, discovered just how highly teachers are regarded by the general public. In an effort to build support for his school choice policies, Dole attacked teacher unions, which oppose school choice. The public interpreted the attack as a criticism of teachers and reacted very negatively. Dole quickly abandoned the strategy. Teachers are surely esteemed for many reasons, not the least of which are personal. Adults know teachers through their childhood memories and through the experiences of their own children, perspectives that tend to be positive.

Teachers are also respected because of careful efforts by their unions to cultivate the image of professionalism. The largest national teacher union, the National Education Association, resisted for many years even calling itself a union, preferring the more honored label of professional association.[27] Since the days of the Progressives, education has been singled out as a special kind of public service. It is typically separated from the rest of local government and from partisan politics. Employment in education requires special certification, outside the routine civil service. Teachers often hold advanced degrees. The people that run the schools, principals

26. A consistent result in annual Gallup poll of trust in American institutions and professions.
27. Unions, as opposed to teachers, are not well regarded by the public. In a Gallup poll in 1996 the public ranked unions twenty-second out of twenty-seven organizations in the levels of confidence they inspire. *Digest*, table 29, p. 33.

and superintendents, are highly educated and specially trained, often holding doctorates. These many credentials send the message that public education is not delivered like other public services, by politicians and bureaucrats. Education is provided by skilled professionals, acting in the best interests of the children they are entrusted to serve.

Professionalism is more than a powerful symbol of what is good about public education. Professionalism is also an important operating principle for the system. Teaching and learning are processes that are difficult to program. Different students learn in different ways. The teacher's job is to be skilled in a range of instructional strategies and to use whatever strategies are necessary to help every student learn. Students do not learn by simply reading a text or listening to a lecture or engaging in any other single learning activity. Students need a mix of activities, and different students may need different mixtures. Teachers must be trained and equipped and then trusted to make the many instructional decisions necessary for every child to learn. Teachers, in other words, must be trained to work as professionals, using their knowledge and experience to make the best decisions for students.

In certain ways the education system has evolved as a professional system. Virtually all teachers, principals, superintendents, and other district officials have been certified for their jobs by the state. Public educators increasingly hold advanced degrees. In 1996, more than 56 percent of all teachers in public education held a master's degree or higher; in 1971 only 28 percent were so well educated.[28] Among principals, 75 percent currently hold a master's or doctorate; the rest have earned a specialist certificate.[29] During the last thirty years, as the public schools have been subjected to steady pressure to improve, educators have at least acquired the credentials to succeed. Fundamentally, the system respects this professional preparation. Teachers are largely free of prescriptive requirements governing how they must teach. From classroom to classroom in a typical school, teachers teach in a

28. Ibid., table 70, p. 80
29. Ibid., table 88, p. 95.

variety of ways, not necessarily differentiated by student needs but by the philosophy or experience of the teacher. Some classes may involve lots of hands-on activities, others mostly lecture. Some teachers may have students working in cooperative groups, others working alone and sitting in traditional rows. Some teachers may be working with district textbooks, others using their own materials. The system treats teachers as professionals in this vital part of their work.

But the system falls far short of functioning as a professional system ought. Most important, the system offers little accountability. A professional system has two hallmarks, autonomy and accountability. Professionals are given tasks when the requirements of doing them well dictate the exercise of ample discretion. The freedom to exercise discretion—autonomy—is then checked by the system with provisions for accountability. These provisions generally focus on the results of the tasks, not on how the tasks themselves are carried out. A professional model of education would recognize that teachers and schools need to decide how best to educate each student. The system would not monitor or particularly care how each school provided education; the system would care about and monitor what students learn.

American education has not done a good job of providing accountability—or autonomy. The system has only recently begun holding schools accountable for results, for what students learn. Until the late 1990s most states and local school systems did not have academic standards; they simply did not specify in any detail what students needed to know or be able to do to be considered well educated. Typical requirements specified what students had to take or pass to graduate from high school or be promoted. But requirements such as "three years of mathematics," for example, allowed students with a wide range of skills, from poor to excellent, to earn high school diplomas. By 2000, every state but Iowa had developed academic standards.[30] Yet these new standards, often hailed as triumphs of education reform, leave much to be desired. The standards, products of committees and political com-

30. Education Week, *Quality Counts 2000*, pp. 62–63.

promise, are often too vague about what students must master to
be of much use. According to one recent rating of the standards, an
evaluation of the potential for the standards to shape education,
only nine states had standards that deserved a grade of A or B.[31]

Of course, standards must also be enforced if they are to affect
schools. Standards must be backed with assessments of what students have learned. The assessments must be backed with consequences—for example, rewards for schools that do well or support
or sanctions for schools that do poorly—if schools are to take the
assessments seriously. At last count, twenty-one states had strong
systems of assessment and consequences.[32] Unfortunately, most of
those systems were not linked to strong academic standards. Most
states carrying out assessments with consequences were adminis-
tering standardized tests, bought "off the shelf," that were not
linked to their academic standards. In these states, schools are trying to get students to pass tests that do not measure most of what
states expect students to know and be able to do. Only five states
have what can be considered strong academic accountability
systems, with both clear academic standards and assessments
designed to measure those standards.[33] Fully forty-five state education systems do not have academic accountability fully in place.

Autonomy is also a significant weakness. Despite the rhetoric of
professionalism that surrounds public schools, the schools display
many of the classic characteristics of bureaucracy. Schools deliver
many specific educational programs—for example, special education, bilingual education, education for the disadvantaged, to
name only the largest—that come with detailed rules and regulations and require many administrators to carry out. Collective bargaining has brought to schools a large number of work rules
protecting teachers from assignments that teachers consider unfair
or excessive. The rules also prescribe how teachers are to be evalu-

31. Finn and Petrilli, eds., *The State of State Standards*, p. 1.
32. Education Week, *Quality Counts 2000*, pp. 62–63.
33. The states with the strongest accountability systems are Alabama, California, North Carolina, South Carolina, and Texas, as described in Finn and
Petrilli, eds., p. 3.

ated, terminated, transferred, and compensated. Whatever the merits of these rules, they also limit the ability of principals to manage schools creatively and flexibly. If, for example, a principal wants to build a team of teachers who share a common instructional philosophy or reward teachers for student achievement or ask teachers to spend more time with parents, she or he will often find obstacles in the teacher contract. Of course, the system does not really expect principals to succeed by being innovative. The system gives principals almost no financial discretion. The principal is expected less to lead the school in creative directions than to manage the school according to the rules set out by the local board and the state. The only leader in the public system expected truly to lead is the superintendent. Yet superintendents are often so limited by the rules of the established system that they cannot lead and, in difficult urban systems, are fired every two years.

The signs of bureaucracy are not only in the rules. School organization is increasingly bureaucratic, relying less on teachers and more on other specialized players, some professional and others not, to provide education. In 1996, only 52.1 percent of all local school district employees were teachers. In 1950, 70.1 percent were teachers.[34] The change is not due mostly to the hiring of lots of central office administrators. Most of the change can be attributed to "support staff"—paraprofessionals, school-site administrators, and a small percentage of other professionals such as social workers and counselors who assist teachers at the school. These people are not generally "pushing paper," as the bureaucratic stereotype suggests; they are delivering specific support services as prescribed in various education programs. These movements toward a less teacher-centered and classically professional model of education and a more prescriptive and bureaucratic model are reflected in school district spending. In 1996, 62 percent of the spending in local school districts went for instruction, including teacher salaries and benefits and instructional supplies. Administration, in the district office and in the schools,

34. *Digest*, table 83, p. 90.

consumed 15 percent, or nearly a fourth of what schools spend on instruction.[35] This is a high rate of administrative overhead for a system that prides itself on its respect for professionalism.

## AN ALTERNATIVE SYSTEM

The inefficiencies, lack of innovation, weak accountability for results, slow pace of improvement, and bias toward the status quo that characterize the current system are prices that are paid for the way the United States has historically chosen to govern and run its schools. There are other ways the country could provide free and universal public education, accountable to democratic authorities. There are other ways that would not subject the schools to the levels and kinds of political and bureaucratic stresses found in the education system today. These other ways would change the fundamental operating assumptions of the current system. The new system would be subject less to the principles of politics and more to the principles of the market.

How might a market-based system of public education work? Very briefly—for other chapters will address this in depth—market control would begin by transferring the authority to operate schools from local school boards exclusively to other providers, approved by democratic authorities. New providers would be funded not by administrative convenience but by enrollment. New providers would need to enroll students to remain in business, pressure that should encourage schools to do whatever is necessary as effectively as possible to attract and maintain students.

Theoretically, this pressure would help schools in a marketplace avoid some of the core problems encountered by schools in the political arena. Schools would better reflect the interests of parents—as opposed to the groups favored by the political process—because parents in a marketplace are empowered to "vote with their feet." This change would in effect restore some of the "local control" that schools have lost over recent years. Schools free from

35. "Administration" includes "instructional services," "general administration," "school administration," and "other support services." Ibid., table 162, p. 174.

the powerful influences of groups wedded to the systemic status quo would be able to change important elements of the system to enhance school performance. Schools could, for example, reform accountability and compensation systems, establishing systems based rigorously on the achievement of results desired by parents, such as academic achievement. Under a market-based system, schools would have strong incentives to innovate themselves, as opposed to waiting for their political or bureaucratic authorities to mandate innovation. Schools would almost certainly spend fewer resources on bureaucracy than the current system spends. Schools would be free to retain leadership long enough to carry out major reforms and to see them to a successful conclusion—unlike in the uncertain political arena where leaders and reforms constantly come and go. Schools would have the ability to allocate resources themselves to meet efficiently the demands of parents and of school success.

Of course, there are no guarantees that markets will yield these benefits. Theoretically there are many ways for markets to fail. Parents might be poorly informed and make poor choices of schools, providing less than ideal pressure for schools to deliver quality. Parents from different socioeconomic backgrounds might make choices of different quality, exacerbating inequality in schools. Schools might not come easily into the marketplace, leaving parents to vie for limited spaces in a small number of decent schools. Schools might deceive parents about their academic quality with advertising. The list goes on. The government could take measures, however, to ensure that the education market works equitably as well as efficiently. The government could provide parents information about schools—school report cards—to help ensure informed choices. Disadvantaged families could be given advantages in the choice process—for example, seats reserved in every school, lotteries to determine school admissions, larger private vouchers.

For years, theory was the major basis for debating the benefits of an educational marketplace. The only empirical evidence of market forces came from private schools or from the residential choices that parents make based on the quality of public schools.

The evidence from these sources arguably supports experimentation with markets for public education.[36] Better evidence of the
workings of market forces in public education now comes from
charter schools, private scholarships, public vouchers for private
schools, and for-profit schools. The evidence from these initiatives
is steadily mounting and should be followed closely. Soon the debate about the merits of markets should not have to rest on specu-
lation and tradition alone.

This is critical, for the existing system of education, despite its
fundamental strengths and historical accomplishments, is a system
with vital weaknesses. The principles on which it is based—local
democratic control, federalism, and professionalism—are fulfilled
more in rhetoric than in reality today. The system itself does not
work consistently in the best interest of schools. The country could
strengthen public education by maintaining what is best about that
system. Democratic control, universal access, full funding at taxpayer expense, high academic standards, tough accountability:
these should be the hallmarks of public education, the principles
on which a stronger system of public education in the future could
rest. The delivery of public education could then be turned over to
a new system, one resting on market principles: choice for parents,
healthy competition among schools, opportunities for new and
different kinds of providers, as well as local boards of education,
with the government overseeing and informing the market's operation. A mixed system of democracy and markets may be the best
system for education, just as it is the best system in so many areas
of American commerce and life.

36. On the effects of choice, see Chubb and Moe, *Politics, Markets, and
America's Schools;* Rasell and Rothstein, *School Choice;* and Peterson and Hassel, *Learning from School Choice.*

# CHAPTER 3

# Achievement in American Schools

*Herbert J. Walberg*

Yield, yield per acre, and crop quality tell agronomists and farmers much about results. Reduction of mortality and morbidity chiefly concern epidemiologists and physicians. Similarly, learning or increases in achievement are or should be the chief aims of educators. Achievement here means the knowledge and skills students learn in the usual school subjects, particularly as measured on standardized multiple-choice, essay, and other examinations.

Parents, legislators, and other educational consumers are concerned with other matters as well, but their views of a school's desirability are usually based substantially on how well they think children learn. Parents know that test scores will often be among the chief determinants of success in gaining admission to selective universities. Firms employ examinations to screen for knowledgeable and skilled workers. Citizens want well-educated young people who contribute to the economy and society and who can competently vote and serve on juries.

Students should be able to read, write, calculate, and reason skillfully; they should possess deep and wide knowledge of standard subject matter. So we need to measure achievement to assess how well students perform and how well schools are preparing them for subsequent education, careers, citizenship, and other aspects of their future lives.

Assessing achievement and where American students stand are big tasks. Should we expect schools to attain higher levels of achievement? Or should we consider how much they progress in a given year? Since poverty and related factors can limit children's learning, how can we compare schools in different communities that contain differing percentages of poor and rich parents?

This chapter answers these and related questions. It shows that standardized tests provide an effective, efficient means for assessing students and schools. For this reason, nations, states, and school districts are turning to such tests to compare schools and evaluate their progress.

Since policymakers, parents, and citizens are keenly interested in achievement, this chapter shows how U.S. students' progress compares with that in other countries and how their achievement levels have changed for roughly the past quarter-century. In addition, we should consider the efficiency of schools in raising achievement in relation to how much they spend and to changing levels of students' abilities.

Unfortunately, as shown below, achievement has remained generally stagnant with occasional, short, and apparently random up-and-down trends despite steadily and substantially rising expenditures and greater levels of potential student abilities. Findings from international achievement surveys, moreover, show that American students compare unfavorably with those in other economically advanced countries in how much they learn in school, despite the fact that American schools expend more money on students than do schools in most other countries. The problem is not attributable to lower school graduation rates in other countries. The United States, once prideful of high school graduation rates, has fallen behind the average graduation rate of affluent countries.

## ACHIEVEMENT STAGNATION IN THE UNITED STATES

A review of how U.S. test scores have been changing reveals little progress in solving the achievement problem. Reading scores, for example, show no upward trend 1984 through 1996 (see chart 1). Similar to the trends in chart 1, compilations of trends in various subjects and grade levels of children on National Assessment of

# CHART 1. READING SCORES OF 17-, 13-, and 9-YEAR-OLDS

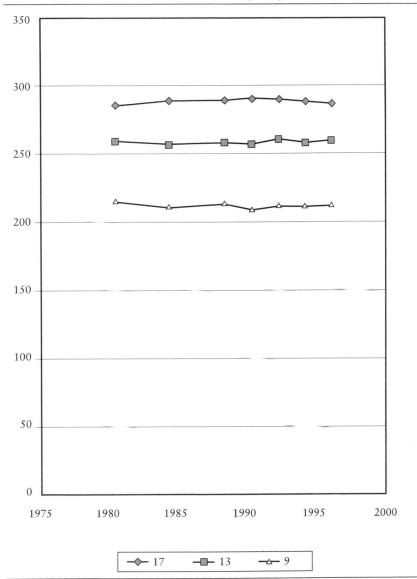

SOURCE: U.S. Department of Education, *Digest of Education Statistics,* 1998, p. 129.

Education Progress scores show the same essentially flat trends. Although a small upward trend may detected for some years and grade levels, small downward trends may be found for others.[1]

In mathematics from 1988 through 1996 for students in schools with high and low concentrations of poverty, achievement scores for both groups of schools has been stagnant for the whole time period (see chart 2).[2] During this period, partly in response to *A Nation at Risk* and other alarming reports, the schools enacted many varied reforms. Yet achievement levels failed to rise. In private sector industries, we expect to see steady improvements and even breakthroughs attributable to competition, improving technology, and other innovations. Quality should rise while costs decline. Why haven't the schools similarly improved?

## Rising Expenditures on K–12 Schools

Rising expenditures on public schools have long failed to increase achievement. The expenditures on public schools have risen substantially and steadily during the period from 1920 through 1997 (see chart 3). They have continued to rise in the recent period when achievement scores for random samples of students have become available and show worrisome generally flat trends of low scores with fitful blips.[3]

### ACHIEVEMENT GAPS

Many studies show that children in poverty often achieve less in school than children in middle-class families. For the past quarter-

1. Source: U.S. Department of Education, *Digest of Education Statistics 1998* (Washington, DC.: Department of Education, 1999), p. 129. See also Stedman's extensive compilations showing similar test score trends discussed in a subsequent section of this chapter (see note 27).

2. The time period chosen was intended to measure results of changes in Title I policy during the period. Office of Planning and Evaluation Service, *Promising Results, Continuing Challenges: The Final Report of the National Assessment of Title I* (Washington, D.C.: U.S. Department of Education Office of the Under Secretary, 1999)

3. Source: U.S. Department of Education, *Digest of Education Statistics, 1998* (Washington, DC.: Department of Education, 1999), p. 35.

CHART 2. TRENDS IN MATH PERFORMANCE AMONG 9-YEAR-OLD
PUBLIC SCHOOL STUDENTS IN LOW- AND HIGH-POVERTY SCHOOLS

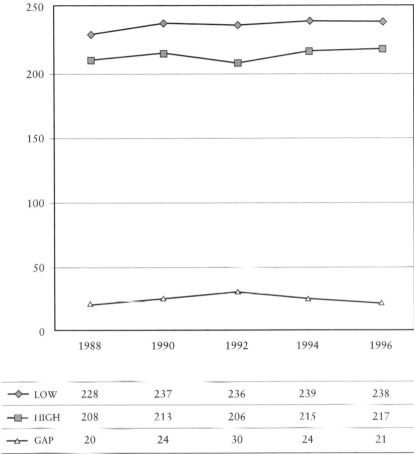

|         | 1988 | 1990 | 1992 | 1994 | 1996 |
|---------|------|------|------|------|------|
| ◆ LOW   | 228  | 237  | 236  | 239  | 238  |
| ■ HIGH  | 208  | 213  | 206  | 215  | 217  |
| △ GAP   | 20   | 24   | 30   | 24   | 21   |

SOURCE: U.S. Department of Education, 1999, p. 6. The scale ranges from 0 to 500; high poverty
schools had 76–100 percent students eligible for free lunch, low-poverty 0–25 percent. *Digest of Education
Statistics*, 1998

century, the federal government has concentrated about $130 bil-
lion on Title 1/Chapter I programs on reducing the gap between
children in poverty and other children. Despite expenditures at a
current rate of about $8 billion, the gap between schools with high
concentrations of children in poverty and other schools has remained the same (see chart 2). The huge expenditures appear to
have done little good in reducing the gap.

# CHART 3. TOTAL PER PUPIL EXPENDITURES IN PUBLIC ELEMENTARY AND SECONDARY SCHOOLS, 1919 TO 1998 IN CONSTANT 1997–98 DOLLARS

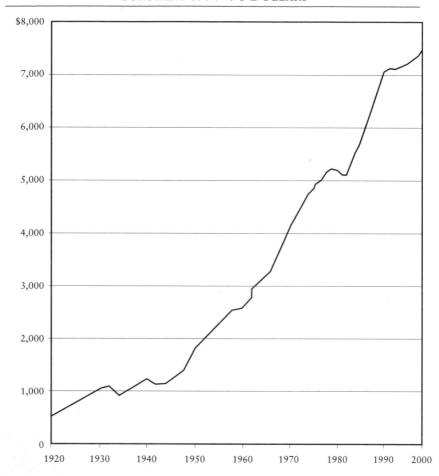

SOURCE: U.S. Department of Education, 1999, p. 35.

## The Black and Hispanic Gaps in Achievement

Since the early 1970s, the National Assessment of Educational Progress (NAEP) and other groups have reported that on average black and Hispanic students have persistently and substantially scored below white students. For any given subject or group, the various trends are flat, encouraging, or discouraging; and no consistent overall trend since 1970 emerges from the many comparisons that have been made. In reading, for example, NAEP data reveal that black seventeen-year-olds had improved to the point that their scores were equal to white thirteen-year-olds by 1990, but there were no further improvements during the decade of the 1990s.[4] The patterns for different subjects and groups are similarly complex and cannot be easily summarized, but scholars agree that the differences among groups are large and enduring.

Scholars have expended much more effort in trying to explain the black gap than the Hispanic gap, but a consensus is yet to emerge. The anthropologist John Ogbu, for example, argued that the gap is ultimately attributable to the forced immigration and slavery of African Americans' ancestors.[5] Others argue that historically deficient education systems in the deep South and inferior schools for rural blacks in southern states harmed achievement, which generation after generation has yet to recover, even after blacks migrated to big industrial cities in the North during the World War I and II years.

In *Losing the Race: Self-Sabotage in Black America*,[6] University of California at Berkeley faculty member John McWhorter reviews some of these possibilities but concludes that black "victimology" is today's primary reason that blacks achieve less than whites. In his view as a black faculty observer at the university, a cult of

4. Jay R. Campbell, Catherine M. Hombo, and John Mazzeo, *NAEP 1999 Trends in Academic Progress* (Washington, D.C.: National Center for Education Statistics, 2000).

5. See, for example, "Variability in Minority School Performance: A Problem in Search of an Explanation," *Anthropology and Education Quarterly* 18, no. 4 (1987): 312–34.

6. New York: Free Press, 2000.

victimology transforms a problem to be solved into a persistent black identity of anti-intellectualism, separatism, and cultural disconnect from learning. Recent letters to the editor of *Wilson Quarterly*, however, have sharply disputed his view.[7]

Large-scale surveys suggest to me that the achievement gap for both blacks and Hispanics may be substantially attributable to poverty and the inefficiency of large-city school systems where minority groups are concentrated.[8] Although there are more poor whites than poor blacks and poor Hispanics, the poverty *rates* among these minority groups are higher. Sociologists have shown that the differences among whites and minority students of the same socioeconomic status (SES) are relatively small,[9] which supports this explanation.

In addition, socioeconomically related differences in achievement-stimulating child-rearing patterns between middle-class parents and those in poverty are huge. In a rare and careful observational study, psychologists found that higher SES parents spent more minutes per hour interacting with their children and spoke to them more frequently. On average, higher SES parents spoke about two thousand words an hour to their children; welfare parents, only about 500. By age four,

> An average child in a professional family would have accumulated experience with almost 45 million words, an average child in a working-class family would have accumulated experience with 26 million words, and an average child in a welfare family with 13 million words.[10]

Higher SES parents, moreover, used

> more different words, more multi-clause sentences, more past and future verb tenses, more declaratives, and more questions of all kinds.

    7. Autumn 2000, pp. 6–7
    8. Herbert J. Walberg and Herbert J. Walberg III, "Losing Local Control, " *Educational Researcher*, June/July 1994, 13 (8), 23–29.
    9. For a recent collection of sociological articles on this complex subject, see Christopher Jencks and Meredith Phillips, editors, *The Black-White Test Score Gap* (Washington, D.C.: Brookings Institution, 1998).
    10. Betty Hart and Todd R. Risley, *Meaningful Differences in the Everyday Experience of Young American Children* (Baltimore, Md.: Paul Brooks Publishing, 1995), p. 198.

The professional parents also gave their children more affirmative feedback and responded to them more often each hour they were together.[11]

The researchers estimated that, by age four, professional parents encouraged their children with positive feedback 750,000 times, about six times as often as did welfare parents. The welfare parents, on the other hand, had discouraged their children with negative feedback about 275,000 times, about two and a half times the amount employed by professional parents.[12] Such parenting behaviors predicted about 60 percent of the variation in vocabulary growth and use of three-year-olds. Vocabulary is the most important single predictor of school success.

A second reason for the minority gaps is inefficiency of big-city school systems that have employed ineffective federal programs such as Title 1/Chapter 1 and bilingual education. Because of their size and greater accountability to federal and state governments than to local citizens and parents, moreover, big-city systems appear relatively indifferent to students and parents. They have gained a well-known and often deserved image of failure. Such big-city achievement gaps, apparent indifference, and inefficiency help explain minority parents' strong desire to choose their children's schools including those in the parochial and independent sectors.

*Achievement Stagnates Despite Children's Rising Abilities*

Long before the era when achievement stagnation was documented, students' *abilities* rose massively and steadily, and they continue to rise. From 1918 through 1995, school children's average IQ steadily rose 25 points.[13] This steep rise put the typical

11. Ibid., pp. 123–24.
12. Ibid., p. 200.
13. James R. Flynn, "IQ Gains over Time," in Ulric Neisser, ed., *The Rising Curve: Long-Term Gains in IQ and Related Measures* (Washington, D.C.: American Psychological Association, 1998), p. 37, figure 2. Test makers renormed IQ tests to make them more difficult over the period to reset them to a population average of 100. Flynn discounted these renormings and adjusted the average IQ estimates to make them comparable throughout the period for which scores are

1995 child at the 95th percentile of the 1918 distribution. These changes plus rising expenditures, better programs, and more skilled teaching should have led to ever-higher levels of academic learning. But, as shown in previous sections, this isn't so. Achievement stagnated.

## INTERNATIONAL COMPARISONS OF ACHIEVEMENT

The 1983 report to the U.S. secretary of education, *A Nation at Risk*,[14] first alerted policymakers and citizens that U.S. students achieve poorly compared to those in other economically advanced countries. Since then, as discussed below, more definitive international surveys have shown that the situation is even graver than originally thought. Not only do American students achieve poorly but they fall further behind the longer they are in school.

### Value-Added Achievement Comparisons

The challenge in comparing schools is like comparing runners who begin a race from different starting points. To know runners' speeds or rates, we would need to measure how far they run in a given time period. Similarly, to compare the effectiveness of schools, we need to ask how much their students improve in achievement over a given time period, which is what is meant by "value-added gains." Children come to one school, for example, already reading, whereas children in another school are far less well prepared. To have the full picture, of course, we should know their gains as well as their scores at the end of any given grade. The gains, however, are particularly important for assessing schools because they are more fully attributable to the school's effectiveness in educating students than are their final achievement levels, which may have been largely determined by their family socioeco-

---

available. Now, as widely reported in psychological journals, the tendency for intelligence test scores to rise is called the "Flynn effect."

14. The National Commission for Excellence in Education (Washington, D.C.: U.S. Department of Education, 1983).

nomic status, child-rearing conditions in the home, and other external factors, especially those that influence the children's development before they start school.

Because of widespread interest in such comparisons throughout the world, the Paris-based Organization for Economic Cooperation and Development (OECD) began comprehensive reporting of such value-added improvements for economically advanced countries in Asia, Europe, and North America.[15] As an example, chart 4 shows the mathematics value-added achievement gains made by students in twenty-four countries from the fourth to the eighth grade.[16] Of the countries surveyed, the United States made the smallest gain.

Unfortunately, this result for U.S. schools is typical of the other comparisons of presently available data. In reading, science, and mathematics through eighth grade, U.S. schools ranked last in four of five comparisons of achievement progress. In the fifth case, they ranked second to last. Between eighth grade and the final year of secondary education, U.S. schools slipped further behind those in other countries. Because they made the least progress, U.S. secondary schools recently ranked last in mathematics attainment and second to last in science, a result that does not accord well with the National Education Goals Panel objective set about a decade ago that American students will be first in the world in mathematics and science.[17] Actually they are last or near last among students in other OECD countries.

Policymakers commission international surveys of achievement

15. As of 1998, all recent value-added comparisons are in my report for the Thomas B. Fordham Foundation, *Spending More while Learning Less* (Washington, D.C.: Thomas B. Fordham Foundation, July 1998). The original data may be found in the periodic reports of the Organization for Economic Cooperation and Development's *Education at a Glance* (Paris: OECD, 1996, 1997, 1998, and 1999). The charts in this chapter illustrating the country comparisons are based on information in the 1997 report, pages 101 and 306.

16. Strictly speaking, these scores are the differences in random samples of students in fourth and eighth grade at a single point in time.

17. For the accomplishment or nonaccomplishment of various national goals, see reports of the panel such as *The National Educational Goals Report: Building a Nation of Learners.* (Washington, D.C.: U.S. Government Printing Office, 1998).

CHART 4. MEAN DIFFERENCE IN MATHEMATICS ACHIEVEMENT
SCORES BETWEEN FOURTH AND EIGHTH GRADERS IN
VARIOUS COUNTRIES

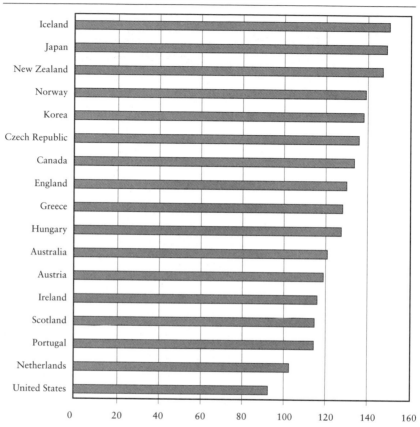

SOURCE: Walberg, 1998, p. 8.

in reading, mathematics, and science because these subjects are
more internationally comparable than, say, civics, history, geography, and literature. Schools in various countries emphasize different aspects of these subjects, which would make the achievement
scores less comparable than the subjects most often compared.
Many policymakers, moreover, believe that mathematics, reading,
and science are particularly important for preparedness for higher
education and the workforce—reading because verbal mastery is

an essential skill in nearly all subjects and economic and social life, mathematics and science because they indicate readiness for further study in demanding fields such as engineering and medicine as well as work in high-tech, fast-growing, competitive sectors of modern economies.

## Graduation and Completion Rates

When international achievement surveys began some thirty-five years ago, U.S. policymakers aimed to graduate all students from secondary school. In fact, greater percentages of U.S. students then graduated from secondary school than those from other economically advanced countries. Because greater percentages of U.S. students remained in school, they were included in the surveys, whereas more students comparable in age in other countries had dropped out, leaving a comparative elite. Thus, it might have been argued that poor American school achievement at the end of secondary school was partly excusable years ago because a less selective American group was being compared with more selective groups in other countries.[18]

In the meantime, however, European and other OECD countries made serious and successful efforts to keep more students in secondary school and graduate them. On average, schools in these countries now succeed better than do U.S. schools. The most recent OECD comparison shows that the United States ranks seventeenth among twenty-three OECD countries in the graduation rates (percentages of secondary school graduates to the total popu-

18. Perhaps the early results were not excusable because the twelfth grade comparisons were somewhat questionable in that they were based on American and other students taking college preparatory mathematics. The U.S. students seemed to be a similarly select group of students to those elsewhere. Some comparisons, moreover, were made of only the top 10 percent of students. Even in these early comparisons, our "best and brightest" still did not do well. In any case, as explained above, recent comparisons of a somewhat more select group of American students with less select groups in other countries show that American students do worst or near worst in secondary school and have fallen furthest behind during the school years.

lation at the typical age of graduation).[19] The average percentages of students aged 14–17 and 18–19 enrolled in education were also higher in OECD countries than in the United States.[20]

Thus, U.S. schools have fallen behind the graduation and enrollment rates of other economically advanced countries. This trend shows that the poor achievement progress of U.S. schools isn't attributable to educating a less selective group of students.

### Productivity: Achievement in Relation to Expenditures

In considering country comparisons of achievement, it is important to know how much they spend on each student. Schools should not only be effective but efficient or productive given the amounts of money they spend. The OECD regularly reports per student expenditures on primary and secondary schools.[21] Among twenty-two countries, U.S. expenditures on primary schools[22] were third highest after Switzerland and Austria (see chart 5). They were also third highest for secondary schools. Thus, U.S. per student expenditures were among the highest, yet our achievement progress was generally worst.

For a country that leads the world in the competitiveness and productivity of many old and new industries, it is shocking that

19. *Education at a Glance* (Paris: OECD), 2000, p. 147. The U.S. percentage of 74 is lower than the average of 79. The average, however, includes several less affluent, recent entrants into the OECD such as Mexico, Portugal, Spain, and Turkey with graduation rates as low as 30 percent.

20. Organization for Economic Cooperation and Development, *Education Policy Analysis* (Paris: OECD, 1997), pp. 14 and 98. OECD, *Education Policy Analysis*, 1998, p. 75.

21. See my previously footnoted report *Spending More while Learning Less* or recent editions of the OECD's *Education at a Glance*. The figures reported are OECD adjusted for purchasing power parity. See Eric Hanushek's chapter in this volume for a detailed analysis of expenditures.

22. In writing on comparative education, the term *primary* usually refers to the first school, aside from preschool, that children usually attend, which is in many countries the first six years of schooling. This roughly corresponds to what Americans often call grade schools or elementary schools, although there are many U.S. variations such as grades 1–6, 1–5, and the more traditional 1–8. Secondary schools are the second schools students attend, which in the United States are usually referred to as high schools, junior high schools, or middle schools.

CHART 5. EXPENDITURE PER STUDENT FOR PRIMARY EDUCATION
IN PUBLIC AND PRIVATE INSTITUTIONS

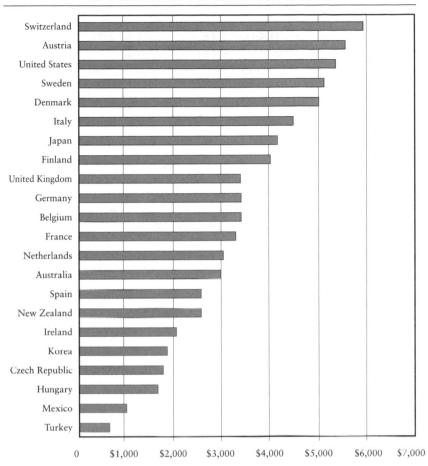

SOURCE: Walberg, 1998, p. 11.

American schools are so inefficient. Among the consequences is that schools fail to pull their weight in improving the quality of American life. Their graduates are less literate, less skillful, less informed as citizens, voters, and workers than they should be. Because they constitute a large sector of the economy, schools are a drag on American progress and wastefully consume resources. Citizens are not receiving value for their tax dollars. In such fields as science, mathematics, engineering, computer science, nursing, and medicine, we must import better-prepared, well-educated workers from other countries, particularly South and East Asia.[23]

## WHY THE DEFENDERS OF THE STATUS QUO ARE WRONG

Scholars originally uncovered the substantial U.S. achievement gap about three decades ago. As discussed above, recent research has confirmed the early findings and suggests that American achievement problems are actually worse than long thought. Despite the huge amount of evidence, three writers have dismissed the validity of the unrelenting findings. Gerald Bracey[24] often takes this view in his monthly column for *Phi Delta Kappan*, a widely circulated education journal. David C. Berliner and Bruce J. Biddle wrote *The Manufactured Crisis: Myths, Fraud, and the Attack on America's Public Schools*.[25]

### *The Positions of the Critics*

Because they have achieved some prominence, these writers deserve to be answered with respect to how their work has been published and their arguments. Gerald Bracey publishes much of his criticism of the achievement surveys in columns and annual education reports in the journal of Phi Delta Kappa, a society with the expressed purpose of promoting and defending public education. Indeed, the title of Bracey's annual reports contains the words "Public Education."[26] Neither his work nor Berliner and

23. Immigration is to be celebrated. We are of course a nation of immigrants and their descendants, and we still benefit much from new arrivals. That does not mean, however, that that American students cannot or should not have to learn or that schools should be excused for poor results.

24. See, for example, "The 10th Bracey Report on the Condition of Public Education," *Phi Delta Kappan*, October 2000, pp. 133–144. In this and other reports, Bracey describes how he has long called reporters to urge on them his dismissal of education research findings critical of public schools.

25. New York: Perseus Press, 1996.

26. Bracey doesn't hesitate to employ ad hominem argumentation. He, for example, has been allowed to give "Rotten Apple Awards" to presidents from both political parties, reporters from nationally circulated newspapers, and prominent scholars for criticizing education. Because Bracey is given the first, last, and regular word in the journal, few people correct his faulty arguments.

Biddle's book has gone through scholarly peer reviewing as would be required in journal publication in education, psychology, and the social sciences.

On the other hand, the data in reports summarized above on achievement changes in the United States over roughly the last thirty years are collected by the Educational Testing Service and similar agencies for the U.S. Department of Education. The plans for data collection and reporting undergo intense scholarly and government scrutiny. The national press covers the reports in detail, often on the front page of such respected papers as the *New York Times* and the *Wall Street Journal*.

The international comparisons come from perhaps the most widely respected international statistical data agency in the world, the Organization for Economic Cooperation and Development, of which about thirty advanced countries in Asia, Western Europe, and North America are voluntary members who seek to learn from one another through cooperative data collection and analysis how to improve the education, medical, industrial, tax, and other systems.

Could or would the many scholars, thirty national governments, and such premiere national and international agencies "manufacture" fraudulent data just to please the alleged nefarious conspirators who seek to make U.S. schools look unjustifiably bad? Would this not result in congressional hearings, exposés, and rolling heads of education malefactors?

## The Substance of the Critics' Arguments

In five refereed publications of the twenty thousand-member American Educational Research Association and in a distinguished publication series of one of the oldest and most prestigious think tanks, the Brookings Institution, Lawrence C. Stedman [27] evalu-

27. "International Achievement Differences: An Assessment of a New Perspective," *Educational Researcher* 26, no. 3 (1997): 4–15; "Incomplete Explanations: The Case of U.S. Performance in the International Assessments of Education," *Educational Researcher* 23, no. 7 (1994): 24–32; "An Assessment of the Contemporary Debate over U.S. Achievement," in D. Ravitch, ed., *Brookings*

ated the contentions of Bracey, Berliner, and Biddle (BBB) that American education is unfairly or even conspiratorially portrayed by the NAEP and international achievement surveys. His many detailed examples showing they are wrong cannot be described here, but several of Stedman's major points are well worth summarizing.

The main flaw in BBB's writings, as Stedman points out, is selective evidence that suits their defense of the status quo for public schools. Actual evidence is crucial to their argument; but, instead of reviewing all of it, they select a few data points for a few years in a few subjects. They fail to point out, for example, that NAEP high school science scores remain lower than they were in 1969. BBB concentrate, moreover, mostly on trends, which they say, correctly, are fairly stable, but they ignore the levels of achievement, which are mostly low, especially the longer American students are in school.

As Stedman further points out, BBB correctly criticized the myth of a very recent general achievement decline, but they left out the sharp 1970s decline on many high school tests and ignored the contradictory evidence of the 1980s. BBB claimed that the current generation of students outperforms prior ones on "virtually all" commercial standardized achievement tests—a contention refuted by major reviews of historical trends on such tests, including Stedman's.

BBB dwelt on Scholastic Aptitude Test comparisons, but these are nearly useless for comparing achievement scores across time. The SAT, as its name implied, is an aptitude test used for college selection, not an achievement test for measuring student progress. Rather than constituting a random sample as in the NAEP, the group taking the SAT is voluntary and the fractions of students that take it at given times and states vary substantially, thereby vitiating any comparisons among them.

*Papers on Education Policy* (Washington, D.C.: Brookings Institution, 1998), pp. 53–121; "Respecting the Evidence: The Achievement Crisis Remains Real," review of "The Manufactured Crisis," *Education Policy Analysis Archives* 4, no. 7: http://olam.ed.asu.edu/epaa/v4n7.html; L. C. Stedman, "The Achievement Crisis Is Real," review of *"The Manufactured Crisis," Education Policy Analysis Archives* 4, no. 1 (1996): http://olam.ed.asu.edu/epaa/v4n1.html.

BBB try to excuse U.S. students' poor performance on the grounds that they don't study what is on the international tests. But, as Stedman points out, they base this contention on only one study of eighth-grade math data from 1981–82, and the data did not support their claim, nor do more recent studies.

Stedman also points out that BBB claim the international assessments improperly compared the broad mass of U.S. students to an overseas elite attending highly selective schools. This is an old criticism from the earliest studies. As discussed above, the average OECD country now has greater percentages of age-eligible youth in and graduating from secondary school than does the United States.

Finally, aside from Stedman's points, BBB do not deal with any of the new research reviewed above. This research shows that, despite greater levels of spending and rising student abilities, achievement has not risen. In addition, recent value-added analyses show American students improve less than do students in other countries despite the generally higher American levels of per student expenditures.

## ACHIEVEMENT TESTS

For those who have long been away from schools, it may be useful to know about the current means of measuring achievement. In keeping with the spirit of this book, it may be useful to overview some of the major means and issues of testing students' achievement.[28]

Considerable research shows that frequent testing with essay questions, short-answer, and multiple-choice tests leads to higher achievement because students prepare more frequently and regularly to be evaluated and because frequent tests provide more information to both teachers and students about their strengths and

28. A forty-one-page booklet further explaining current testing policies is Herbert J. Walberg, Geneva D. Haertel, and Suzanne Gerlach-Downie, *Assessment Reform: Challenges and Opportunities* (Bloomington, Ind.: Phi Delta Kappa, 1994).

weaknesses.[29] Teachers may also observe and rate their students' performance in class. They may assign, for example, laboratory exercises in science, physical measurements in geometry, and essays in history and literature. Then they may judge or rate the quality of the resulting work. For additional assessment and feedback, teachers may also check their students' homework and either grade or comment on it. Such assessments may be termed *teacher-aligned* or integrated with instruction because they correspond to content of the immediate lessons being taught.

## Standardized Tests

For several reasons, such teacher assessments do not serve well in large-scale surveys of achievement intended to provide information on how students, schools, districts, state, and even nations compare with one another, how they compare with established standards, or how achievement is changing over time. Tests intended for this purpose are "standardized" in that the conditions and timing of the tests are nearly identical for all students. Many sports and the international Olympics employ similar standardized conditions so that athletes' performances can be fairly compared no matter where they are and whatever the date of their performances.

Standardized tests widely sample the subject matter. In this respect, they are like national voter and consumer surveys that sample, say, a thousand people, to provide information on the entire adult population with a probable sample error of less than several percentage points.[30] Sample surveys provide information quickly,

29. With a colleague, I compiled 275 effect sizes of frequent testing, homework, mastery learning, direct instruction, and other educational methods and conditions. They serve as indicators of which methods and conditions have the largest impacts on achievement. Along with costs and other considerations, such effects can serve as the basis of formulating policies likely to improve achievement. See Herbert J. Walberg and Jin-Shei Lai, "Meta-Analytic Effects for Policy," in Gregory J. Cizek, ed., *Handbook of Educational Policy* (San Diego, Calif.: Academic Press), pp. 419–52.

30. This refers only to sampling error with respect to the time of the survey and the question asked. If the questions differ or the times differ from the intended forecast, such surveys, of course, may be grossly inaccurate.

efficiently, and cheaply. So, too, can thirty to sixty multiple-choice questions about a broad subject constituted by thousands of facts and ideas.

Sample surveys differ from a census aimed at getting information from every single member of the population. Analogously, test designers usually cannot take an achievement census by asking all conceivable questions about a subject. So they may divide the subject into various skills and areas of content, then sample within each, just as survey designers employ stratified sampling, that is, sampling within cities, suburbs, and rural areas in the several geographic regions of the nation.

## Objective, Multiple-Choice Tests

So that aspects of the subject may be sampled in a short time, achievement surveys generally employ multiple-choice examinations. Thirty items may be administered in the amount of time required to answer a single essay question. Multiple-choice questions afford a much larger sample of students' knowledge and skills than do essay questions. They are also fairer to students because their scores do not depend heavily and arbitrarily on whether they happened to have concentrated or not on only one narrow aspect of the subject.

Standardized tests are fairer in another sense: skilled essayists can write impressively on many topics without really having mastered them. We may, of course, be interested in writing ability and require an essay to measure it, although multiple-choice tests can even provide a quicker, more objective, and, some argue, more accurate estimate of writing ability.[31]

Other things being equal, essays in neat handwriting get better

31. A obstacle in measuring writing ability is getting agreement from experts on definitions, especially for anything that goes beyond the conventional matters of spelling, grammar, and appropriate word usage. If there were greater consensus about cohesion, coherence, concision, organization, and elegance as components of style, graders and computers might more reliably and validly mark essays. See Joseph M. Williams, *Style: Ten Lessons in Clarity and Grace* (Reading, Mass: Addison-Wesley, 2000).

grades. Also, the same essay may be given wildly different marks by different graders or the same grader on two occasions. On the other hand, with perfect objectivity, machines can quickly and cheaply score thousands of multiple-choice tests and also produce detailed diagnostic reports on individual and group strengths and weaknesses.

A final reason that multiple-choice tests are preferred in large-scale achievement surveys is that "constructed response" tests requiring essays, laboratory equipment, calculators, and the like usually add little information value to students' scores on objective tests. The score on the multiple-choice test often serves as a better predictor of an essay grader's mark than another essay grader's mark of the same examination. So, for large-scale surveys, the large extra cost of essay examinations is usually unwarranted by the marginal information they may provide (except, as pointed out above, possibly when educators want to encourage and measure essay writing as separate from knowledge and skills in a subject such as history, literature, or science).

## Test Criticism

Defenders of the status quo often wrongly criticize multiple-choice tests as "multiple-guess tests." On a test with four options per item, we would, for example, expect students to guess about 25 percent of the answers correctly if they knew nothing about the subject. Guessing, however, can be taken into consideration in scoring, either by various guessing corrections or grading relative to other students. In any case, this criticism is beside the point since standardized test scores are rarely reported as the percentage of items correct.

Some critics attack multiple-choice tests for measuring recognition rather than recall or construction of the right answer. New objective test formats allow answer-sheet recording of recalled or constructed answers that may be objectively machine scored. In any case, recognition, recall, and construction are usually very highly correlated. It may be impossible to find someone who can correctly recognize the facts in a subject such as biology or history but can neither recall any nor reason about them. An old colleague of mine once asked Einstein's collaborator, who disliked objective tests, to find the student among a national sample of several hundred who had best answered a high school physics problem set. It turned out that that student had also attained the highest score on the objective test of physics knowledge and skills.

Little wonder that even our oldest professions such as law and medicine employ multiple-choice tests for admission and certification, as do graduate colleges and MBA programs for admission decisions. If these demanding fields employ multiple-choice tests, to what do schools aspire that cannot be similarly measured?[32]

## PROMISING SOLUTIONS FOR RAISING ACHIEVEMENT

For the reasons stated above, politicians, businesspeople, citizens, and parents are greatly concerned about the inefficiency of the public schools and their threat to the economy and society. Many business leaders describe their problems in getting competent workers, capable of reading, calculating, and learning new material.

The crisis is most acute in technology, an important growth area of the economy. The Information Technology Association of America reported that 1.6 million new information workers would be needed by the end of the year 2000 but that 850,000 positions will go unfilled. According to its survey, technical-support representatives, database developers, and programmers are the three positions in greatest demand.[33]

### Achievement Standards

In response to the continuing education crisis, legislators are setting forth two kinds of accountability, both employing achieve-

32. Many examples of multiple-choice items that measure both knowledge and "higher order cognitive skills" can be found in textbooks on testing such as Anthony Nitko's *Educational Assessment of Students* (Englewood Cliffs, N.J.: Prentice-Hall, 1996).

33. Rachel Emma Silverman, "Employers Face Dearth of IT Workers as Demand Exceeds Supply, Data Shows," *Wall Street Journal*, April 10, 2000, p. A1.

ment tests to measure results. The first is more rigorous state standards with achievement tests as indicators of success and failure. Students who cannot meet these standards may be retained in grade or fail to graduate from high school. Schools with sufficiently high failure rates risk being closed. States are phasing in these standards and giving schools some time to gear curricula and instruction to the standards. Because the effects of poverty and other factors are difficult to overcome, it would also seem wise to use value-added achievement scores in any index of a school's success, at least for a time.

Such "high-stakes" achievement test schemes, however, are hardly foolproof. The tests may be technically flawed. The standards may be arbitrarily high or low. Test security may be breached. Schools may teach narrowly to the tests or only to the types of content or problems known to be tested; they may ignore other worthy education goals. Better design and administration of testing programs can overcome these problems but may require steadfastness, money, and experience.

## School Choice

The second form of accountability makes schools more directly accountable to parents rather than school boards who may not represent citizens and parents well or have management skills to hold educators accountable. Among the variations of this form are charter schools that give private boards public funds to educate students that come to them. In another form, scholarships are given directly to parents, who may spend them at parochial, independent, and for-profit schools of their choice. Charter schools and scholarships provide a greater diversity of curricula, approaches to education, and means of instruction. They also provide for greater competition among providers and choice for customers, that is, parents, children, and youth.

The ideals of choice and competition have led to wondrous results for consumers in nearly all other sectors of the economy in the United States and elsewhere. Since funds for charter schools and public scholarships come from public sources, it is reasonable, perhaps even necessary during the experimental period of, say, the next five years, to employ achievement tests to measure their progress.

Legislatures or their appointed commissions might insist that, to continue, charter schools and schools that receive publicly funded scholarship students meet a minimum level of standards as measured by independently designed achievement tests. So as to avoid the deadening hand of government regulation, the standard might be the average achievement test scores of public schools in the state in the usual school subjects plus knowledge of the Declaration of Independence, the U.S. Constitution, and important state documents.

Alternatively, the marketplace provides the ultimate accountability to customers. Unhappy ones can walk away. They can avoid providers of goods and services that make them dissatisfied. For this reason, charter and scholarship schools might only be required to engage in state-mandated testing for a limited period—say, five years—until their worth is clearly demonstrated in achieved results.

## CONCLUSION

Despite huge amounts of research over many years on what best promotes learning, American schools lurch from fad to fad. They fail to make evidence the basis of practice in the manner of business, medicine, agriculture, law, and other fields. As a consequence, American schools produce the worst achievement results at the third-highest expenditures among economically advanced countries. Achievement scores have remained stagnant, moreover, despite substantially rising expenditures, rising children's abilities, and many reforms. Substantial amounts of money for special programs, more than $120 billion, have failed to reduce the achievement gap between poor and middle-class children. The schools fail to employ new technologies for learning or even to employ traditional technologies well. Current demands for standards, accountability, incentives, and choice described briefly in this chapter and at length in the other chapters are clearly warranted.

# CHAPTER 4

# Spending on Schools

## Eric A. Hanushek

Public opinion generally supports the conclusion that our public schools face serious problems. Common views, supported by a variety of media stories about poor performance of students, provide the backdrop for much of school policy. But, even if concern about schools is a prevalent view, the precise causes of problems are less clear. Some hold that student preparation for schools—resulting from increasing family problems, more immigrants, more poverty, or whatever—has declined over time, leading to falls in student performance. Others hold that support for schools has fallen. Budgets are turned down; pressures to lower taxes take precedence over schools; an increasingly older population has less interest in schooling. And, to the extent that teachers or other personnel contribute to any problems, it is poor pay and lack of resources that make teaching an undesirable occupation. In short, resources are the key, either directly to deal with the needs of schools or indirectly to compensate for the poorer preparation of students. Unfortunately, these common conceptions—oft-repeated in the press, in legislatures, and even in courtrooms—are for the most part simply wrong. Resource support for schools has been high, and the problems of performance—which are real—result from other forces.

A related issue centers on equity concerns. Long-standing concerns about the distribution of income, about the extent of poverty, and about intergenerational transmission of well-being frequently point to increased schooling as the key. Providing increased skills for the poor has been seen as a viable way to ameliorate distributional concerns while improving the performance of the economy as a whole. The translation of this argument into policy has largely centered on the quality of schools serving the poor and the rest of society. And the arena for debate and change has been first the courts and second the state legislatures. In fact, considerable change in the funding of schools has occurred, but it appears to have had little effect on student outcomes.

This chapter describes the resources and financing of schools. The interpretation of this, of course, depends largely on the results of resource patterns—an element highlighted here and discussed in detail in another chapter.

## BACKGROUND

Expectations about the outcomes of educational policy have been high for several decades. The recent era of concern about the quality of U.S. public schools can be traced to reactions about the launch of the Soviet *Sputnik* in the late 1950s. At that time attention was focused on the failure of U.S. schools to keep up with Soviet schools in terms of math and science performance. This concern was amplified with attention to the distribution of outcomes in the mid-1960s when the War on Poverty was launched. A key element of alleviating poverty was providing better schooling for the poor.

The reality has not matched the expectations. In a series of international comparisons of math and science performance that began in the 1960s, U.S. students scored in the lower half of the distribution. The exact position has varied with the specific test and precise set of countries taking each test.[1] The education sum-

1. U.S. Department of Education, *Pursuing Excellence: A Study of U.S. Eighth-Grade Mathematics and Science Teaching, Learning, Curriculum, and Achievement in International Context* (Washington, D.C.: National Center for

mit of the nation's governors in 1989 set the goal for U.S. students to be first in the world in math and science by the turn of the century, but the 1995 results of the Third International Mathematics and Science Study (TIMSS) placed U.S. students—particularly high school students—well down in the world rankings.

The international comparisons have mirrored performance on the National Assessment of Educational Progress (NAEP) that has permitted comparisons of U.S. students since the early 1970s. Performance in 1999 of seventeen-year-olds was roughly the same as that in 1970 across math, reading, and science.[2] Thus, whatever concerns about overall performance that existed three decades ago still exist.

On the distributional side, some improvement was seen during the 1980s. White students have consistently scored above black or Hispanic students, but the gap narrowed noticeably during the early 1980s.[3] This narrowing, however, stopped by 1990 and perhaps reversed somewhat.

The trends in performance have led some to call for a redoubling of efforts. Both the level and the distribution of resources to schools are seen as inhibiting reaching the desired goals. This discussion concentrates on what has happened with resources for schools.

## THE OVERALL PATTERN OF PUBLIC SCHOOL RESOURCE USAGE

The United States recognized the importance of schooling long ago and moved more aggressively during the twentieth century than all countries of the world to educate its population. Through much

---

Education Statistics, 1996). Eric A. Hanushek and Dennis D. Kimko, "Schooling, Labor Force Quality, and the Growth of Nations," *American Economic Review* 90, no. 5 (December 2000): 1184–1208.

2. There are some nuances. Math and reading scores are slightly up while science is down for the entire period. Performance on each test has also followed somewhat varying patterns from the earliest testing to today.

3. See, for example, Christopher Jencks and Meredith Phillips, eds., *The Black-White Test Score Gap* (Washington, D.C.: Brookings Institution, 1998).

of the century, a primary emphasis was expansion of access to schools. At the beginning of the twentieth century, just 6 percent of the population graduated from high school. This percentage grew steadily until more than half the school-age population finished high school by 1950. Of course, younger cohorts systematically attained more schooling than the entire adult population. Thus, while the average levels of schooling for the entire population have continued to rise (as younger and more schooled cohorts replace older cohorts), the median school completion rates of the youngest cohorts have been constant since the mid-1970s.

With constancy of completion rates, much of the attention has switched to quality issues (i.e., the amount of learning per year of schooling). The main thrust of this has been to provide extra resources to support a deepening of schools. Before considering recent resource movements, however, it is useful to put spending and resources into the larger picture of the twentieth century.

Real spending per student—that is spending per student adjusted to remove general inflation—has grown steadily and dramatically. From a spending of $164/student in 1890, the average for the United States quintupled roughly every fifty years, reaching $4,622/student in 1990 (see figure 1). (All spending is expressed in 1990 dollars.) Such increases over such an extended period of time represent truly amazing growth, growth that is hard to find in any other sector. For example, popular accounts suggest widespread hostility to increases in health care costs, but, by some measures, the rate of inflation in health care has been less than the inflation in education. Indeed, the contrast to health care is remarkable. Many indicators suggest overall improvement in the quality of life from improvements in health care, something that cannot readily be said for performance in the education sector. Yet the popular conception is that health care costs have risen too much, while education costs are too low.

Over the long period, three factors have pushed up the spending per pupil. First, pupil-teacher ratios have fallen. Second, teacher salaries have risen. And, third, expenditures for other than instructional salaries have grown more than proportionately. An important part

FIGURE 1. REAL SPENDING PER PUPIL IN U.S. PUBLIC SCHOOLS, 1890–1990

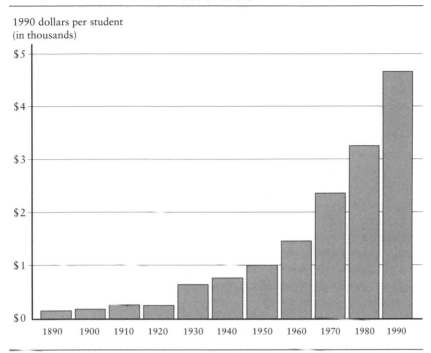

1990 dollars per student
(in thousands)

of the story is the consistency of these forces over the century. The precise importance of each component has moved up and down some during the century, but each has provided steady pressure on overall spending.

Recent experiences coincide with those of the larger picture. The major changes of the quarter-century from 1970 to 1995 are summarized in table 1. The average pupil-teacher ratio fell by roughly a quarter. The percentage of teachers with at least a master's

TABLE 1. RESOURCES IN U.S. PUBLIC SCHOOLS, 1970 AND 1995

|  | 1970 | 1995 |
|---|---|---|
| Pupil-teacher ratio | 22.3 | 17.3 |
| Teachers with a master's degree or more | 27.5% | 56.2% |
| Median teacher experience | 8 years | 15 years |
| Real expenditure per pupil (1997 $) | $3,645 | $6,434 |

degree has more than doubled, so that a majority of teachers have a high level of education. Median teacher experience, which is largely driven by hiring cycles related to student demographic swings, almost doubled over this period. Finally, real spending per pupil—which is directly influenced by the preceding and other factors—increased by three-quarters over the period.

Contrast these resource changes—that reflect the general prescriptions many advocate—with the patterns of flat student performance. These data suggest on the surface real problems but not the resource shortages that many popular arguments conjure up. The large resource increases appear to be simply a reflection of the policies commonly advocated. The implied lack of relationship of resources and performance seems implausible. Could it be true? Or is something else going on below the surface?

### BENIGN EXPLANATIONS OF SPENDING GROWTH

Two concerns about external cost pressures have arisen and been offered as possible mitigating factors for the bad resource outcome: the pressures of competing for skilled workers and the pressures of demands for special populations. The competition for labor, particularly teachers, can be expressed in a variety of ways including issues about the calculation of real expenditure or about quality shifts in the teacher labor markets. The concern about increased demand and requirements on schools, while possibly covering a wide variety of factors, has largely focused on the role of special education.

#### Measuring Cost Increases and Competition for Labor

To understand the increase in expenditures over time, it is obviously important to adjust for inflation. Most typically, expenditure in any year is adjusted by the consumer price index, or CPI. For example, table 1 showed the spending on schools in 1970 when adjusted to 1997 purchasing power. After this adjustment, the real expenditure figures reflect the resources that society is giving up to run its schools. But the adjusted dollars may misstate the changes in resources that schools effectively have for their educational program.[4] Schools must compete for teachers with other industries. If productivity gains in other sectors of the economy permit firms to pay more for college-educated workers, schools must also pay more for teachers or run the danger of having good people go elsewhere. Thus, the costs to schools will go up, since they must pay more for workers even though they do not produce any more (i.e., even though productivity improvements are not occurring).[5] This in turn implies that use of a general deflator for inflation like the CPI does not reflect the change in actual costs faced by schools.

As is well known, the wages of college graduates have soared since the mid-1970s. Whereas the typical college graduate earned about 35 percent more than the typical high school graduate in the mid-1970s, this premium grew to more than 75 percent by

---

4. The effect of using alternative price deflators in the context of schools is raised by Richard Rothstein and Karen Hawley Miles, *Where's the Money Gone? Changes in the Level and Composition of Education Spending* (Washington, D.C.: Economic Policy Institute, 1995). The more general conceptual issues related to productivity differences are highlighted by William J. Baumol and William G. Bowen, "On the Performing Arts: The Anatomy of Their Economic Problems," *American Economic Review* 55 (May 1965): 495–502, in the context of the performing arts.

5. Many people assume that productivity changes are essentially nonexistent in schools because instruction is largely provided by one classroom instructor with a relatively fixed number of students. In reality, the number of students is not fixed, as described previously. In the face of increasing salaries for teachers, schools have actually moved to hire additional teachers. Thus, schools have operated very differently than suggested by the productivity model. Specifically, the productivity model of William J. Baumol, "Macroeconomics of Unbalanced Growth: The Anatomy of Urban Crisis," *American Economic Review* 57, no. 3 (June 1967): 415–26, suggests that the low-productivity firm must either face higher costs or decrease quality in the face of wage pressures from other industries. If this were the reaction of schools, they would either hold pupil-teacher ratios constant or increase them. For a more complete discussion of salaries, see Eric A. Hanushek and Steven G. Rivkin, "Understanding the Twentieth-Century Growth in U.S. School Spending," *Journal of Human Resources* 32, no. 1 (winter 1997): 35–68.

1990. This phenomenon is usually interpreted as the increased demand for skilled workers, propelled by industries that have developed production methods that emphasize skills. Many take pride in recent developments of the American economy, but an implication is that schools must compete with other industries to obtain college-educated workers as teachers.

A related phenomenon is that opportunities for females in the workforce have greatly expanded over the past three decades. Although the professional jobs of women were at one time largely restricted to teaching or nursing, such is no longer the case. Wages for college-educated women have risen rapidly, and career paths have altered accordingly. Thus, the captive labor force of schools has escaped, leaving schools to compete even more broadly for teachers.

One way to adjust for this changing labor market is to deflate expenditure increases by measures that reflect how rapidly wages of college workers are increasing (as opposed how rapidly prices for products purchased by a typical consumer are increasing). Doing this suggests that the rate of increase in expenditure has been somewhat less than appears from the CPI, but it is not all that different.[6] In other words, while the precise answer differs somewhat over different periods of time, this alternative approach does not make a huge change in the picture of expenditure changes for schools.

## Patterns of Teacher Salaries

An alternative approach, however, may be more telling. Workers with a college education actually earn quite varying amounts. Although it is common to quote the averages, salaries for workers of the same age and education fall across a broad range. One expla-

6. Eric A. Hanushek, "The Productivity Collapse in Schools," in *Developments in School Finance, 1996*, ed. William J. Folwer Jr., pp. 185–95 (Washington, D.C.: National Center for Education Statistics, 1997), compares alternative deflators.

nation for this distribution is that workers with the same schooling levels actually have widely varying skills and abilities. Building on this idea, one indication of the quality of teachers at any point in time comes from considering where the typical teacher falls in the overall salary distribution for college-educated workers. Specifically, if individuals are deciding on careers based on salaries and if the most able can command the highest salaries, the comparison of average teacher salaries with other workers can give a rough "quality" measure.

In fact, the changes in salaries relative to other occupations, depicted in figure 2, have been dramatic. Teacher salaries for females—which represented some of the best options for women in the 1940s—have fallen steadily until today. The pattern is even

FIGURE 2. COLLEGE-EDUCATED EARNING LESS THAN AVERAGE TEACHER, BY GENDER AND AGE, 1940–1990
(in percent)

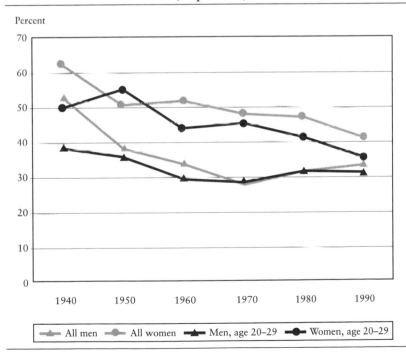

more exaggerated for young women. Male teachers, who comprise approximately one-third of the teacher force, saw relative earnings fall from 1940 to 1970 but hold steady (or maybe increase) subsequently.[7] By 1990, men and women teachers were coming from quite similar places in the overall salary distribution. Taken together, however, the story is that teacher salaries have not kept up with those of college graduates, suggesting that the average quality of teachers may have slipped over time.

The interpretation of this, nonetheless, requires caution. To begin with, overall salaries for college graduates may not be a good index of the specific skills required for teaching. But, beyond that, it is not inevitable that schools make these choices. In particular, schools could decide to match the rate of increase of other salaries in the economy. They did not, implying that the observed expenditure increases are held down in the sense that schools allow teacher salaries to deteriorate at the time that they have had rapid increases in overall spending. Had the choice not been made to let relative teacher salaries fall, expenditure increases would have been even more rapid. The choice that schools made involved reducing pupil-teacher ratios, while letting relative salaries fall.

The simple comparisons of teaching salaries with those elsewhere in the economy have led to general calls for increasing teacher salaries. These calls have, in part, been supported by stories of specific shortages—of math and science teachers, of special education teachers, of language and bilingual teachers. Indeed, raising the average salaries of teachers may be a course that eventually should be pursued, but the simple aggregate data are insufficient to make that case. First, detailed studies of teacher quality and salaries do not indicate that there is much relationship between the two within the current structure of schools. Importantly, salaries are generally determined by teacher experience and teacher education levels (i.e., having an advanced degree or not)

7. See Hanushek and Rivkin, "Understanding the Twentieth-Century Growth in U.S. School Spending," for a discussion of relative salary changes for teachers.

and not by any demonstrated performance in the classroom.[8] Raising salaries across the board for current teachers would equally reward both good and bad teachers without changing student achievement by much. Second, the argument for increasing salaries is based on attracting different people into teaching, but those effects would take many years to be felt. Each year a relatively small proportion of teachers is replaced through the natural processes of retirement and leaving teaching. So, even if college students today reacted immediately to the promise of increased rewards in teaching, it would take many years to see substantial change in the teaching force. Third, if the pool of teachers were to expand, schools must still be able to select the best from this group. Analysis of current hiring processes[9] does not present an optimistic assessment of the prospects for good hiring from an expanded pool.

Thus, the idea of increasing average teacher salaries without other, more fundamental changes in the hiring, retention, and salary determination processes appears to be a dubious policy interpretation from the existing data on teacher salaries.

## Special Education

Concerns about the education of children with both physical and mental disabilities were translated into federal law in 1975 with the Education for All Handicapped Children Act. This act prescribed a series of diagnostics, counseling activities, and services to be provided for handicapped students. To implement this and subsequent laws and regulations, school systems expanded staff

8. For a general discussion of the relationship between resources and student performance, see Hanushek, "The Productivity Collapse in Schools," and Eric A. Hanushek et al., *Making Schools Work: Improving Performance and Controlling Costs* (Washington, D.C.: Brookings Institution, 1994).

9. For example, Richard J. Murnane, Judith D. Singer, John B. Willett, James J. Kemple, and Randall J. Olsen, *Who Will Teach?* (Cambridge: Harvard University Press, 1991); Dale Ballou and Michael Podgursky, *Teacher Pay and Teacher Quality* (Kalamazoo, Mich.: W.E. Upjohn Institute for Employment Research, 1997).

and programs, developing entirely new administrative structures in many cases to handle "special education." The general thrust of the educational services has been to provide regular classroom instruction where possible ("mainstreaming") along with special-ized instruction to deal with specific needs. The result has been growth of students classified as the special education population even as the total student population fell. Between 1977 and 1994, the percentage of students classified as disabled increased from 9.7 to 12.2 percent. Moreover, the number of special education teachers increased much more rapidly than the number of children classi-fied as disabled. The average cost of special education is estimated to be in excess of twice the cost of regular education, putting cost pressures on schools.

From the standpoint of interpreting trends in expenditure and performance, the concern about the recent emphasis on special education is that these students tend not to take standardized tests. Thus, even if special education programs are effective, the in-creased expenditures on special education will not show up in measured student performance.[10]

The magnitude of special education and its growth, however, are insufficient to reconcile the cost and performance dilemma. Using the best available estimate of the cost differential for special education—2.3 times the cost of regular education—the growth in special education students between 1980 and 1990 can explain less than 20 percent of the expenditure growth.[11] In other words,

10. The laws governing special education clearly provided advantages to the special education children, some of whom are believed to be spared from exclu-sion to schools in addition to getting enriched programs. Nonetheless, little atten-tion has been devoted to assessing special education outcomes. See Eric A. Hanushek, John F. Kain, and Steven G. Rivkin, "Does Special Education Raise Academic Achievement for Students with Disabilities?" National Bureau of Eco-nomic Research, working paper no. 6690, 1998.

11. Cost estimates can be found in Stephen Chaikind, Louis C. Danielson, and Marsha L. Brauen, "What Do We Know about the Costs of Special Educa-tion? A Selected Review," *Journal of Special Education* 26, no. 4 (1993): 344–70. As they indicate, costs vary widely by type of disability. The calculation of impli-cations for school spending are found in Hanushek and Rivkin, "Understanding the Twentieth-Century Growth in U.S. School Spending."

while special education programs have undoubtedly influenced overall expenditures, they remain a relatively small portion of the total spending on schools.

Direct estimates of exogenous programmatic changes resulting from other academic aspects of schools such as language instruction for immigrants or nonacademic programs such as sports, art, or music are not readily available. Nonetheless, no evidence suggests that these can explain the magnitude of spending growth.

## Conclusions about Overall Expenditure Growth

A significant overall policy issue facing U.S. public education is why dramatic increases in resources for schools do not appear to translate into enhanced student performance. Some have suggested that the answer lies in the data: measured expenditure on schools does not reflect a number of realities faced by schools. The two leading candidates are external cost pressures—making it increasingly more difficult to hire high-quality teachers—and the necessity of providing costly programs for special education. Each has some merit, implying that the measured expenditure increases do overstate the effective resource growth for regular education students. But allowing for these does not change the overall picture of striking resource improvements matched with flat student performance.

The suggestion of a disconnect between spending and student performance has actually been reinforced by detailed studies at the school and classroom level. The studies, which have been controversial largely because of their findings, indicate no systematic relationship between resources and outcomes once one considers families and other factors that determine achievement.[12] The studies, of course, do not indicate that resources never make a difference. Nor do they indicate that resources could not make a difference. Instead they demonstrate that one cannot expect to see

12. See Hanushek et al., "Making Schools Work"; Hanushek, "The Productivity Collapse in Schools."

much if any improvement simply by adding resources to the current schools.

## INEQUALITY IN EXPENDITURE

Although the previous discussion highlighted the level of average spending, there is wide variation around the average. And considerable concern and policy attention have focused on the distribution of spending.

Overall spending represents a combination of spending by federal, state, and local agencies. For the past two decades, the shares of expenditures by each level of government have been relatively stable, with the federal government contributing 6–8 percent and state and local governments roughly evenly splitting the remainder. This stability in shares did, however, occur after some significant changes in the prior two decades. During the 1960s, the federal government's share doubled. During the 1970s, the traditional majority spending role of localities declined to equality with state governments. (These averages mask wide variation across the states, however, with some states leaving no role for localities in determining spending and others strongly emphasizing the local responsibility for spending.)

The federal government has concentrated on funding compensatory programs for schools. These programs primarily include Head Start preschool programs, Title I compensatory education programs, and special education funding. In these programs, funds are targeted on disadvantaged students or special needs students.

Evaluations of the effectiveness of federal programs in improving student performance do not suggest much overall success. Title I, which has changed form repeatedly over its history, has never indicated success in boosting general performance of disadvantaged students.[13] Head Start has evolved into a health and nutrition program and has historically been dubbed as having limited

13. See, for example, George Farkas and L. Shane Hall, "Can Title I Attain Its Goal?" in *Brookings Papers on Education Policy 2000*, ed. by Diane Ravitch (Washington, D.C.: Brookings Institution, 2000).

educational effectiveness, with any gains in early performance eroding over time.[14] Special education programs have never received any overall evaluation, making it difficult to assess this 20 percent of federal education spending.[15] In sum, there is little reason with existing evidence to believe that federal actions as a whole have had much effect on student achievement for their targeted populations.

Schools are, nonetheless, the primary responsibility of the states, so the lack of systematic federal impact might not be altogether surprising. The states have pursued a variety of programs that affect equality in schools. Most significantly, states operate independently, implying substantial differences in spending, regulations, and operations across states. Although the compensatory federal spending has some equalizing effect, it is small relative to the overall disparities in funding. Figure 3 shows the distribution of mean expenditure across states. The spending data, while unadjusted for any cost of education differences, show a remarkable spread.

Differences in average spending across states are the largest component of inequality in resources available to students. When comparing differences in spending across states to that across districts within a state, the basic finding is that two-thirds of the differences in school spending come from between-state differences.[16]

It is interesting that, while federal spending has focused on purely distributional issues in terms of disadvantaged (low-income) populations, there is little equalization of overall spending across

14. See W. Steven Barnett, "Benefits of Compensatory Preschool Education," *Journal of Human Resources* 27, no. 2 (spring 1992): 279–312.

15. Hanushek, Kain, and Rivkin, "Does Special Education Raise Academic Achievement for Students with Disabilities," find some evidence of positive effects on achievement for special education, but this investigation does not consider variations in either state or federal funds for special education.

16. The most systematic study of spending patterns is Sheila E. Murray, William N. Evans, and Robert M. Schwab, "Education-Finance Reform and the Distribution of Education Resources," *American Economic Review* 88, no. 4 (September 1998): 789–812. They employ various approaches to identify the source of variations in spending across schools, but all suggest the dominance of state differences.

FIGURE 3. DISTRIBUTION OF SPENDING PER PUPIL BY STATE, 1995

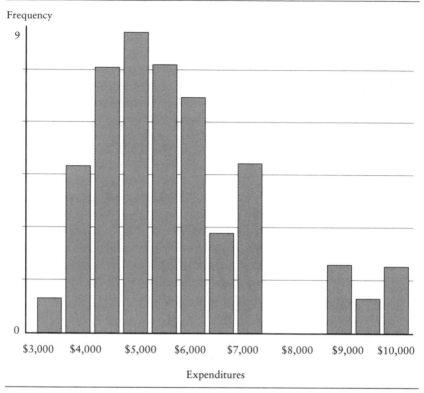

states. Federal spending has done little to disturb existing spending differentials across states, even though this large variation in spending is negatively related to the education and income of the state.

A variety of other programs and financing incentives is designed to promote more equality in schools. The growth in state shares during the 1970s is at least partially related to school funding court cases or attempts of legislatures to deal independently with the issues raised in those cases. Beginning in the late 1960s, a wave of school finance cases has swept the nation. The origins of these cases are typically traced to the California case of *Seranno v. Priest*. The underlying legal theory was that children in property-poor school districts with their commensurately limited taxing power were being discriminated against because the ability of the school to raise funds depended on the wealth of the students' neighbors.[17] This suit, originally brought under both state and U.S. constitutions, became the model for similar suits in a majority of the states. Although the U.S. Supreme Court ruled that existing state school financing plans did not violate the equal protection clause of the Fourteenth Amendment, most state constitutions explicitly define a state role in the provision of elementary and secondary schooling, and they have been the focus of suits.

State courts have split on whether or not their financing arrangements violate the state constitution, but one overall effect of the court action has been the relative increase in state funding that has come from the state. The general thrust of these suits has been that states should take a larger responsibility in school funding so as to ameliorate if not eliminate the funding advantages that certain districts have. This by itself leads to an increase in state share. Moreover, since there is frequently a significant amount of redistribution of funding called for by court orders and by legislative "equity" initiatives, it appears frequently to be more feasible to increase the total spending while changing the pattern (i.e., it is easier to redistribute a larger pie than a constant pie). Considerable heterogeneity exists across states, however, and such generalizations fit the aggregate better than individual states.

The primary focus of the court cases has been equity (although it may be changing). If there is a wide disparity in the funding and quality of schools, the argument goes, there will be subsequent disparities in earnings and other outcomes. And, while quality is the general rubric of concern, most of the court cases have focused attention on purely fiscal and expenditure aspects of schools. The prevailing evidence suggests that court cases have tended to pro-

17. The original arguments were made by John E. Coons, William H. Clune, and Stephen D. Sugarman, *Private Wealth and Public Education* (Cambridge, Mass.: The Belknap Press of Harvard University Press, 1970), and have been modified.

mote a more even distribution of spending across districts, although the effects have not been large on average.[18]

The new version of state school finance cases has focused on "adequacy," or whether state funding is sufficient to meet state educational goals. Although ambiguity exists in the exact definition, this set of school finance cases appears to address both the distribution and the level of spending across districts. The argument tends to begin with a focus on student outcomes but then is quickly translated into pure resource terms. Again, if spending is not closely related to performance, it is difficult to specify what level of spending would be needed to achieve any desired level of outcomes that might be determined to be adequate. In other words, while introducing the idea of concern about outcomes, the adequacy discussions inherently face the same issues as the traditional equity discussions—with the difference that the level of spending also becomes a concern.

Surprisingly, there has been little study of the effects of equalization of spending in the states. There is, as suggested above, reason to believe that overall levels of spending have little impact on student outcomes, and this might reasonably be thought to generalize to the results of changing the spending patterns within states. The little evidence that does exist confirms this: there is no reason to believe that equalizing expenditure also tends to equalize student performance.[19] Nonetheless, since the school finance court cases have been such a significant element of funding discussions over

18. James H. Wyckoff, "The Intrastate Equality of Public Primary and Secondary Education Resources in the U.S., 1980–1987," *Economics of Education Review* 11, no. 1 (March 1992): 19–30, and Murray, Evans, and Schwab, "Education-Finance Reform," provide evidence on the court cases. Murray, Evans, and Schwab show that states under court order have moved more toward equality that those not under order, although most states have not made dramatic changes.

19. Thomas A. Downes, "Evaluating the Impact of School Finance Reform on the Provision of Public Education: The California Case," *National Tax Journal* 45, no. 4 (December 1992): 405–19, looks at variations in student test scores after equalization in California and finds no relationship. Hanushek and Somers (forthcoming) relate variations in school spending to variations in subsequent labor market rewards and similarly find no relationship.

the past three decades, one might expect more attention to the outcomes.

## SOME CONCLUSIONS

The patterns of expenditure on schools tell a fairly simple story. Real spending on schools has been increasing for a long time. The spending has in broad-brush terms been happening in the ways that is commonly advocated: teacher education has been increasing, teacher experience has been increasing, and pupil-teacher ratios have been falling. Yet, at least for the past three decades when student performance has been measured, there is little indication that these increases in resources have led to discernible improvements in student outcomes.

Consideration of other factors that might distort the resource outcome picture does not change the conclusions. Although cost pressures on teachers and special education have had some influence on the resource flows into school, they do not change the overall conclusions.

Beyond the level of resources, concern about their distribution has been an important focus of policy. Coincident with increases in the level of resources has been a shrinking of the variations of spending across districts. A portion of this has driven by court cases about spending equity, although the most important issues are variations in resources across states. With this movement toward spending equity, however, there is no evidence that outcomes have become more equalized.

All this suggests that resources per se are not the issue. And there is little reason to believe that future resource flows will have the desirable impact on student outcomes unless other, more fundamental factors change.

The puzzle of why resources do not systematically affect performance remains. The most consistent explanation is that the current incentives within schools do not push schools to concentrate on student performance.[20] A good teacher can expect roughly the

20. Hanushek et al., *Making Schools Work*.

same salary pattern, employment opportunities, and other job outcomes as a poor teacher. The same holds for virtually everybody
within schools. Thus, it is not particularly surprising that added
resources are not consistently translated into improved student
performance. Improving the incentives in schools appears to be the
most important task if resources are to be used more effectively in
the future.

# CHAPTER 5

# If Families Matter Most, Where Do Schools Come In?

## *Caroline M. Hoxby*

### FAMILIES AND SCHOOLS

Most people believe that a child's family is the most important determinant of his or her life outcomes—not just family-related outcomes like marriage but also achievement outcomes like test scores, whether the child graduates from college, and wages later in life. Most people are right: the widespread belief in families' importance is amply supported by statistical evidence, some of which I review in this chapter. Nonfamily influences on children have much less powerful effects on childrens' outcomes—by at least an order of magnitude.

Some people find such evidence profoundly discouraging because they would like children's outcomes to be largely independent of family circumstances. Such people tend to react to the evidence in one of two ways. Some resist the statistics and hope that, by combining the numbers in some new way, they will find that families are not very important (and that nonfamily factors, such as schools, are). Others decide that policy efforts should be focused on improving family circumstances (through income transfers, antidrug programs, and so forth) instead of reforming schools or other institutions that affect children more directly. Neither of these reactions is very productive. On the one hand, family effects are of such great magnitude that varying how statistics are computed has little effect on the central conclusion that families are extremely important. On the other hand, a key family factor that affects children is parents' own education, so that it is hard to improve one generation's achievement without having first improved the achievement of the previous generation!

Moreover, both of these reactions are misguided because it is wrong to think of families and schools as *alternative* influences on children—so that, if families are important, schools are not. In fact, one of the ways in which "good" families benefit their children is by choosing good schools for them. On the one hand, it is right to attribute this "good school" effect to families because school quality is a resource that they choose to provide (like nutritious meals or comfortable living space). On the other hand, if no good schools were available, a family's ability to benefit its children would be limited. Moreover, well-planned school reforms can exploit the power of families, making their influence better. Essentially, the logic of such a reform is to improve parents' influence by giving them incentives to be better, more informed, more active consumers of education. Reforms can also make parents better consumers by eliminating arbitrary constraints on their choices. Finally, a reform can improve parents' effects by raising their incentives to make investments in their children's education that are complementary to schools.

An example unrelated to schools may help with the essential logic. Families produce good nutritional status by being good consumers at the grocery store and by preparing food wisely. If a change in the grocery store industry—say, better labeling of food and availability of nutritious recipes—made families into better grocery consumers and better producers of meals, nutritional status would increase. The improvement in nutrition would take place even though the vast majority of nutritional status was determined within the family, both before and after the change in the industry.

This chapter is about the links between families and schools. I explore the importance of families for children's outcomes, paying particular attention to the school-related channels through which family effects work. I also describe how family effects work better under some schooling institutions than under others. This description naturally leads toward some discussion about school reform, but the primary purpose of the chapter is evidentiary.

## The Importance of the Family

From precolonial times onward, observers of American children have seen widely differing levels of achievement, regardless of whether the measure was literacy, numeracy, familiarity with literary and scientific works, or the ability to prepare and write sophisticated arguments. Observers attributed the variation in achievement to several sources: differences in children's ability and motivation, differences in the schooling resources available to children, and differences in children's home environments.[1] By the early 1960s, however, many people who were concerned about disparate achievement had become focused on the idea that schooling *resources* accounted for most of the disparity. In particular, they believed that differences in resources accounted for most of the achievement disparities among ethnic groups and income groups. For instance, they thought that, although there were more- and less-able white students and more- and less-able black students, the difference between the achievement of the *average* white student and the *average* black student was largely attributable to the black students' attending schools with lower spending, fewer textbooks, fewer teachers, and so on.

1. The United States Bureau of Education (later the Office of Education and then the Department of Education) published numerous studies comparing the persistence, promotion, educational attainment, and achievement of different groups of students, especially urban, rural, black, white, and immigrant children. The Bureau of Education also published studies comparing resources (spending, buildings, books, teachers, and so on) across different schools. See the *Bulletins* of the Bureau of Education—for instance, no. 39 (1916).

Into this (rather complacent) belief system was dropped, in 1966, the Equality of Educational Opportunity Commission (EEOC) report. The EEOC report revealed that, once researchers controlled for differences in students' family backgrounds, differences in school resources accounted for almost *none* of the disparity in achievement. That is, the report concluded that families mattered a lot and that schools hardly mattered at all:

> It is known that socioeconomic factors bear a strong relation to academic achievement. When these factors are statistically controlled, however, it appears that differences between schools account for only a small fraction of differences in pupil achievement.[2]

Reviewing the EEOC report, Mosteller and Moynihan noted that, if anything, the above statement greatly understated the results:

> The pathbreaking quality of the EEOC had to do with its analysis of the relation of variation in school facilities to variation in levels of academic achievement. It reported so little relation as to make it almost possible to say there was none.[3]

Because the report had been expected to verify existing beliefs, its conclusions were shocking to the very groups that had proposed that it be commissioned: educators, civil rights leaders, and much of the United States Congress. (The 1964 Civil Rights Act included the commission for a study which became the EEOC project. Because the survey and analysis was conducted by a team headed by James Coleman of Johns Hopkins University, the report is often called the "Coleman Report.")

The basic statistics contained in the Coleman Report were valid.

2. James S. Coleman, Ernest Q. Campbell, Carol J. Hobson, James McPartland, Alexander M. Mood, Frederic D. Weinfeld, and Robert L. York, *Equality of Educational Opportunity* (Washington, D.C.: United States Government Printing Office for the National Center for Education Statistics, 1966), pp. 21–22.

3. Frederick Mosteller and Daniel P. Moynihan, "A Pathbreaking Report: Further Studies of the Coleman Report," in Frederick Mosteller and Daniel P. Moynihan, eds., *On Equality of Educational Opportunity* (New York: Random House, 1972), p. 15.

In fact, when the report was issued, a number of scholars scrambled to reanalyze the EEOC data and found (somewhat to their surprise) that their analyses broadly confirmed the statistics in the report.[4] Moreover, the report's statistics remain largely valid: a researcher could generate similar statistics today using up-to-date educational surveys. Despite the general accuracy of its statistics, however, the Coleman Report created untold confusion about families and schools. This was because James Coleman misinterpreted the statistics. Unfortunately, Coleman's problems with interpretation were followed by nearly everyone who commented on or reanalyzed the EEOC data in the fifteen years following the report's release.

The interpretation problem began with the fact that Coleman (and his followers and critics) largely failed to recognize (and certainly did nothing to account for) the fact that school resources are not randomly assigned to families. The school that a child attends is determined by her or his own family's income, job location, tastes, knowledge about educational opportunities, and so on. In 1964, it was no accident that the children of bankers and educators tended to attend schools replete with resources, while the children of poor farmers tended to attend schools with meager resources.

One consequence of not recognizing that family characteristics determine children's schools was that Coleman *underestimated* the importance of families relative to schools! That is, it is not enough to compare two families who appear to be similar but whose children attend schools with widely different resources. The family whose child attends the well-financed schools is likely to, say, have

4. See, for instance, Eric Hanushek and John F. Kain, "On the Value of *Equality of Educational Opportunity* as a Guide to Public Policy," in Mosteller and Moynihan, eds., *On Equality of Educational Opportunity;* David J. Armor, "School and Family Effects on Black and White Achievement: A Reexamination of the *USOE* Data," in Mosteller and Moynihan, eds., *On Equality of Educational Opportunity;* and Marshall S. Smith, "*Equality of Educational Opportunity*: The Basic Findings Reconsidered," in Mosteller and Moynihan, eds., *On Equality of Educational Opportunity.*

more wealth (a variable not measured by the EEOC survey) than the family whose child attends the poorly financed one. In other words, Coleman and his contemporaries attributed the effects of many unobserved *family* characteristics to *schools*.

This first flaw in Coleman's interpretation did not greatly alter reception of the EEOC report because readers were already shocked by the degree to which families, instead of schools, accounted for the variation in achievement. If a thoughtful critic had revealed that Coleman's statistics understated the importance of families and overstated the importance of schools, it is doubtful whether he would have intensified the (already strong) reaction to the report.

The second consequence of Coleman's neglecting the fact that family circumstances determine children's schools was far more serious. He (and his followers and critics) ignored the fact that one of the key ways in which families affect their children is through choosing or determining the schools that they attend. What are the implications of this fact?

- First, giving parents information and resources that enable them to choose schools more wisely is likely to improve student achievement significantly.

- Second, relaxing arbitrary institutional or resource constraints on parents that prevent them from sending their children to the school they prefer is likely to improve student achievement significantly.

What Coleman's evidence *did* show was that simply giving more resources to schools (in the absence of interaction between families and those resources) was unlikely to improve student achievement significantly.

Put another way, Coleman (and those who followed him) framed the question as families *versus* schools, perhaps because their implicit agenda was to find support for policies that worked by imposing resources on schools, regardless of the cooperation of local families. They therefore ignored the implications of evidence that families who sought high achievement consistently sought good schools as a mechanism for achieving their goals. If achievement-prone families could have attained their goals without schools, it is not likely that they would have consistently sought out some schools and avoided others. A better way to have framed the question would have been to hypothesize that there is (1) some achievement that a school can create without any interaction with families; (2) some achievement that families can create without using a school as a learning device; and (3) some achievement that is created in a school when the families it serves are "invested" in it, help determine how its resources are used, and support its activities. It is the goal of this chapter to focus on the last of these three channels by which achievement can be improved. I describe the interactions between families and schools and point out policies that are likely to improve such interactions. In this, the chapter departs from much of the ongoing literature on families and schools, which is still (unproductively) obsessed with families *versus* schools.

There is substantial evidence that his or her family is the most important determinant of a student's outcomes. In practice, social scientists rely on a limited number of relatively crude measures of family background: parents' education, family income, number of children in the family, race/Hispanic ethnicity, parental involvement with the school, and availability of learning-related resources (like books) in the home. It is possible to augment this list, of course, but even this short list of variables explains far more variation in student outcomes than is explained by school input variables, such as per-pupil spending, class size, teachers' salaries, teachers' credentials, books per student, and computer availability in the school. Indeed, the *combined* explanatory power of school input variables and neighborhood variables (such as the educational, income, and racial composition of the local population) does not come close to matching that of family background variables.

Some of the most recent evidence on this point comes from the National Educational Longitudinal Survey (NELS), which began following a group of 24,599 eighth-graders in 1988.[5] The students are still too young to have finished their education or earned wages that reflect their likely careers, but they were tested in May 1992 (at the end of the twelfth grade for the typical student) in four subjects: reading, mathematics, history, and science. One can use regression to apportion the explained variation in the students' test scores among family background variables, school input variables, and neighborhood variables. I used a regression that included, specifically:

*Family variables:* the maximum of parents' years of completed education, family income, indicators for race and Hispanic ethnicity, number of siblings; indicators for parents' having attended a school event, parents' having planned courses with child, parents' knowing graduation requirements, having more than 50 books at home, having a calculator available for child's use with homework, family having used the library, family having visited a museum.

*School input variables:* per-pupil spending, average class size, minimum teacher salary, average teacher salary, maximum teacher salary, percentage of teachers who are certified in their teaching area, percentage of teachers who have masters' degrees, average experience of teachers, number of books per student, number of computers per student, number of counselors per student.

*Neighborhood variables:* in addition to indicators for census region in which the family lives, the following variables are used, both at the level of the school district in which the family lives and at the level of the metropolitan area in which it lives: mean household income, an index of income inequality, percentage of households below poverty, percentage of households with incomes above $50,000, percentage of population who are black, percentage of the population who are Hispanic, percentage of the population who are Asian, percentage of the adult population with a high school degree, percentage of adult popu-

---

5. The NELS used a complex sampling scheme, which called for purposeful dropping of some students and "freshening" the sample with other students. As a result, the 1988 wave of the survey contained 24,599 eighth-graders, but the 1990 wave contained 19,402 students and the 1992 wave contained 16,315 students.

lation with some college education, percentage of adult population with a baccalaureate degree.[6]

In the regression just described, the family variables account for 34 to 105 times as much variation as the school input variables do. (There is a range of estimates because family variables account for different amounts of variation on different subject tests.) Family variables account for 12 to 24 times as much variation as neighborhood variables (income, educational attainment, and racial composition of the school's district population; region of the country) do.[7] Put another way, family variables explain 11 to 14 times as much variation in students' test scores as school inputs and neighborhood variables *combined*. See figure 1 for a summary of how the explained variation in students' mathematics scores is apportioned among family, school, and neighborhood variables.

Of course, test scores have their limitations as outcomes. The advantage of using test scores is that they are available for people who were students only a few years ago. The disadvantage of test scores is that they are an intermediate outcome—that is, one cares about test scores not so much for themselves, but because they are good predictors of other, later outcomes about which one cares more directly: a student's ultimate educational attainment, occupation, income, and so on.

To examine some later outcomes, I turn to the National Longi-

6. There are nine census regions. The Gini coefficient is the index of household income inequality.

7. Author's calculations using United States Department of Education, National Center for Education Statistics, *National Education Longitudinal Study, 1988: Third Follow-up*, restricted access computer file (Washington, D.C.: National Center for Education Statistics, 1996). It may be useful to know that the $F_{14,8345}$-statistic for the hypothesis that the family variables are jointly equal to zero is 146 for reading and language arts, 213 for mathematics, 157 for history, and 178 for science. The $F_{11,8345}$-statistic for the hypothesis that the school input variables are jointly equal to zero is 5 for reading and language arts, 6 for mathematics, 5 for history, and 8 for science. The $F_{30,8345}$-statistic for the hypothesis that the neighborhood variables are jointly equal to zero is 2 for reading and language arts, 7 for mathematics, 4 for history, and 3 for science.

FIGURE 1. VARIATIONS IN TWELFTH-GRADERS' MATH SCORES
THAT ARE EXPLAINED BY FAMILY, SCHOOL INPUT, AND
NEIGHBORHOOD VARIABLES

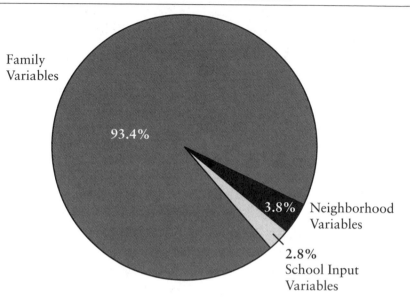

Family
Variables

93.4%

3.8% Neighborhood
Variables

2.8%
School Input
Variables

tudinal Survey of Youth (NLSY), another representative survey
that began following 12,686 young Americans in their teens and
has continued through their middle thirties.[8] I examine their outcomes at age thirty-three, by which age most have completed their
education and settled into a job that is reasonably indicative of
their career prospects. The two later outcomes that are most often
examined are income and completed years of education. If one
uses regression to explain these two outcomes with the family,
school, and neighborhood variables described above, one finds
that family variables explain fourteen times as much variation in
income as school input variables do and that family variables explain twenty-three times as much variation in income as neighbor-

8. Specifically, the NLSY began in 1979 with 12,686 young people between
the ages of 14 and 21 (inclusive). The NLSY respondents have been resurveyed
every year since then, and the most recent available data are from the 1998 survey, when the respondents were aged 33 to 40.

hood variables do.[9] Also, one finds that family variables explain nineteen times as much variation in educational attainment as school input variables do and that family variables explain twenty-four times as much variation in educational attainment as neighborhood variables do.[10] Summarized another way, family variables generally account for nine to eleven times as much variation in later outcomes as school inputs and neighborhood variables *combined*. See figures 2 and 3 for how the explained variation in students' later income and educational attainment is apportioned among family, school, and neighborhood variables.[11]

If one is interested in school reform, is it useful to know how much of the variation in outcomes is accounted for by family effects? The answer is yes if school reform can affect the relationships between families and schools and can thereby alter family effects. Because family effects explain so much more variation in outcomes than do school effects, a small improvement in family conduct that comes about through school reform may be much more useful than a relatively large change in school inputs. In other words, family effects are so important that school reformers are neglectful if they do not attempt to partly improve family effects.

### CHANNELS FOR FAMILY EFFECTS

One can distinguish between three types of family variables: (1) those that are not under the family's control (race, ethnicity); (2)

9. Author's calculations using United States Department of Labor, Bureau of Labor Statistics, *The National Longitudinal Survey of Youth, 1979–1998*, release 10.0, restricted access computer file (Columbus, Ohio: Center for Human Resource Research, Ohio State University, 1999).

10. For the regression in which completed years of education is the dependent variable, the F-statistic for the hypothesis that the family variables are jointly equal to zero is 205, the F-statistic for the hypothesis that the school input variables are jointly equal to zero is 3, and the F-statistic for the hypothesis that the neighborhood variables are jointly equal to zero is 3.

11. The NLSY does not have a twelfth-grade test, but its respondents did take the Armed Services Vocational Aptitude Battery (ASVAB) set of tests. It is interesting to note that if one takes students' standardized scores on the language arts and mathematics components of the ASVAB tests and regresses these scores

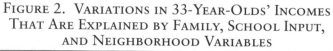

FIGURE 2. VARIATIONS IN 33-YEAR-OLDS' INCOMES
THAT ARE EXPLAINED BY FAMILY, SCHOOL INPUT,
AND NEIGHBORHOOD VARIABLES

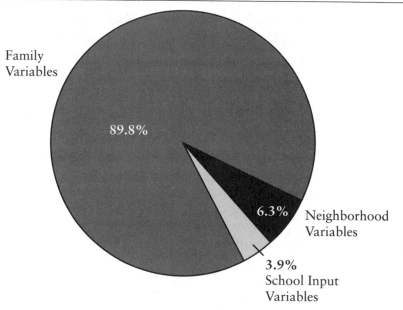

those that are partially under the family's control but are unlikely to be affected directly by the family-school relationship (parents' education, family income); and (3) those that describe family conduct that is intimately related to schooling or learning (visiting the school, planning courses with the child, using the library, and so on). School reform—or, more broadly, the way that schools operate—can change the family effects associated with all three types of variables. Most obviously, if school reform affects family conduct (measured by variables of the third type), it can change family effects. In addition, the effects of variables of the first and second type may be related to schools. For instance, if racial discrimina-

on the family, school, and neighborhood variables, one obtains results that are similar to the NELS results described above. The similarly suggests that the results are not unique to the NELS or NLSY but are general across time, specific tests, and samples.

FIGURE 3. VARIATIONS IN 33-YEAR-OLDS' EDUCATIONAL
ATTAINMENT THAT ARE EXPLAINED BY FAMILY, SCHOOL INPUT,
AND NEIGHBORHOOD VARIABLES

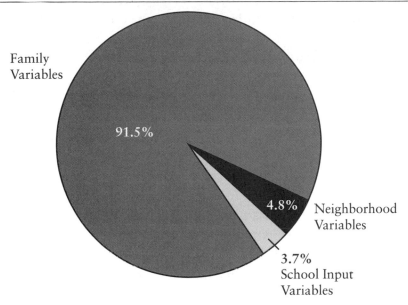

tion has traditionally limited the residential choices of some race—
and thereby limited their ability of choose among schools—then a
school reform that affects the relationship between race and school
choice may alter the effect of race. Similarly, if income has traditionally limited families' ability to choose among schools, then a
school reform that affects the relationship of income and school
choice may alter the effect of family income.

Finally, one should not forget that school reform may have indirect effects on the second type of variable (parents' education,
parents' income) because a reform that affects one generation's
schooling can change the educational and income "inheritance" of
the next generation.

Naturally, one would like to know the exact mechanism by
which each family variable affects student outcomes, but—for the
purposes of this chapter—is it *necessary* to know the exact mecha-

nisms? The answer to this question is no because it turns out that, on the whole, the reforms that are likely to improve some family effects are also likely to improve other family effects. The fact that various family effects are affected in the same direction is not pure coincidence. Intuitively, a reform will tend to improve family effects of many kinds if it makes parents more informed, more active, and less constrained by arbitrary factors.

Nevertheless, we may be interested in the family characteristics that are associated, statistically, with a child's being successful academically. Although the effect of a given characteristic does vary slightly with the outcome that one uses to measure a child's success—test scores, educational attainment, income, and so on—the family characteristics that are important statistically for one outcome are important statistically for other outcomes. All the family characteristics included in the regression described above are typically statistically significant predictors of outcomes.[12]

Parents' completed years of education is the family characteristic that typically has the greatest statistical significance in regressions like that described above. Family income has less importance but is another significant predictor of a child's achievement.[13] Not surprisingly, parents who are more educated and families with higher incomes tend to have children who are higher achievers. Family *conduct* variables that are statistically significant predictors of good student outcomes include owning an atlas, owning a dictionary, owning more than fifty books, having a computer for child's use with homework, having a calculator for child's use with

12. In a regression, t-statistics are commonly used to measure the statistical significance of effects. If an effect has a t-statistic with an absolute value of 1.96, then it has only a 5 percent probability of being a zero effect. A t-statistic that is larger than 1.96 in absolute value has an even smaller probability of being a zero effect.

13. For instance, when test scores are the outcome, parents' education has a t-statistic between 19 and 22 while parents' income (which is also important) has a t-statistic between 9 and 11. When students' later educational attainment is the outcome, parents' education has a t-statistic of 29, while parents' income has a t-statistic of 2. When students' later income is the outcome, parents' education has a t-statistic of 8 while parents' income has a t-statistic of 5.

homework, having attended a school event, parents' checking that homework is done, parents' planning course-taking with child, using the library, visiting science or history museums, parents' knowing what courses child is taking, parents' knowing how well child is doing in school, and parents' knowing graduation requirements.[14]

Does it really matter if each of the above-mentioned family conduct variables has an independent, causal effect on children? For instance, it may be that using the library and having a calculator available are symptoms of parent's knowing more about their children's schooling. For the purposes of this chapter, it does not matter *which* family conduct variables have a causal effect so long as *some* alterable behaviors or attitudes have a causal effect. Why does it not matter? First, in each case in which I present evidence that schools can affect family conduct, I rely on a source of variation in schools' operation that does *not* depend on the decisions of individual families. This is an important distinction that will become clear through examples. Second, when I present evidence that schools' operations foster a particular family behavior (such as attending school events), I am not attempting to focus attention on that particular behavior. Indeed, the conduct variables are

---

14. The t-statistics for these family characteristics are owning an atlas, t-statistic of about 3; owning a dictionary, t-statistic of about 5; owning more than fifty books, t-statistic of about 5; having a computer for child's use with homework, t-statistic of about 3; having a calculator for child's use with homework, t-statistic of about 5; having attended a school event, t-statistic of about 4; parents' checking that homework is done, t-statistic of about 4; parents' planning course-taking with child, t-statistic of about 7; using the library, t-statistic of about 11; visiting science or history museums, t-statistic of about 9; parents' knowing what courses child is taking, t-statistic of about 4; parents' knowing how well child is doing in school, t-statistic of about 3; and parents' knowing graduation requirements, t-statistic of about 3.

The effects described come from regressions in which the explanatory variables are the relevant family conduct variable plus all the other family, school input, and neighborhood variables listed on pages 95–96. The dependent variables are twelfth-grade reading scores, twelfth-grade mathematics scores, educational attainment at age 33, and income at age 33. The t-statistics are approximate because they vary slightly with the outcome.

highly correlated, and the effect is probably on several related behaviors.

## Parents' Choosing Better Schools

Some commentators doubt whether most families make intentional choices about their children's education. Other commentators assert that, to the extent that families do make intentional
choices, they are guided by superficial characteristics such as the
appearance of buildings or success in sports.

Survey evidence suggests that the majority of parents *do* make
intentional choices about schools. Among nonrural parents surveyed in the 1996 National Household Education Survey (NHES),
15.0 percent chose their child's school by selecting a private
school, another 16.8 percent chose their child's school by selecting
a magnet school or other public school of choice (that is, some
form of public school choice was available in their area and they
took advantage of it), and the remaining parents sent their children
to the school assigned to their residence. Within this last category
of parents, however, 54 percent exercised some choice among
schools by choosing their residence partly in order to choose a
school. All in all, 68.6 percent of parents made an intentional
choice about their child's school.[15] See figure 4 for a summary of
these statistics.

Another type of evidence—and a type that suggests that parents
care about achievement and not just buildings or sports—comes
from the amount that families are willing to pay for schools that
produce better educational outcomes. House prices are the main
form by which such payments are made in the United States. When
the price of a house reflects the quality of the school associated
with it, it is evidence of a demand for school quality among parents

15. Author's calculation using United States Department of Education, National Center for Education Statistics, *National Household Education Survey,
1996,* restricted access computer file (Washington, D.C.: National Center for Education Statistics, 1998). I exclude rural parents from this analysis because, in
many rural areas, there is only one school that is reasonably nearby.

FIGURE 4. PARENTS' VARIOUS FORMS OF INTENTIONAL CHOICE
AMONG SCHOOLS (in percent)

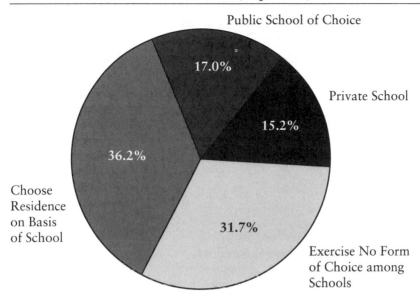

that is widespread. Why? If just a few families were willing to pay for schools that produced better educational outcomes, then their choices would have little effect on house prices. A systematic relationship between house prices and public school outcomes associated with them is evidence of a widespread parental interest in schools.

The best house price evidence on parents' willingness to pay for schools that produce good educational outcomes comes from neighboring houses that are situated on the boundary of different schools' attendance districts. Black (1999) considers physically similar, neighboring houses in Massachusetts that are in the same school district but on opposite sides of a boundary dividing two school attendance areas.[16] Such houses differ only in the school

16. Sandra E. Black, "Do Better Schools Matter? Parental Valuation of Elementary Education," *Quarterly Journal of Economics* 114, no. 2 (May 1999): 577–600.

that their residents' children must attend; they share the same neighborhood, the same property tax rates, and local public goods other than schools (such as police, fire, and recreation services). She finds that a house associated with school that has test scores that are 5 percent higher carries a market price that is 2.5 percent higher. She does not find evidence that people are willing to pay for superficial characteristics of schools such as newer buildings.

Other evidence from house prices comes from school finance equalization programs, some of which force districts to invest in fewer school inputs than local taxpayers are willing to purchase. In districts that are constrained to spend less than they voluntarily spent, the response to the imposition of an equalization program is a fall in house prices—showing that local families valued the ability to choose (and pay for) the resources in their school.[17] Moreover, Brunner and Sonstelie show that, in such districts, foundations arise that solicit donations from local families and pay for the school inputs banned by the school finance equalization programs.[18] In short, the evidence from the housing market suggests that many parents do value their ability to choose better schools—and are willing to pay for them.

Although the survey and house price evidence suggests that many parents do make intentional choices about schools, the evidence does not imply that all parents are equally able to exert a "good" family effect by making the investment in their child's education that they would like to make. A better school costs more—within the public sector as well as the private sector. Families may have restricted school choices because they can afford only a limited range of housing, because they would face racial or

17. See Caroline M. Hoxby, "All School Finance Equalizations Are Not Created Equal," *Quarterly Journal of Economics*, 2001. Such districts exist especially in states like California and New Mexico that effectively imposed binding restrictions on per-pupil spending as part of their school finance equalization programs.

18. Eric Brunner and Jon Sonstelie, "Coping with Serrano: Voluntary Contributions to California's Local Public Schools," in *1996 Proceedings of the Eighty-Ninth Conference on Taxation*, held under the auspices of the National Tax Association, 1996, 372–81.

ethnic discrimination outside of a limited range of housing, because they cannot afford private school tuition, or simply because there are few public school districts and/or few private schools in their area.

For instance, in the NHES survey, the probability that a family exercised some choice over their child's school varied with the family's income and race. For instance, among nonrural families with incomes between $10,000 and $15,000, 5.3 percent selected a private school, 21.4 percent took advantage of a local public school choice program, and 26.6 percent chose their residence partly on the basis of the school. In contrast, among nonrural families with incomes of $75,000 or more, 28.8 percent selected a private school, 10.4 percent took advantage of a local public school choice program, and 42.2 percent chose their residence on the basis of the school[19] (see figure 5).

Controlling for income, black and Hispanic families are *more* likely than white families to make intentional school choices by selecting a private school or a public school of choice, but they are less likely than white families to make intentional school choices by choosing their residence on the basis of the school. This suggests that discrimination that differs across residential areas may indeed be a constraint on black and Hispanic families. That is, their ability to exercise choice among public schools may be limited by residential housing patterns. For instance, consider a relatively narrow income band such as $30,000 to $35,000—that is, examine racial differences in school choice while effectively holding income constant; 14.8 percent of black families, 14.1 percent of Hispanic families, 4.6 percent of Asian families, and 12.1 percent of white families with incomes of $30,000 to $35,000 use private schools. Within the same income band, 25.6 percent of black families, 17.0 percent of Hispanic families, 36.4 percent of Asian families, and 10.3 percent of white families use public schools of choice. Finally, within the same income band, 29.9 per-

19. These calculations and those in the next two paragraphs are author's calculations using the NHES, United States Department of Education, 1998.

FIGURE 5. PARENTS' VARIOUS INCOME RANGES WHO EXERCISE
FORMS OF CHOICE AMONG SCHOOLS (in percent)

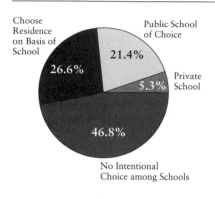

Family Income $10,000–$15,000

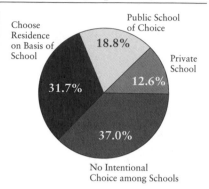

Family Income $25,000–$30,000

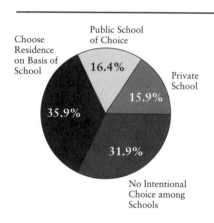

Family Income $40,000–$50,000

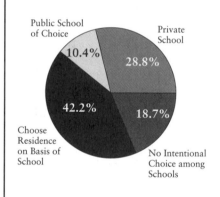

Family Income $75,000 or More

cent of black families, 30.4 percent of Hispanic families, 31.8 percent of Asian families, and 48.4 percent of white families choose
their residence on the basis of the school (see figure 6).

Of course, income constraints and discrimination do not account for all the parents who make no intentional choices about
schools. For instance, when one looks just at white parents with
incomes of $35,000 to $40,000, one finds that parents who have
more education are more likely to make intentional school choices:

## FIGURE 6. PARENTS OF VARIOUS RACES/ETHNICITIES WHO EXERCISE FORMS OF CHOICE AMONG SCHOOLS
(in percent)

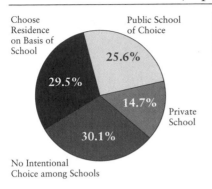

**Black Families with Income
$30,000–35,000**

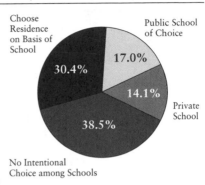

**Hispanic Families with Income
$30,000–35,000**

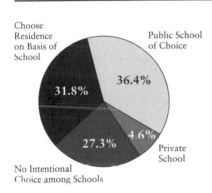

**Asian Families with Income
$30,000–35,000**

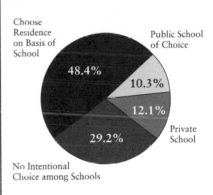

**White Families with Income
$30,000–35,000**

55 percent of parents who have only a high school degree do so while 63 percent of parents with a baccalaureate degree do so. Perhaps more educated parents are more informed or more motivated to purposefully choose a school for their children. One must be cautious, however, before jumping to the conclusion that parents who do not currently seek much information about various schools' quality have little inclination to choose good-quality

schools. Many families that appear to be disinclined to focus on school quality are also families that have a restricted set of choices. A family with a restricted set of schools from which to choose has little incentive to invest in information about schools.

In short, some family effects that appear to be income effects or racial/ethnic effects are probably not direct effects of income or race/ethnicity but indirect effects of parents' limited ability to choose a school for their children. Can one measure the share of family income and race/ethnicity effects that is related to schools through this channel? It is difficult to get a perfect measure, but a crude measure of the public school choice available to a family is a count of the number of districts in its metropolitan area where the family would be likely to be able to afford housing and the family would not be more than twice as racially/ethnically isolated as its racial/ethnic group generally is in its metropolitan area.[20] If one controls for just this crude measure of ability to exercise choice among public school districts, the explanatory power of family income and race/ethnicity drops by a third.[21] Thus, a good share of the family effect of income and race/ethnicity is probably related to schools. A reform that extended school choice to families who currently have restricted choice would likely decrease the negative effect (on achievement) of coming from a low-income or a minority family.

20. Specifically, one counts the number of districts that a family could choose if it were restricted to choose districts in which at least 20 percent of the housing is such that the annual rent or estimated annual mortgage payments would be no more than 0.3 of the family's annual income. One also counts the number of districts that a family could choose if its racial group in the district has at least 0.5 of the share of the district population that it would have if its racial group were spread evenly over the metropolitan area. For instance, if blacks represented 10 percent of a metropolitan area's population, then a district in that metropolitan area would be counted as "available" to black families if the district's population were at least 5 percent black. If blacks represented 12 percent of a metropolitan area's population, then a district would be counted as "available" to black families if the district's population were at least 6 percent black.

21. Author's calculations using the NELS, United States Department of Education, 1996.

## Parents' Influence on Curriculum and Pedagogy

Family effects also work through parents' choosing schools partly based on curriculum and pedagogy. What are parents' preferences? The evidence suggests that parents are results-oriented (their liking for a pedagogical technique depends on how their child reacts, not on the educational theory that underlies it) and skeptical about pedagogical and curricular innovations. For instance, Hess shows that, in schools where parents effectively exercise choice, they forestall the rapid introduction and discarding of curricular and pedagogical fads.[22] Center city schools (over which local parents have little influence) are likely to have "policy churn," Hess's term for frequent and erratic changes in pedagogy, curriculum, and school rules. Even the best school policies are likely to be ineffective if introduced with little consistency. Thus, one means by which parents can have a good family effect on their children is by preventing them from being subjected to policy churn.

In addition, parents are a force that tends to keep schools oriented toward student outcomes, rather than educational theories. Some evidence about parents' being results-oriented comes from surveys. For instance, Redfield describes a survey of parents, teachers, students, and principals in a school district.[23] Among these groups, only the parents favored evaluating a school on achievement outcomes such as standardized test scores, the dropout rate, and the share of students who attend college. The "teachers were more concerned with non-academic outcomes that might be attributable to themselves," and the principals were too worried about

22. Frederick M. Hess, "Policy Churn and the Plight of Urban School Reform," in *Learning from School Choice*, ed. Bryan C. Hassel and Paul E. Peterson (Washington, D.C.: Brookings Institution, 1998).

23. Doris L. Redfield, "A Comparison of the Perspectives of Teachers, Students, Parents, and Principals Concerning the Influences of Teaching on Students and the Use of Student Outcomes to Evaluate Teaching," Kentucky Department of Education Research Report, 1987 (available through EDRS, accession number ED290765).

the legitimacy of various tests to favor their use.[24] Redfield's findings are confirmed by the NELS parent surveys in which the majority of parents reported that they wanted a greater role in deciding whether schools, teachers, and administrators were meeting standards. In contrast, most parents were content to let schools manage themselves internally with regard to textbooks, teaching strategies, and so on.[25]

Additional evidence about parents' preferences, however, comes from schools that have incentives to submit to parents' preferences because they (the schools) are affected by parents' choices. This is evidence based on parents' *revealed preferences*—that is, the preferences revealed by their behavior. If we compare metropolitan areas in which parents exercise little choice (because there are only a few school districts, given the size of the metropolitan area) to those in which parents exercise significant choice (because there are many school districts, given the size of the metropolitan area), we can learn about the average parent's preferences. Choice among school districts is particularly good to examine because, though a limited form of choice, it is by far the most pervasive form of choice in the United States. Also, different metropolitan areas have very different amounts of this form of choice—mainly due to accidents of history and geography. The diverse experiences of different metropolitan areas provide variation that is useful empirically. Finally, choice among *districts* is important because districts are autonomous, both in control and finance. This means that they have to compete for parents in a meaningful way.[26]

24. Apparently, the students perceived the questions somewhat differently from the other groups since they were mainly worried about random factors (such as illness) that might have affected *individual* performance.

25. Author's calculations using NELS base year and second follow-up parent surveys, United States Department of Education, 1996.

26. For instance, consider the extremes—metropolitan areas with no choice among school districts and metropolitan areas that given their size have the maximum amount of district choice that is available in the United States. A good measure of school choice is an index equal to the probability that two randomly selected students in a metropolitan area attend the same district. Of course, in a metropolitan area like Miami that has only one district, the index is equal to 1. In a metropolitan area like Boston that has more than 90 districts, the index is

Compared with schools in metropolitan areas with minimal choice among districts, schools with maximum choice are 35 percent more likely to have a curriculum that fulfills the New Basics criteria in English, math, science, social studies, and foreign language.[27] Such schools are also more likely to "emphasize discipline" (an increase of 0.6 on a scale of 1 to 3), have classroom activities that are "highly structured" (an increase of 1.2 on a scale of 1 to 3), and have principals who are evaluated (in part) on students' standardized test scores (an increase of 0.4 on a scale of 1 to 3). In summary, according to their revealed preferences, the average parent prefers a curriculum that is oriented toward core subjects like reading, writing, mathematics, history, and science; uses outcomes like test scores to evaluate school administrators;

---

approximately equal to 0.01. The source of these statistics is the United States Department of Education, *School District Data Book: 1990 Census School District Special Tabulation,* computer file (Washington, D.C.: National Center for Education Statistics, 1995).

One can compare metropolitan areas with varying degrees of choice among public school districts—minimal, average, maximal. Moreover, one can guarantee that the variation among metropolitan areas is generated by local geography, rather than a layout of school districts designed in response to parents' behavior. One guarantees this by instrumenting for the choice index with the metropolitan area's number of *natural* boundaries—streams and rivers turn out to be the most important natural boundaries, in practice. Instrumenting for choice is important because it allows us to see the long-term, *causal* effect of school choice on parental behavior. Instrumenting prevents us from mistaking an association between choice and parental behavior for a causal effect of choice on parental behavior. Intuitively, the instrumenting identifies the causal effect of choice because natural boundaries can (through choice) affect parent behavior but parental behavior cannot affect the existence of streams, rivers, or other natural boundaries. In this chapter, the effect of choice among public school districts is always estimated using the index of choice, instrumental variables based on natural geographic features, and numerous variables that control for metropolitan area characteristics such as population, land area, and demographics. Hoxby (2000) contains much more detail about the empirical strategy that is briefly described here, including details on data sources, measures of public and private school choice, and the effects of using instrumental variables.

27. The New Basics standard in question is equivalent to that used for the National Assessment of Educational Progress (NAEP). To attain the standard, a school's high school curriculum must contain four Carnegie units of English, three Carnegie units of mathematics, three Carnegie units of science, three Carnegie units of social studies, and two Carnegie units of foreign language.

and has a school environment that provides structure and discipline.[28]

### Parents' Interacting with and Controlling Their Child's School

One means by which parents can have a good "family effect" on their child is by judicious control of their child's experience at school. Parents know a substantial amount about their child's abilities and how their child is reacting to school, and a child's school experience is likely to be better if the school makes use of parents' knowledge. For instance, a parent may be able to help a school identify a child's learning style, interests, or disability. In addition, parents can reinforce their child's teacher—for instance, by emphasizing the importance of the subject that the teacher has identified as most needing work. Finally, parents can get directly involved in their child's schooling—by participating in school activities, steering their child away from incompetent teachers, planning their child's course of study, being an advocate for their child's needs, and so on.

To interact successfully, parents and schools must communicate effectively and share a sense of common purpose. Why are communication and common purpose more prevalent in some schools than others? Both logic and evidence suggest that decentralization of school decision making is one prerequisite for communication and common purpose. Simply put, parents *can* effectively interact with decision makers at their child's school, particularly if it is a reasonably small school. Most parents *cannot* effectively interact with decision makers who preside over many schools because they (the parents) have little or no direct access to such high-ranking

---

28. In fact, there is evidence that parents may like good grades to a fault. That is, there is more grade inflation (measured by the relationship of a school's letter grades to its scores on national, standardized tests) in schools that face significant parental choice. It may be, however, that parents are not fooled by the inflated letter grades but believe that college admissions officers or employers will be fooled.

administrators. In short, if a school is not allowed to make important curricular or other decisions because authority is centralized, then parents have little incentive to interact with the only school staff to whom they have access (school-level staff).

It is possible that another prerequisite for communication and common purpose is parents' being at least somewhat able to choose their child's school. Choice may matter for two reasons. First, when families are able to choose among schools, they are more likely to end up in a school with other families who share their preferences. Such schools naturally have more community feeling and shared purpose. Second, families who have to make choices among schools tend to force schools to communicate information to them that is relevant to their decision making. Naturally, a school prefers to inform parents about its (the school's) successes and prefers to remain silent about its failings. If parents need to decide how well a school is performing relative to the other local schools, they are more likely to insist upon the school's communicating information like performance on statewide tests, college admissions, and so on. Moreover, because schools are more likely to listen to parents in an environment where schools have to remain attractive to parents, parents are more likely to speak up in such an environment.

Evidence on the relationship between parental interaction and school decentralization comes from data on school consolidations. For instance, consider school consolidations in the state of Connecticut between 1988 and 1992. Parent surveys before and after the period show that parental involvement fell and parent-school communication deteriorated in schools that were consolidated or otherwise reorganized so that they grew substantially (an enrollment increase of at least 25 percent). Relative to parents in the *same* schools in prior years, parents in the consolidated schools were 12 percent less likely to respond to questionnaires from the school, 7 percent less likely to say that their school "communicate[d] well" with them, 10 percent less likely to participate in parent-teacher organizations, 10 percent less likely to attend a school open house, and 5 percent less likely to check their children's homework.[29]

Evidence on the relationship between parents' being able to choose a school and parents' being involved with a school comes from comparing metropolitan areas in which families have more and less choice among school districts. Compared with parents who have no choice among districts, parents who live in metropolitan areas with maximum choice are 70 percent less likely to be ignorant of the courses their children are taking and 59 percent less likely to be ignorant of the graduation requirements of their child's school. Compared to parents with no choice, parents with maximum choice are also 16 percent more likely to be sent standardized test scores whenever the school administers a test, 43 percent more likely to have attended a meeting at their child's school, 19 percent more likely to have attended a school event, and 50 percent more likely to plan their child's courses with him over multiple conversations.[30]

As additional evidence, people often cite differences in parental conduct between regular public schools and private schools—since parents *must choose* private schools. On the one hand, the differences in parental conduct are striking. For instance, 47 percent of parents visit their child's regular public school, while 85 percent of parents visit their child's private school. On the other hand, it is difficult to interpret this evidence because parents who would interact more with schools under *any* circumstances may be more likely to send their child to a private school. Therefore, it is hard to give much weight to such evidence, intriguing though it is. Much more convincing evidence on this front comes from comparing parents who are "lotteried in" and "lotteried out" of voucher programs: see Paul Peterson's chapter in this volume.

29. Author's calculations, based on Strategic School Profiles 1992 through 1998 and Town and School District Profiles 1987 through 1992, Connecticut State Department of Education, Bureau of Research, Evaluation, and Student Assessment, *Strategic School Profiles, 1992–93 through 1997–98,* computer file (Hartford, Conn.: Connecticut State Department of Education, 1999).

30. The calculations in this and the following three paragraphs are author's calculations using the NELS, United States Department of Education, 1996.

Finally, can parents be sufficiently informed about their child's school to be a force for good? Consider, for example, whether parents can discern a school's value added—that is, how much the school is adding to children's learning each year, taking account of their learning at the end of the previous year. In the NELS survey, parents rate their school on whether it "places a high priority on learning," whether they are "satisfied" with the education, and whether "the teaching is good." There is a correlation between parents' rating and their school's value added. In the NELS, a school's value added is based on a school-level average of individual students' value added—specifically, the difference between a student's tenth- and eighth-grade knowledge in reading and math, as measured by standardized tests. For instance, in schools with value added in the lowest quartile, only 19 percent of parents "strongly agree" that their school places a priority on learning and 25 percent of parents "disagree" or "strongly disagree." In contrast, in schools with value added in the highest quartile, 32 percent of parents "strongly agree" that their school places a priority on learning and only 10 percent of parents "disagree" or "strongly disagree." In schools with value added in the lowest quartile, only 15 percent of parents are "very satisfied" with the education; but, in schools with value added in the highest quartile, 44 percent of parents are "very satisfied."

Interestingly, the correlation between parents' ratings and schools' value added is much higher in metropolitan areas where parents have a high degree of choice among districts. In fact, regression results support the hypothesis that the correlation between parents' rating and schools' value added *only* exists in metropolitan areas with an above-average degree of choice. There is no evidence of a correlation in metropolitan areas with little of no choice among districts. For instance, in metropolitan areas with maximum choice, raising a school's value-added from the lowest to the highest quartiles raises its "teaching is good" rating 2 categories (from "disagree" to "strongly agree" or from "strongly disagree" to "agree") and raises its "satisfied with education" rating 3 categories (from "very dissatisfied" to "very satisfied"). In metropolitan areas with no choice among districts, raising a school's value-added has no statistically significant effect on its rating.[31]

*Homes That Complement School Activities*

Even if one compares families that are equally supportive of their children's emotional well-being and equally ready to devote resources to their children, one still finds differences in the degree to which families create home environments that actively complement their children's school activities. Parents may create study space or play space for their child; may provide their children with books or with toys; may spend time with their children at libraries or shopping malls; and so on. For instance, compared with children who score in the bottom quartile on reading and math tests, children who score in the top quartile are more likely to use libraries with their parents (79 percent versus 48 percent) and visit science museums with their parents (63 percent versus 27 percent). They are also more likely to come from homes with more than fifty books (96 percent versus 76 percent), with an atlas (81 percent versus 55 percent), with a calculator (98 percent versus 89 percent), and with a computer (60 percent versus 27 percent).

Clearly, parents differ in the degree to which they create a home environment that complements a child's schooling. The relevant question is, then, are there schools that increase parents' inclination to create an environment that complements school? One hypothesis is that parents who have made a personal investment in their child's schooling are more likely to complement the school at home, in order to increase the value of the investment they have already made. Evidence that supports this hypothesis comes from two main sources: parents who are aware of having made a per-

31. The results described are from regressions of the parental ratings on a measure of district choice, an interaction of the choice measure with the school's value added, the school's value added, and a number of metropolitan-level demographic variables. The choice measure and its interaction are instrumented using measures of natural boundaries in the metropolitan area.

sonal investment because they have just shifted their children from public to private school, and parents who are aware of making a personal investment because they have a lot of choice among public school districts (and, thus, are aware of paying—either through their house price or through their local taxes—for a better school).

Parents who shift their children from public to private schools tend to be especially aware of making an investment in their children's education—simply because they have to start paying tuition. It is interesting to see whether families alter their home environment at the same time. Moreover, it is useful to look *within* the same family over time (rather than across private school and public school families at a point in time) in order to hold the family's underlying characteristics constant. In the NELS, 192 families switched their children from public to private schools over the course of the survey (that is, between eighth and twelfth grades). Although this is a small sample of families and we observe only a small number of variables both before and after the school move, it is nevertheless possible to see some statistically significant changes in family behavior. After switching to private schools, the families are 4 percent more likely to own an atlas and 5 percent more likely to have a specific place for their children to study.

In metropolitan areas where families have a lot of choice among school districts, parents are aware of making a personal investment when they choose to live in a high-performing district. This is because, as described above, they have to pay for the district—through their house price, their property taxes, or both. Are parents in such metropolitan areas more likely to make their home environments complement their children's schools? Data from the NELS suggest that they are. Compared to metropolitan areas with minimal choice, in metropolitan areas with maximum choice 8 percent more parents provide a home environment that supports their children's school experience—according to their school's principal. In addition, 14 percent more parents use libraries with their children, 5 percent more visit science museums with their children, 4 percent more have an atlas, 4 percent more have a calculator, and 18 percent more have a computer.[32]

## FAMILY INFLUENCE, NOT THE FORCE FOR GOOD THAT IT COULD BE

This chapter is by no means the first work to note the importance of families in student outcomes or to suggest that school reform can be most efficacious when parents are "co-opted." There is a long tradition of trying to involve parents in their children's education. These attempts often take the form of parent training. The Title I program, for instance, attempts to train parents so that they can be school aides. The Comer school program uses moral suasion to get parents to learn along with their children.[33] Another approach to "co-opting" parents is getting them into the school to talk about their careers, help with projects, or accompany extracurricular activities. It is not the purpose of this chapter to dismiss such approaches to parents, but it is important to recognize that they essentially try to expand the school to include parents—making them into "extension students" of a sort. It is natural that schools should try to extend themselves in this way—after all, some parents have plenty to learn and teaching is what schools do. But we have seen that school effects on students are not very strong. Should we suppose that school effects will be much stronger on parents, who cannot spend much time at school and whose habits may be more fixed?

School reforms can only exploit family effects in a significant way if they concede the primacy of families as consumers of schools and investors in their children's education. If a reform concedes such primacy, how does it operate? It gives parents incen-

32. All these estimates control for family background characteristics, control for metropolitan areas' demographic characteristics, and use instruments for public school choice based on natural boundaries.

33. James P. Comer, *School Power: Implications of an Intervention Project* (New York: Free Press; New York: Maxwell Macmillan International, 1995, ©1993).

tives to be savvy, demanding consumers of schools by making the reward for wise decisions greater and by reducing barriers that constrain parents' choices arbitrarily. In other words, if parents can gain a lot in terms of their children's education by engaging in wise conduct, they have incentives to conduct themselves well. If, on the other hand, the system is such that the school that can be obtained by even the best consumer parent is only slightly better than the one obtained by the worst, parents will not have much incentive to alter their conduct. In summary, a school reform that unreservedly tries to exploit the power of family effects does so by allowing families that conduct themselves well to earn big rewards. This is essentially different from a reform that tries to exploit the power of school effects by extending schools into the parental domain.

Even within reforms that give parents incentives to exert positive family effects, one can differentiate among a few types of reform. Some simply give parents a greater range of choices; some go further and make parents more aware of their investment in education; and some go even further and pressure schools to be responsive to parents. The first type of reform—for example, decentralization of authority—increases parents' incentives to be good consumers by adding variety to their menu of schools. The second type of reform—for example, a voucher supplied by a private foundation (so that no money is withdrawn from the regular public school budget when a student takes a voucher)—increases parents' incentives to compare schools' efficiency. That is, parents should begin comparing schools on the basis of their value added for cost. The second type of reform also gives parents incentives to make investments that are complementary to school, such as family visits to libraries or a computer for their child's use. The third type of reform—for example, a charter school program in which charter fees come from the regular public school district that loses the students—makes parents' more likely to be heard when they have concerns and, therefore, increases parents' incentives to be demanding consumers, even in regular public schools.

Currently, not all parents are able to earn better education for their children by engaging in wise conduct. As described above, parents currently differ substantially in their ability to exercise choice, and the evidence suggests that these differences account for at least some—possibly a substantial minority—of the effects of family income and family race/ethnicity. There is no structural reason why poorer families should not be able to choose among numerous schools, just as richer families do. To be sure, without drastic changes in school finance, richer families may always be able to spend more on their children's education than poorer families do. But it is essentially arbitrary that richer, nonminority families are more likely to face numerous, small districts while poor and minority families tend to face huge districts from which it is costly to move. Even under a scenario in which families get permanently stuck with the level of per-pupil spending that they currently have, the degree of choice available to poor and minority families could be made much more similar to that of richer, nonminority families. All that would be required is the breaking down of the residentially based monopoly power of huge school districts—through district partition or (more easily) charter schools or vouchers.

Systematic differences by family income and race account, however, for only some of the many limits on parents' ability to choose among schools—and, thus, account for only some of the weakness in the incentives for parents to be good consumers and investors. Many well-off, nonminority families have limited choice because they live in metropolitan areas with only a few districts. Moreover, choice among public school districts is a weak form of choice, even in metropolitan areas with the maximum amount of such choice. It is a weak form of choice because families have limited flexibility once they have made an initial residential decision and because the mechanisms for rewarding effective schools and penalizing ineffective ones are indirect at best.[34] Also, public schools are controlled

34. The mechanisms, such as they are, operate through the property tax. See Caroline Hoxby, "The Effects of School Choice on Curriculum and Atmosphere," in *Earning and Learning: How Schools Matter*, ed. Susan E. Mayer and Paul E. Peterson (Washington, D.C.: Brookings Institution, 1999), for a discus-

politically, and parents are a less concentrated (and thus less effective) interest group than teachers, especially if teachers are unionized. In areas where regular public schools are constrained by regulations or unions, they may be so much of a kind that parents' do not face meaningfully different alternatives. Many of these limits on parents' ability to be good consumers are relaxed by school reforms such as vouchers and charter schools.

Finally, it is currently difficult for a parent to be an informed consumer. Schools retain as much control of their students' outcome data as they can. Even schools that face incentives to supply parents with information prefer to release performance information selectively. Parents will not be really informed consumers until schools have incentives to provide information *and* states (or parent coalitions) create consistent standards about the sort of information that schools should release. In fact, it appears that the information environment is currently improving because of a recent upsurge in mandatory, statewide testing and statewide publication of school "report cards" and "profiles." Such state initiatives are consequences of public frustration over achievement, evinced in statehouses (where there is increasing discussion of school accountability) and in federal commissions like Goals 2000.

One may be wary of reforms that attempt to improve family effects by giving parents greater choice because one might worry that, while the reform would make many parents better consumers, it might give other parents greater opportunities to make school-related choices that are unwise or that have negative spillovers. For instance, one might worry that a minority of parents have bizarre ideas about curriculum and would give their children little knowledge of core subjects if they were allowed more choice. To take another simple example, one might worry that parents would leave a school that was financially burdened because it contained disabled students, without giving any consideration to

---

sion of rewards and penalties for regular public schools that operate through the property tax.

whether their behavior would induce flight by still other parents. Happily, choice-based reforms *lend* themselves to mechanisms that control such potential problems. In particular, the prices in choice-based reforms (such as the size of the voucher or the charter school fee) can be set to discourage choices that have negative spillovers or are otherwise undesirable, while still allowing latitude for a range of desirable consumer behavior on the part of parents.[35] In fact, command-and-control programs that attempt to command parents tend to fail because parents find ways to sidestep regulations. Parents do not even feel guilty about contraverting regulations if they think the regulations ignore the information that they (parents) have about the children's needs. Programs that work through parents' choices but make parents face the "social prices" of their actions may be the most efficient, least resisted way to manage problematic family behavior.

Ultimately, the argument that school reform needs to make the best use of families does not rely on reformers' *liking* families' preferences. Instead, the argument is practical. While a reformer may—in a deep sense—prefer schools to families as sources of in-

---

35. The price mechanisms in question are the subject of other work, but an example may be helpful. Consider a school district that is going to implement a charter school program that will be available to all its students. Suppose that the district is afraid that its schools will become more segregated and that it has a target for racial/ethnic desegregation in its schools. Its target might be the racial/ethnic composition of the district as a whole—say, 20 percent African American, 15 percent Hispanic, and 65 percent white non-Hispanic. The following price mechanism will allow charter schools to be widely available and will also encourage schools to reach the segregation target. The per-pupil payment to a charter school should be set at a level that is adequate so long as the school does not diverge egregiously from the district's target. The payment should, however, increase substantially as a school gets closer to the target. With such payments, the district effectively sets a price that parents and school staff have to pay if they make choices that cause their school to deviate from the target. Charter school staff have an incentive to reach out to (and make their program attractive to) students who would make their school more desegregated. Parents can obtain better funding for their children by moving them from schools where their race is overrepresented to schools where their race is underrepresented. Schools have an incentive to keep working toward the target but do not go out of business if they fall short in a particular year.

fluence on children, she or he might still choose reforms that improve family effects for the practical reason that a small, plausibly obtainable improvement in family effects would swamp a large, hopelessly optimistic improvement in school effects. According to the estimates described above, a reform that improved family effects by 5 percent would probably do more for students' outcomes than a reform that improved school effects by 70 percent. It is likely that school reform is capable of achieving at least small improvements in family effects because some of the key channels through which families affect their children are related to schools: choice of schools, pressure on schools to be achievement oriented, control of their children's school experiences through interacting with teachers and administrators, and creation of home environments that complement school.

# CHAPTER 6

# Getting Better Teachers—and Treating Them Right

## Chester E. Finn Jr.

American teachers do not get the respect, the freedom, the compensation, or the rewards that many of them deserve. At the same time, U.S. schools are not producing satisfactory results, a problem that is not likely to be solved until our classrooms are filled with excellent teachers. The key to well-educated children and strong schools is a top-notch teaching staff. Every child needs—and deserves—a knowledgeable, dedicated, and effective instructor, well grounded in academic content, expert at imparting knowledge and skills to children, and passionate about this calling. Unfortunately, while U.S. schools have many fine teachers today, they don't have enough. Complicating matters further, as many as two million of today's teachers will quit or retire over the next decade, creating a large need for qualified people to replace them—and for even more to accommodate the country's dual trends of enrollment growth and class-size shrinkage.

About this nest of intertwined quality and quantity problems there seems to be a national consensus. How to get from here to a suitable set of solutions, however, is the subject of far less agreement. My purpose in this chapter is to suggest a promising path that is very different from the one most policymakers and education reformers are presently following.

## BACKGROUND

In round numbers, U.S. public and private schools employ three million teachers. Many other Americans—estimates run in the neighborhood of four million—were trained to become teachers but for various reasons are not working in classrooms today. In addition, an unknown number of individuals who did not originally plan to teach would now consider doing so if the terms of employment—and entry—were different.

Private schools, for the most part, are free to hire anyone they like, without regard to specialized training or state certification. In some jurisdictions, public charter schools enjoy similar flexibility. With rare exceptions, however, standard public schools are permitted to employ only people who have been "certified" as teachers by the state.

Certification procedures and requirements vary, but typically they oblige the would-be public schoolteacher to attend a state-approved training program, ordinarily in a college of education, where the candidate must study a prescribed curriculum. Many of the required courses involve pedagogy, child development, the "foundations of education," "classroom diversity," "study of self (teacher) as learner," and so on.[1] Practice teaching is ordinarily required (and is the part that teachers generally find most valuable). There may be a test of basic skills. It is also common, at some point along the way, to test teaching candidates for their knowledge of pedagogy and, sometimes, knowledge of the subject in which they will be certified (which may or may not be the subject they end up teaching). States award teaching certificates to those who survive this cluttered, protracted, and irksome proc-

1. The number of required units varies from six semester units in Texas to thirty-six in some states. C. Emily Feistritzer and David T. Chester, *Alternative Teacher Certification: A State-by-State Analysis 1998–99* (Washington, D.C.: National Center for Education Information, 1998). Requirements for individual states can be found in the National Association of State Directors of Teacher Education and Certification (NASDTEC), *Manual on the Preparation and Certification of Educational Personnel, 1998–1999.*

ess.[2] That does not, however, mean that everyone holding such a certificate is well educated himself, much less that he will prove effective at imparting what he knows to the children in his classroom.

The length and complexity of these procedures depend on the state, as well as on the subject or level of schooling that the would-be teacher seeks to be certified in. For most, however, it becomes the driving force in their undergraduate education and, often, at the postgraduate level, too.

If an individual gets through college without having subjected herself to this regimen, and then seeks to become a public schoolteacher, it's usually necessary to return to college for a year or longer. Some states have developed "alternative" certification programs that make it possible to begin teaching without completing the standard preparation sequence in advance, although often it's mandatory to jump through the remaining hoops during evenings, weekends, and summers.

This marriage of "approved" teacher-training programs and state certification requirements has been the subject of criticism for many years. Two main objections are commonly voiced. First, that the content of these preparation sequences and certification requirements is banal and pointless stuff beloved of educationists but not very valuable to actual school practitioners; that it's minimally linked to subject matter mastery; and—most research indicates—that it can muster scant evidence of a relationship to classroom effectiveness. The second complaint is that this training-and-certification cycle is so burdensome—and full of "Mickey Mouse" courses and requirements—that it discourages able would-be teachers from making their way into the public schools.

These are problems that the nation needs to solve, for teacher quality matters a great deal. We know this from decades of research and the experience of millions of families. Recent studies in

2. In an average state (Missouri), seventy-three different certificates are available. Dale Ballou and Michael Podgursky, "Teacher Training and Licensure: A Layman's Guide," in *Better Teachers, Better Schools* (Washington, D.C.: Thomas B. Fordham Foundation, 1999), p. 34.

Tennessee, Boston, and Dallas, inter alia, find dramatic differences between the performance of youngsters who are assigned the best teachers and those entrusted to the worst classroom practitioners.[3] No matter how well intentioned, U.S. school reform efforts will surely falter unless essentially all teachers have the knowledge and skills necessary to help essentially all their pupils meet high standards.

Children who face high-stakes tests for promotion and graduation will need instructors with more knowledge and skill than ever before. But today's system for recruiting, preparing, licensing, and deploying teachers is not up to the dual challenge of quality and quantity.

No wonder many U.S. teachers do not feel ready for the challenges they encounter in their classrooms. According to a recent survey, only 36 percent of them feel well prepared to implement high district or state standards.[4]

Training and certification aren't the whole story, either. The personnel practices of the teaching field are archaic and bureaucratic. Licensure is often followed by a hiring sequence in which the likeliest openings for a novice are in the worst schools, there to be hurled into a classroom and left pretty much alone with a bunch of demanding kids and little opportunity for colleagueship, professional growth (apart from more Mickey Mouse "staff development" programs), or mentoring by expert teachers.

On top of that, the expert teachers themselves get no tangible rewards; they're paid exactly the same as ordinary (and weak) instructors. Longevity and paper credentials bring more money, but effectiveness does not. Nor does it matter whether one is a high

3. William L. Sanders and Joan C. Rivers, "Cumulative and Residual Effects of Teachers on Future Student Academic Achievement," 1996; Heather Jordan, Robert Mendro, and Dash Weerasinghe, "Teacher Effects on Longitudinal Student Achievement," 1997; and Boston Public Schools, "High School Restructuring," March 9, 1998. These research studies were all cited in Kati Haycock, "Good Teaching Matters a Lot," *Thinking K-16*, a publication of the Education Trust, 3, no. 2 (1998).

4. National Center for Education Statistics, *Teacher Quality: A Report on the Preparation and Qualifications of Public School Teachers* (Washington, D.C.: U.S. Department of Education, January 1999), p. iii.

school chemistry teacher whose other job opportunities pay $100,000 or a middle school social studies teacher whose non-teaching options are far less lucrative. Their salaries remain identical. The same spurious equality holds for teachers in tough inner-city classroom situations and those in cushier environments. So long as they work in the same school system, they're paid the same. (If the cushier setting is a suburban school system, it likely pays more.)

## DISPELLING SOME MYTHS

Some of the bizarre practices of the teaching field are ubiquitous, but others are more localized. Consider today's much-ballyhooed teacher shortage. True, some school systems have had difficulty recruiting fully certified teachers in certain fields. Yet others have dozens of applicants for virtually every classroom opening. Where there are shortages, they are at least partly created by the certification bottleneck itself and exacerbated by the silly uniformity of a compensation system that bears no relationship to the labor marketplace. In the aggregate, U.S. colleges of education actually produce more teaching candidates than our schools need; of the 142,000 college graduates prepared to teach in 1992–93, for example, more than half did not even apply for teaching jobs in the year following graduation.[5] Pennsylvania alone confers some 20,000 new teaching certificates each year yet hires only 5,100 teachers annually.[6]

Another surprise is that most "new hires" in American schools are not young people fresh from university preparation programs; roughly one-third of them are former teachers returning to the classroom, and another quarter are people who trained to teach at an earlier time but then changed their minds.[7] Of the 5,100 teach-

5. C. Emily Feistritzer and David T. Chester, *Alternative Teacher Certification: A State-by-State Analysis 2000* (Washington, D.C.: National Center for Education Information, 2000), p. 10.

6. Robert P. Strauss, "Who Gets Hired to Teach? The Case of Pennsylvania," in *Better Teachers, Better Schools* (Washington, D.C.: Thomas B. Fordham Foundation, 1999), 105.

7. Feistritzer and Chester, *Alternative Teacher Certification*, p. 9.

ers hired in Pennsylvania in each of the past several years, only 1,300 were newly certified. There's a vast "reserve pool" of teachers in America today. This also means that changing preparation programs today will not transform the teacher workforce tomorrow.[8]

There are shortages in certain specialties, to be sure. Math, science, foreign languages, and special ed face shortfalls in many places. High-poverty schools often encounter difficulty hiring enough good teachers. And turnover is rapid. It is estimated that one-third of all new teachers leave the field within five years, a rate that rises to half in high-poverty schools.[9] This would not necessarily be cause for concern if those who stayed were the ablest and most effective, but there's mounting evidence that the teachers who leave are the most promising. A recent study of college graduates found that novice teachers who scored in the top quartile on college entrance exams were almost twice as likely to exit the field as those who scored lower.[10]

Many people assume that paltry pay causes the attrition. And it's true that teacher salaries in the United States lag behind wages in some other careers. The average pay for a twenty-two to twenty-eight-year-old teacher with a bachelor's degree was $21,792 in 1999–2000, while pay for a forty-four to fifty-year-old teacher with a master's degree averaged $43,313.[11] But these averages mask wide variations. In Riverdale, New Jersey, for example, salaries start at $32,140 and peak at $56,415, while in

    8. C. Emily Feistritzer, "The Truth Behind the 'Teacher Shortage,'" *Wall Street Journal*, January 28, 1998.

    9. National Association of State Boards of Education Study Group on Teacher Development, Supply, and Demand, *The Numbers Game: Ensuring Quantity and Quality in the Teaching Workforce* (Alexandria, Va.: National Association of State Boards of Education, October 1998), p. 23.

    10. Ulrich Boser, "A Picture of the Teacher Pipeline: Baccalaureate and Beyond," *Quality Counts 2000—an Education Week/Pew Charitable Trusts Report on Education in the 50 States*, January 13, 2000, p. 17.

    11. Lynn Olson, "Sweetening the Pot: Policymakers Offer Enticements but Rarely Target Their Efforts." Ibid., p. 30.

nearby Mahwah, salaries start at $28,482 and top out at $85,075.[12]

The top pay in many places isn't bad, especially for a 180-day workyear. (Most Americans work about 240 days.) Within a given district, however, salaries are based almost entirely on seniority and academic degrees completed. Former New Jersey governor Thomas Kean has noted that "it's the only profession I know where you don't get a penny more for being good at what you do."[13] We should look forward to the day when great teachers, teachers in scarce fields, and teachers who shoulder difficult challenges are paid six-figure salaries. But this is not apt to happen so long as mediocre practitioners and superb instructors are harnessed to uniform pay scales.

Although it's surely true that meager starting salaries pose a barrier to attracting able people into teaching and holding them there, the training sequence, certification process, and school system personnel practices also bear much of the blame. They levy opportunity costs that deter talented individuals—young, middle-aged, and old—from even trying public school teaching and impose procedures and rules that strike many promising would-be teachers as irrelevant if not ridiculous. They also create wrong incentives for just about everyone up and down the line.

## Two Solutions

In crafting solutions to the problems outlined above, policymakers may choose between two basic approaches, briefly sketched in this section and then elaborated below.

One, which can fairly be termed the "conventional wisdom" of the teaching field itself, is most prominently associated with the National Commission on Teaching and America's Future (NCTAF),

12. Neil H. Reisner, "Pay Varies Widely Among Districts," in a special quality of life report by the *Record* staff, *Bergen Record*, December 14, 1995 (http://www.bergen.com/ed/95/salaries.htm).

13. David Glovin and John Mooney, "An Advancing Class: Many Teachers Making $70,000." Ibid.

led by Stanford education professor Linda Darling-Hammond. It is, essentially, a regulatory strategy that seeks to restrict entry into the classroom and that relies heavily on greater inputs, uniform practices, and more peer judgments as sources of quality control.

The other, which I'll term the *commonsense approach*, was set forth in the April 1999 manifesto *The Teachers We Need and How to Get More of Them*, issued by the Thomas B. Fordham Foundation on behalf of several dozen governors, state education chiefs, prominent scholars and analysts, and veteran practitioners. It was elaborated in *Better Teachers, Better Schools*, a research volume published in July 1999. It is, essentially, a *deregulatory* strategy that opens entry into classrooms and, for quality control, depends primarily on students' learning as evidence of their teachers' effectiveness.

Why do we need such an alternative? Because the regulatory strategy is fatally flawed. In fact, some shortcomings of the present teaching force are themselves caused or worsened by regulatory policies that rely on state bureaucracies and ed school professors for quality control. Hence the need to try something very different: unbar the doors into U.S. classrooms while holding every school accountable for its students' performance. Instead of mandating a list of university courses and degrees, examine future teachers on their subject knowledge and classroom prowess. Allow principals and their school teams to hire the teachers they need (and replace those who don't work out). Focus relentlessly on whether students are learning. Let anyone teach who demonstrates the capacity to produce the desired results and reward them accordingly.

This path to teacher quality is modeled on the approach that almost every successful modern enterprise has adopted to boost its performance and productivity: set high standards for the results to be achieved, identify clear indicators of progress toward those results, and be flexible and decentralized about the means for reaching them. Other organizations have recognized that regulating inputs and processes is counterproductive. There is little reason to believe that it will work better when addressing the teacher quality problem. It certainly hasn't in the past.

The alternative outlined here is also the way that most other professions work. Consider college professors or members of the clergy. They don't rely on government regulation to control entry. They rely on outstanding education, demonstrated performance, and the quality control afforded by the marketplace.

At the end of the day, what I am urging is open-mindedness, experimentation, and empiricism. Nobody today is certain how best to solve the teacher quality-and-quantity problems. It would be a mistake to put all our eggs in any one policy basket. The country, in fact, should try *both* these approaches—and others yet to be devised. It's premature to lock ourselves into any single system for boosting teacher quality. We don't yet know enough.

## THE ROMANCE OF REGULATION

As we have seen, the dominant theory of quality control for U.S. teachers relies on state regulation of entry into the profession. This approach has led to a cadre of people half drowned in pedagogy but not necessarily drenched in content. Indeed, the inability of today's licensure system to ensure that teachers can stay afloat in the subjects they teach is one of its gravest failings—and suggests an antiknowledge bias in the field that is scarcely compatible with attracting and retaining the best and brightest. Amazingly, state certification does not always insist on deep college-level study of the subjects to be taught, nor does it employ rigorous exams to verify the adequacy of a teacher's knowledge of his field. Most state-mandated tests of teachers' subject knowledge are so rudimentary that they can be passed by anyone with a decent high school education. "Why should prospective teachers go to college if this is all they need to know?" ask the authors of a recent study of licensing tests published by the Education Trust.[14]

Exacerbating the problem of weak subject mastery is the lamentable fact that teachers often find themselves assigned to courses

14. Ruth Mitchell and Patte Barth, "How Teacher Licensing Tests Fall Short," in *Not Good Enough: A Content Analysis of Teacher Licensing Exams,* spring 1999 issue of *Thinking K-16*, published by the Education Trust.

outside their own fields of expertise as cost-saving measures or administrative convenience or because of instructor shortages in advanced subjects such as math and science. "Foreign education ministers who visit me are just stumped when I try to explain this practice," notes Education secretary Richard Riley. "Their translators simply have no words to describe it."[15]

It appears, for example, that more than half of U.S. history teachers did not major—or even minor—in history itself.[16] More than half of the youngsters studying physics in American schools have teachers with neither majors nor minors in physics.[17] (Is it any wonder that U.S. high school seniors trail the world when it comes to *their* knowledge of physics?) More troubling still, children attending school in poor and urban areas are least likely to find themselves in classrooms with teachers who engaged in deep study of their subjects. Since most teachers merely follow the rules that their states set for certification, these shortcomings in the preparation of our teaching force must be laid at the feet of the regulators, not the teachers.

Yet states are now tightening the regulatory vise, making it even harder to enter their public school classrooms by piling on new requirements for certification. Many are following the lead of California, which requires a five-year preparation sequence.

On the advice of high-profile groups such as the National Commission on Teaching and America's Future, states are hiking their admissions criteria for training programs and insisting that these programs be accredited by the National Council for the Accreditation of Teacher Education (NCATE). That organization is currently revising its own standards to make accredited programs

15. Richard W. Riley, U.S. secretary of education, "New Challenges, a New Resolve: Moving American Education into the 21st Century," Sixth Annual State of American Education Speech, Long Beach, Calif., February 16, 1999.
16. Richard M. Ingersoll, "The Problem of Underqualified Teachers in American Secondary Schools," *Educational Researcher*, March 1999, cited in Tyce Palmaffy, "Measuring the Teacher Quality Problem," in *Better Teachers, Better Schools* (Washington, D.C.: Thomas B. Fordham Foundation, 1999), 25.
17. Ibid.

longer, more demanding, and more focused on avant-garde education ideas and contemporary social concerns.

Recent news that the Education Testing Service will align its widely used Praxis teacher tests to NCATE's standards is the latest in the effort by teacher organizations to monopolize control over entry into the classroom, restricting it to a single, heavily regulated path through ed schools that are pressed to become ever more similar and to produce ever more uniform products. The profession's chosen solutions to the teacher quality problem will further centralize and standardize the certification process, curbing diversity in the sources and pathways followed by teachers and throwing more barriers in front of able people who would like to try teaching if only it weren't so hard to make one's way through the door.

## SHORTCOMINGS OF THE REGULATORY STRATEGY

The regulatory strategy has failed even at its most basic task of screening out ill-prepared candidates. Although some states have exit exams (from their university-based training programs) that appraise the skills, knowledge, and competence of fledgling teachers, in many others "quality control" occurs only on initial entry into the training program, where requirements are notoriously low. In a state with no exit exam, completing the prescribed courses and earning the requisite degree are all that's needed to get a teaching license.

State regulation also values the wrong things. Researchers have struggled to identify the key traits that distinguish good teachers from bad. Insofar as there are links between teacher characteristics and classroom effectiveness, the strongest of these involve verbal ability (and, in some fields, subject matter knowledge). This has been known since the famed Coleman Report of 1966, when teacher scores on a verbal test were the only school "input" found to have a positive relationship to student achievement.[18] Recent

18. Christopher S. Jencks, "The Coleman Report and the Conventional Wisdom," in Frederick Mosteller and Daniel P. Moynihan, eds., *On Equality of Educational Opportunity* (New York: Random House, 1972), p. 101.

studies in Texas and Alabama have confirmed the tie between teacher verbal facility and pupil achievement.[19] Such evidence suggests that recruiting smarter and better-educated people into teaching will do more to improve school results than requiring more or different preservice training.

Yet outstanding candidates are often deterred by the hurdles that the regulatory strategy erects. Burdensome certification requirements deflect eager individuals who might make fine teachers but are put off by the cost of completing a conventional preparation program. One college senior writes, "What discourages us most are the restrictive paths to the classroom and the poor reputation of schools of education—and as a result, of teaching itself. . . . It is the certification process, then, and not a lack of interest, that steers us away from teaching."[20] The best and brightest of today's young Americans have bountiful career options; if the costs of becoming a teacher are too high, they will do something else.

The most insidious hurdles involve lengthy training in pedagogy. Although some policymakers and parents view "certified" teachers as synonymous with qualified teachers, being certified generally means little more than having endured state-approved training at a school of education. Yet there's little evidence that this leads to effective teaching.

Telling evidence can be found in studies comparing teachers who were trained and licensed through traditional programs with teachers who bypassed these programs. Alternative certification streamlines the classroom entry of a growing number of prospective teachers in some states. Such programs normally require a bachelor's degree, passage of a competency test, and an intensive

19. Ronald F. Ferguson, "Can Schools Narrow the Black-White Test Score Gap?" in Christopher Jencks and Meredith Phillips, eds., *The Black-White Test Score Gap* (Washington, D.C.: Brookings Institution, 1998). Ronald F. Ferguson and Helen F. Ladd, "How and Why Money Matters: An Analysis of Alabama Schools," in *Holding Schools Accountable: Performance Based Reform in Education* (Washington, D.C.: Brookings Institution, 1996).

20. Elizabeth Greenspan, "No Thanks," *Teacher Magazine*, April 1999.

(but compressed) regimen of specialized preparation, often undertaken while on the job. Studies of alternative certification find that students of such teachers perform at least as well as pupils of conventionally licensed teachers.[21]

The conventional wisdom within the field holds that traditional training programs would be more effective if only they were lengthened or required to become accredited. Yet research does not support this claim, either. Studies comparing graduates of accredited and nonaccredited programs find little difference between them.[22] Nor has research found graduates of five-year teacher training programs to be any more effective in the classroom than the alumni/ae of four-year programs.[23]

We also see much evidence that traditional training programs are not a prerequisite for good teaching, hence ought not enjoy monopoly control over classroom entry. Where personnel decisions have been deregulated, schools rush to hire well-educated persons whether or not they possess standard certification. In New Jersey, the first state to implement alternative certification, roughly 20 percent of all teachers now enter the field via that route.[24]

Private schools, which are free to hire anyone they like and which have a strong market-driven incentive to engage the best instructors they can, hire a large proportion of unlicensed teachers;

21. Stephen D. Goebel, Karl Ronacher, and Kathryn S. Sanchez, *An Evaluation of HISD's Alternative Certification Program of the Academic Year: 1988–1989* (Houston: Houston Independent School District Department of Research and Evaluation, 1989), ERIC Document No. 322103. Susan Barnes, James Salmon, and William Wale, "Alternative Teacher Certification in Texas," paper presented at the annual meeting of the American Educational Research Association, March 1989, ERIC Document No. 307316. Michael Kwiatkowski, "Debating Alternative Teacher Certification: A Trial by Achievement," in *Better Teachers, Better Schools*, p. 228.

22. Dale Ballou and Michael Podgursky, "Teacher Training and Licensure: A Layman's Guide," in *Better Teachers, Better Schools*, p. 46.

23. Ballou and Podgursky, "Teacher Training and Licensure," in *Better Teachers, Better Schools*, p. 49.

24. Leo Klagholz, *Growing Better Teachers in the Garden State: New Jersey's "Alternate Route" to Teacher Certification* (Washington, D.C.: Thomas B. Fordham Foundation, 2000), p. 17.

65 percent of teachers at secular private secondary schools are un-licensed.[25] Such teachers are more likely to have graduated from selective colleges and universities than the certified teachers hired by public schools.

## Teaching versus Medicine

Those who assert that a licensure system based on preservice pro-fessional training in a college of education is key to producing good teachers often make a medical analogy: You wouldn't trust an unlicensed brain surgeon to open your skull, so why trust an unlicensed teacher to teach your kid? That formulation is seduc-tive but wrong. It postulates that teaching, like doctoring, rests on a solid foundation of specialized professional knowledge that is scientifically buttressed by reliable, replicable research. In medical school, doctors acquire—and are tested on—this body of scien-tifically robust knowledge and methods. Unfortunately, this is not the case in education.

As the late Albert Shanker, longtime president of the American Federation of Teachers, wrote in 1996, "Many of the attributes that characterize a profession are not hallmarks of today's teach-ing profession." He continued, "To be considered a true profes-sion, an occupation must have a distinct body of knowledge—acknowledged by practitioner and consumer alike—that under-girds the profession and forms the basis of delivering high-quality services to clients."[26] But the knowledge base that colleges of edu-cation seek to impart is uneven, incomplete, highly disputed, and vulnerable to ideological and interest-group manipulation. This lack of grounding of teaching methods in solid research fosters the faddism that lurks in most colleges of education. We should not be surprised that there is no reliable link between their coursework and their graduates' eventual prowess in the classroom.

25. Ballou and Podgursky, "Teacher Training and Licensure," in *Better Teachers, Better Schools*, p. 50.
26. Albert Shanker, "Quality Assurance: What Must Be Done to Strengthen the Teaching Profession," *Phi Delta Kappan*, November 1996.

Without a solid body of basic knowledge, the regulatory approach has no foundation on which to rest. So it turns instead to fashionable opinions of the day within the field. For example, NCATE, the major accrediting body for ed schools, embraces the subject matter standards of the International Reading Association and the National Council of Teachers of Mathematics. Yet these organizations support highly disputed classroom practices of dubious value for children, such as "whole language" reading in the primary grades, early use of calculators in math class, and the downplaying of basic computational skills. If these are the academic foundations on which accreditation rests, attempts to raise the quality of ed schools by obliging all of them to become accredited could have the perverse effect of forcing all teacher training to adopt the same misguided approaches.

The problem with the regulatory strategy goes beyond its enchantment with pedagogy. As in any field, the regulations inevitably focus on inputs rather than results: on courses taken, requirements met, time spent, tests passed, credentials acquired, and activities engaged in, rather than actual evidence of classroom effectiveness, particularly as gauged by student learning. Yet such input measures are sorely inexact approximations of how good a teacher one will be. Indeed, decades of research into the connection between teachers' input qualities and their eventual effectiveness in actual classrooms (as gauged by pupil learning gains) yield few linkages. Even the aforementioned connection between verbal ability and subject knowledge, on the one hand, and effective teaching, on the other, is not robust. Taken as a whole, today's regulations concentrate on inputs that have scant bearing on classroom success. Hence "reforms" that would change the type and amount of inputs needed for certification will only limit access to teaching for no good reason.

## OTHER APPROACHES

Would a different kind of regulation work better, one that relies, say, on expert judgments rather than paper credentials? Peer review of teacher performance has become popular in recent years.

Instead of input measures, it assumes that good teaching is best detected via observation by other practitioners. Thus the National Board for Professional Teaching Standards (NBPTS) has designed an elaborate method for appraising teacher performance and certifying outstanding instructors. This process is costly and time-intensive. It can lead to sizable rewards, such as the $30,000 bonus that California governor Gray Davis has recommended for NBPTS-certified teachers. Yet today we have no idea whether teachers vetted by NBPTS are in fact the best teachers as judged by how much and how well their pupils learn. Here as elsewhere, peer review consists mainly of judging quality by observing processes, that is, appraising a teacher's skill in using conventional (and popular) classroom practices.

Another approach favored by prominent education groups as a way of linking licensure requirements more closely to performance is to develop "teacher standards" that spell out what good teachers should know and be able to do. This sounds promising, yet most such "standards" turn out to be empty slogans. "Teachers organize and manage a social structure in the classroom that enables students to be active participants in literate communities," reads one standard proffered by the Interstate New Teacher Assessment and Support Consortium (INTASC). It is hard to imagine that a "standard" so woolly could ever be of use as a licensing tool, much less a predictor of classroom prowess. How could a state bureaucrat tell which candidates for certification had met it and which had not?

NCATE's accreditation standards are not very different. "Candidates . . . use the comprehensive nature of students' physical, mental, and social well-being to create opportunities for student development and practice of skills that contribute to good health," reads one. Such standards often specify that good teachers understand some important concept, such as "how children grow and develop." Absent a solid research base for most of what is "known" by teacher educators, however, it is not clear what the correct answer is. The weakness of these standards is self-evident, yet there has been no real effort to demonstrate that they are valid gauges of teacher effectiveness.

We would be better off to acknowledge that nobody can systematically measure the elusive qualities that good teachers have. Teaching is a complicated art and there are many ways to be good at it. (As a profession, in fact, it's more like university teaching or ministering to a congregation than it is like law or medicine.) Teachers with very different teaching styles and approaches can be equally effective.

Despite the inability of the regulatory approach to assure good teaching, a redoubling of regulatory zeal remains the field's preferred solution to the quality problem. The idea that more—and more homogeneous—training is the key has innate appeal for states seeking to do something. Peer review sounds terrific, the unions love it, and it has the added virtue of shifting the burden of difficult personnel decisions from state policymakers to the profession itself. That shift is even more profound in states that cede all power over licensure and certification to "independent professional standards boards," another favorite union device for gaining control over entry into teaching and one that is now spreading from state to state.

Regulation is contagious. Thus a number of governors and legislators have clambered onto this bandwagon. But it isn't likely to work. We certainly cannot be sure that it will work. It's premature and imprudent to clamp this approach onto all fifty states, hence the need to experiment with other strategies.

## A COMMONSENSE ALTERNATIVE

Instead of using degrees earned, standards met, or the opinions of other teachers as indexes of quality, we should evaluate teachers based on the only measure that really matters: whether their pupils are learning. Although good teachers do many other worthwhile things besides add to student learning—they help other teachers, for example, serve as moral role models, work with parents, and so on—nothing they do is as important as academic achievement. The more of it they produce, the greater will be society's admiration for them and the more open-handed will be the attitude of policymakers and taxpayers regarding their compensation.

Gauging the student learning that individual teachers produce is no pipe dream. Careful statistical analysis can identify the gains that students make during a school year and then estimate the effects of individual teachers on their progress. This "value-added" technique is precise and its results are statistically robust. Used today in several states and many school districts, it allows principals, policymakers, taxpayers, and parents to see for themselves how much individual teachers are helping students to learn.[27]

Judging teachers by the results they produce is the core of the commonsense strategy. The rest is straightforward: states should allow individual public schools to employ teachers as they see fit and then hold those schools to account for their results.

Since good teachers can be found in many places, prepared in many ways, and channeled into schools via many pathways, states should scrap nearly all the hoops and hurdles that discourage good candidates from entering the classroom. Deregulating teaching in this way will not only expand the pool but also raise its quality. The role of the state should be to ensure that teachers do no harm. All other key personnel decisions should be devolved to the school itself. In return for this autonomy, schools should be held accountable for producing results. (Monitoring those results is another state responsibility.)

Such an approach recognizes that there is no "one best system" for preparing and licensing good teachers. This argues against mandating any single path into the profession. Education schools certainly ought not to control the only route, especially considering how many teachers report that the best place to learn their craft is on the job in the company of other good teachers.

Rather than buttressing an orthodoxy that does not work, the

27. Organizing an education system on the basis of student achievement requires better measures of student achievement than most states have today (in particular, annual assessments of students in every grade), though a number of jurisdictions are moving in that direction. Implementing this "commonsense alternative" will mean more such movement. We also recognize, of course, that student test scores can never be a full or perfect measure of teacher effectiveness; teachers add many valuable things to students that cannot be captured by any test.

commonsense approach embraces pluralism. In a deregulated environment, good teacher education programs will thrive and prosper. Those that do a poor job will not, once they lose the protection that the regulatory cartel confers. Principals and their school teams will decide whether to hire teachers who have been trained in certain pedagogical methods and theories. They will do so if they see proof that those methods are effective and those theories lead to student achievement.

The popularity of such programs as Teach for America, which places liberal arts graduates without formal education coursework in public school classrooms in poor rural communities and inner cities, indicates that the prospect of teaching without first being obliged to spend years in pedagogical study appeals to some of our brightest college graduates. More than three thousand people annually apply for five hundred Teach for America slots. Since 1994, several thousand veterans of the armed forces have also transited from the military to K–12 classrooms through the Troops to Teachers program.

Several dozen states today have alternative certification programs designed to recruit and train liberal arts graduates and people who have been following other career paths. In most jurisdictions, however, these yield small numbers of teachers. In Ohio, the Internship Certificate Program has produced a grand total of one certified teacher since its 1990 inception–and even that miniscule rip in the regulatory fabric will be sewn tight if Ohio goes ahead and creates an "independent" teacher standards board.[28] In other states, however, alternative paths have begun to draw significant numbers of talented and enthusiastic individuals toward the classroom. Teachers who possess alternative certification are more likely to have bachelor's degrees in math and science, both fields with chronic shortages. They are more apt to be members of minority groups.[29] As an added bonus, alternative cer-

28. C. Emily Feistritzer and David T. Chester, *Alternative Teacher Certification: A State-by-State Analysis 2000* (Washington, D.C.: National Center for Education Information, 2000), p. 303.

29. Jianping Shen, "Has the Alternative Certification Policy Materialized Its Promise? A Comparison Between Traditionally and Alternatively Certified Teach-

tification teachers also have lower attrition.[30] Yet the regulatory strategy would shut down such programs or force them to mimic conventional education programs.

## NOT ALL REGULATIONS ARE EVIL

Trading accountability for autonomy does not mean sloughing off every single regulation. Every child should be able to count on having a teacher with a solid general education, one who possesses deep subject area knowledge and has no record of misbehavior. The state has an obligation to ensure that all its teachers meet this minimal standard. Thus states should perform background checks. To boost the likelihood that those who teach our children are themselves well educated, states could reasonably insist that teaching candidates have at least a bachelor's degree in some academic subject.

States should also ensure subject matter competence. Although knowing one's subject isn't the only important quality for effective teaching, it is surely a prerequisite. There are two ways to do this: requiring teachers either to major in the subjects that they teach or to pass challenging tests in those subjects. Neither is faultless as a means of assuring that teachers possess the requisite knowledge and will be good at delivering it. But either strategy beats today's widespread disregard of subject matter mastery.

## POWER TO THE PRINCIPALS

For principals and school teams to shape their own membership in such a way as to shoulder accountability for school results, they must not only be free to select from a wide range of candidates but must also have the flexibility to compensate staff members

ers in Public Schools," *Educational Evaluation and Policy Analysis* 19, no. 3 (1997): 276–83. Klagholz, *Growing Better Teachers in the Garden State.*

30. Michael Kwiatkowski, "Debating Alternative Teacher Certification: A Trial by Achievement," in *Better Teachers, Better Schools*, p. 228. Ellen Schech, director, Alternate Route Program, New Jersey Board of Education, in "No Thanks," *Teacher Magazine*, April 1999. Klagholz, *Growing Better Teachers in the Garden State.*

according to marketplace conditions (and individual performance), and they must be able to remove those who do not produce
satisfactory results. Everyone who has studied effective schools at-
tests to the importance of a cohesive team that shares a common
vision, and almost everyone who has studied current teacher personnel systems has witnessed the danger of tying the school team's
hands when it comes to deciding who will join (or remain in) it.[31]
The only way to help effective teams to form is to allow them to
choose their own members.

That means flexible pay, too. Common sense argues that teachers of subjects in short supply should be paid more than those in
overstocked fields, that teachers working in hard-to-staff schools
should earn more than those in schools with hundreds of applicants, and that outstanding teachers should be paid more than
mediocre ones. Yet today the typical public school salary schedule
(and teachers' union contract) allows for none of these common-
sensical practices. In only twelve states can teacher pay vary at all
based on performance or marketplace conditions.[32]

As for the occasional incompetent teacher, the more freedom a
school has in initial hiring, the more flexibility it needs with respect
to retention. That's common sense, too. Some people will be hired
who don't work out, at least not as part of a particular school's
team, and the school should not be burdened with them. Yet today
most public school teachers are awarded permanent job tenure

31. The importance of the power to remove teachers is emphasized by the
most mainstream research in the field. Gordon Cawelti, former executive director
of the Association for Supervision and Curriculum Development, concludes in a
recent study of what makes schools effective: "A school seeking a turnaround
in student performance must seek out teachers who want to work in such an
environment. A school must also be able to remove teachers who are unwilling
to commit the energy and dedication needed to make sure that a productive and
challenging education is provided to all children who attend. This policy issue
must not be overlooked. Without committed teachers, you are unlikely to raise
student achievement significantly." Gordon Cawelti, *Portraits of Six Benchmark
Schools: Diverse Approaches to Improving Student Achievement* (Arlington, Va.:
Educational Research Service, 1999), pp. 64–65.

32. Chester E. Finn Jr., Marci Kanstoroom, and Michael J. Petrilli, *The Quest
for Better Teachers: Grading the States* (Washington, D.C.: Thomas B. Fordham
Foundation, November 1999), p. 45.

after just a few years of service; thereafter, they are almost never dismissed (or involuntarily relocated) for ineffectiveness. Although teachers should of course be safeguarded from abusive and capricious treatment at the hands of administrators, they cannot be protected from losing their jobs for cause. Union contracts often have "seniority" provisions that allow veteran teachers to transfer into a school regardless of their instructional prowess, the school's actual needs, or their impact on the school team. Such policies will also need to be changed so that principals can be empowered and made accountable.

School-level executives and veteran teachers are in the best position to know who teaches well and who teaches badly in their school. They have access to far more significant information than state licensing boards and government agencies. They should be authorized (and, if need be, trained) to appraise each teacher's singular package of strengths and weaknesses rather than having distant bureaucracies decide who will be on their team. Once hired, teachers should be evaluated based on the only measure that ultimately matters: whether their pupils are learning.

## CONCLUSION

For too long, policymakers have tackled the teacher quality problem by tightening regulation and expanding pedagogical requirements, even though this approach shrinks the pool of candidates while having scant effect on their quality. Forty years of experience suggest that this strategy has not worked. It probably cannot work. It's reminiscent of the heavy drinker who proposes to cure his hangover by imbibing more of the strong spirits that gave him the headache in the first place. As with the alcoholic, a "hair of the dog that bit you" approach to teacher quality reform can be counted on to make the problem worse. Indeed, it has already compounded today's dual crisis of quality and quantity and weakened the impulse to turn teaching into a true profession. True professions, after all, don't hide behind government regulations, tenure laws, and uniform pay scales.

States that want to persist with this approach will naturally do so. Based on today's evidence, one would have to say that most states will continue in this mode. But I suggest that others try something different. I predict that states that reduce barriers to entry will find not only that their applicant pool is larger but also that it includes many more talented candidates. The key is to shun excessive and ill-conceived regulations and focus instead on student outcomes.

Flexibility in return for results is the approach that many states are now employing for schools themselves. After a series of none-too-successful attempts in the 1980s to boost academic achievement by clamping additional regulations on the public schools—three years of high school science instead of two, so many minutes a day of homework, new reading curricula, and so on—America is now experimenting with freedom, pluralism, and competition for its schools, all joined to accountability for their results.

In this spirit, many jurisdictions have scrapped the "one best system" view of education reform; instead, they encourage schools to be different, encourage individual schools to make their own decisions about schedule, instructional style, and curricular focus, and empower families to select the schools that best suit their children, all the while monitoring academic performance and making that information public. The country's two thousand (and counting) charter schools are perhaps the most vivid example of our willingness to solve the school-quality problem via deregulation. This approach trusts principals to run schools worth attending and parents to be astute consumers in the education marketplace, although it also uses statewide academic standards and tests to audit and report on actual achievement and to keep the consumers well informed.

A similar approach should be tried for teacher quality. Yet today the conventional wisdom pushes the other way: pressing for greater uniformity and micromanagement of inputs and processes instead of concentrating on results.

Still, there are welcome signs of receptivity to change. In his February 1999 State of American Education speech, for example,

Secretary Riley proclaimed, "We must make sweeping efforts to make teaching a first-class profession. And, then, we must hold schools accountable for results."[33] He later added, "What else can we do? We can create rigorous alternative paths to give many more Americans the opportunity to become a teacher."[34] I agree.

33. Richard W. Riley, "New Challenges, A New Resolve."
34. Ibid.

# CHAPTER 7

# Teachers Unions and the Public Schools

## Terry M. Moe

On the surface, it might seem that teachers unions would play a limited role in public education, fighting for better pay and working conditions for their members, but otherwise having little impact on the structure and performance of the public schools. Yet nothing could be further from the truth. The fact is, the teachers unions probably have more influence on the public schools than any other group in American society.

Their influence takes two forms. First, they shape the schools from the bottom up, through collective bargaining activities that are so broad in scope that virtually every aspect of the schools is somehow affected. Second, they shape the schools from the top down, through political activities that give them unrivaled influence over the laws and regulations imposed on public education by government. In combining bottom-up and top-down influence, and in combining them as potently as they do, teachers unions are unique among educational actors—and absolutely central to an understanding of America's public schools.

Despite their importance, the teachers unions have been poorly studied by education scholars. Indeed, in the hundreds of governmental and academic reports on school reform over the last few decades, many of them providing the intellectual basis for new legislation at both the state and national levels, the teachers unions have almost always been completely ignored, as though they are simply irrelevant to an assessment of problems and solutions.[1]

This is a remarkable state of affairs. My purpose here is to provide a simple, informative overview of the pivotal roles that teachers unions actually play in public education, and to suggest why, if Americans want to understand and improve their public schools, the unions can no longer be overlooked.

## THE RISE OF TEACHERS UNIONS

Most of the nation's K–12 public school teachers belong to a union. Of those that do, almost all belong to a local affiliate of either the National Educational Association (NEA) or the American Federation of Teachers (AFT).[2]

The NEA is by far the bigger of the two. It was established in 1857 as a professional organization for public educators, and for the first hundred years of its life (and more) was controlled by superintendents and other administrators rather than by teachers, even though teachers made up most of its membership. By the mid-

1. For prominent examples, see National Commission on Excellence in Education, *A Nation at Risk* (Washington, D.C.: Government Printing Office, 1983); Twentieth Century Fund, *Making the Grade* (New York: The Fund, 1983); Carnegie Task Force on Teaching as a Profession, *A Nation Prepared* (Washington, D.C.: Carnegie Forum on Education and the Economy, 1986).

2. As I note later on, it is very difficult to get precise, reliable figures on union membership and collective bargaining for public school teachers. Perhaps the best measures are provided by the School and Staffing Survey (SASS), 1993–94, a national data set on public and private schools, school districts, and teachers collected by the National Center for Education Statistics within the federal Department of Education. According to the SASS, 80% of public school teachers nationwide belonged to a union in 1993–94, and this figure rises to 89% when we exclude the South (which is largely a right-to-work region). Evidence from other surveys suggests that union membership among public school teachers has not changed much since the 1980s, so these figures are probably fairly accurate for today's system as well. Precise breakdowns for the NEA and the AFT are not possible, largely because the AFT does not provide data on how many of its members are actually K–12 teachers (as many as half, apparently, are not: a fact the union would prefer to keep to itself). A good estimate, based on surveys, is that the NEA organizes perhaps four times as many teachers as the AFT, and that only a small percentage of organized teachers do not belong to one of these two unions.

1950s, the NEA had extended its reach to virtually all areas of the country, and could claim about half of all public school teachers as members (some of them joining because local school boards required them to). Throughout this entire hundred-year period, however, the NEA did not function as a union, and indeed was antiunion, reflecting the management interests of the administrators who controlled it.[3]

The AFT was a union from the beginning, and a socially radical one at that. Around the turn of the century, activist teachers formed their own unions in several big cities, and in 1916 four of these unions came together to form the national-level AFT, which then quickly affiliated with the American Federation of Labor as part of the mainstream labor movement. Over the decades, the AFT grew rather steadily as new cities were unionized and new members added, but by the early 1960s it had still only organized perhaps 5 percent of the nation's public school teachers, almost all of these clustered in large urban areas, notably Chicago, New York, and Atlanta.

The watershed event for the teachers union movement came in 1961, when the AFT won a representation election in New York City, giving it the right to represent that city's teachers in collective bargaining negotiations. This victory set off an aggressive AFT campaign to organize teachers in other cities, putting the NEA on notice that, if it didn't convert itself into a union and compete for teachers, the AFT was going to take hold of the entire constituency. Such a move was not easy for the NEA. With administrators at the helm and their interests incompatible with unionism, the organization was riven with conflict over the matter. Institutional imperatives soon won out, however, and the NEA took on the challenge of organizing teachers for collective bargaining.

Throughout the 1960s and into the 1970s, the NEA went head-

3. Basic historical material on the rise of the teachers unions and specifics on both the NEA and AFT can be gleaned from many sources. Here, I just give a brief summary account. See, e.g., Myron Lieberman, *The Teacher Unions* (New York: Free Press, 1997); Marjorie Murphy, *Blackboard Unions: The AFT and the NEA, 1900–1980* (Ithaca: Cornell University Press, 1990); and Maurice R. Berube, *Teacher Politics* (New York: Greenwood Press, 1988).

to-head with the AFT in disputed urban districts, where the two often fought on relatively equal terms. In the meantime, though, the NEA used its nationwide presence in the full range of districts—a presence the AFT did not have—to give it a huge advantage in representing teachers outside the major urban centers. Both organizations grew tremendously. But it was the NEA that emerged triumphant from their early competitive struggle, gaining control over the lion's share of teachers and school districts and maintaining its stature as the leading force in American public education. From this point on, however, its leadership would reflect the interests of a labor union, rather than those of an eclectic professional association.

During this twenty-year period, the American education system underwent a massive transition. Until the early 1960s, only a tiny percentage of teachers were unionized, and school boards and other democratic authorities made all the key decisions about schools. Aggressive organization by the NEA and the AFT, accompanied by waves of teacher strikes and labor unrest, brought thousands of school districts under union control. By the early 1980s, just twenty years or so after the AFT's initial victory in New York City, the transformation of the system was largely complete. The turbulence of institutional change had largely subsided, dramatic increases in union membership had started to level off, and a new equilibrium had taken hold in which (outside the South) unionization and collective bargaining had become the norm.

As of the year 2000, this new equilibrium still prevails and is quite stable, protected by union power. The NEA, which claimed a membership of 766,000 in 1961, now claims to have some 2.5 million members, about 2 million of whom are practicing K–12 teachers. It has affiliates in all fifty states, and is politically active and powerful throughout the country. The AFT has expanded (by its own count) from 70,821 members in 1961 to roughly 1 million members today. Only about half of these are teachers, but the organization's growth has obviously been considerable. As in the past, AFT strength is concentrated in a fairly small number of urban areas. Although it has affiliates in forty states, most of them are much smaller and less influential than the NEA affiliates. Only in New York and Rhode Island is the AFT the dominant teachers union.[4]

These sorts of figures are helpful in giving us a sense of how unionization and collective bargaining have taken hold in American education, and how the two unions compare in size and strength. It is important to recognize, however, that precise data on the actual levels of union membership and the prevalence of collective bargaining are surprisingly difficult to come by. Even the simplest questions must often be answered through sketchy information that is patched together from various data sources. The Department of Education, the Bureau of Labor Statistics, the Census Bureau, and other standard sources of information have done a poor job of collecting data on matters related to teachers unions.

Those of us who want to understand developments in unionization and collective bargaining, then, must do the best we can with limited information. The basic developments are reasonably clear, but the details are difficult to document in a comprehensive, systematic way. This is something that will doubtless change in future years, as the teachers unions attract more attention and study.

### TEACHERS UNIONS AND THE GROWTH OF PUBLIC SECTOR UNIONS

Any effort to gain historical perspective on the rise of the teachers unions must recognize that it was not an isolated development in the American labor movement. It was an integral part of a much broader phenomenon: the spectacular growth of public employee unions generally.

Several factors were responsible for this phenomenon, but one of the most important, it appears, is simply that the laws changed. Prior to the 1960s, states did not authorize public employees (including schoolteachers) to engage in collective bargaining, and sometimes prohibited them from doing so. In 1959, Wisconsin be-

4. See Lieberman, *The Teacher Unions; NEA Handbook* for 2000; and the AFT website at www.aft.org.

came the first state to enact a collective bargaining law for public
sector workers, and over the next two decades most states followed suit, usually by adopting legal frameworks similar to the
National Labor Relations Act, which had long structured labor-
management relations in the private sector, and still does. These
laws created rights, duties, and procedures that made it easier for
unions to organize public workers, get government employers to
bargain with them, and win contracts and concessions.[5]

The new laws were not solely responsible for union gains. The
states that adopted public sector bargaining laws the earliest
tended to be states in which the union movement as a whole was
already politically powerful, and in which teachers and other public employees were already beginning to unionize with some success under the old laws. Still, the shift in legal framework gave
their efforts a boost, and helped fuel a surge in public sector unionism.[6] By the early 1980s, the percentage of unionized workers in
government had skyrocketed from trivial levels just two decades
earlier to a robust 37 percent—where, as with teachers, it stabi-
lized in what appears to be new equilibrium. In 1999, union den-
sity in the public sector remained at 37 percent. [7]

At the very time that unions were succeeding so dramatically in
the public sector, they were stumbling badly in the private sector,
in what was nothing short of an organizational catastrophe for
the labor movement. The percentage of unionized workers in the
private, nonagricultural workforce fell precipitously and continu-

5. For an overview of these developments in public sector unionism generally,
see James L. Stern, "Unionism in the Public Sector," in Benjamin Aaron, Joyce
M. Najita, and James L. Stern, eds., *Public Sector Bargaining*, 2nd edition (Washington, D.C.: Bureau of National Affairs, 1988).

6. See especially Gregory M. Saltzman, "Bargaining Laws as a Cause and
Consequence of the Growth of Teacher Unionism," in David Lewin, Peter Feuille,
Thomas A. Kochan, and John Thomas Delaney, eds., *Public Sector Labor Rela-
tions* (Lexington, Mass.: Lexington Books, 1977); and Gregory M. Saltzman,
"Public Sector Bargaining Laws Really Matter: Evidence from Ohio and Illinois,"
in Richard B. Freeman and Casey Ichniowski, eds., *When Public Sector Workers
Unionize* (Chicago: University of Chicago Press, 1988).

7. Figures are taken from Barry T. Hirsch and David A. Macpherson, *Union
Membership and Earnings Data Book* (Washington, D.C.: Bureau of National
Affairs, 2000).

ously across the decades, from a high of roughly one-third in the early 1950s to less than 10 percent in 1999.[8] Why did teachers unions and other public sector unions do so well, when private sector unions—which had long benefited from the same sorts of union-promoting legal frameworks—fared so poorly?

Experts disagree on the precise causes and their relative importance. It seems clear that, to some extent, specific changes in the economy and government are responsible. One change, of course, is that governments adopted new bargaining laws that stimulated public sector unionization. Another is that employment in the private sector shifted over time from manufacturing (highly unionized) to services (poorly unionized) and from the rust belt (highly unionized) to the sun belt (poorly unionized), which had the effect of draining members from private sector unions and making their organizational missions more difficult. Another is that public sector workers may have changed their perspectives and adopted a new militancy.[9]

Specifics aside, however, there are generic—and fundamental—differences across the two sectors that need to be appreciated, and that have surely had profound influences on the developments of the last few decades. The simple fact is that, even with common legal frameworks, the two sectors offer starkly different contexts for union activity.[10]

In the private sector, most employers know that they will lose business to competitors if their costs increase, and this prompts them to resist unionization. Similarly, unions cannot make costly

8. See Leo Troy and Neil Sheflin, *Union Sourcebook: Membership, Structure, Finance, Directory* (West Orange, N.J.: Industrial Relations Data and Information Services, 1985) for data on the early period, and Hirsch and Macpherson, *Union Membership and Earnings Data Book*, for data on the later period. The Troy and Sheflin figures are based on the entire private workforce, and not just the private nonagricultural workforce, but their percentages for comparable years are very close to those of Hirsch and Macpherson.

9. See, for example, Richard B. Freeman, "Why Are Unions Faring Poorly in NLRB Elections?," in Thomas A. Kochan, ed., *Challenges and Choices Facing American Labor* (Cambridge: MIT Press, 1985), and John F. Burton, Jr., and Terry Thomason, "The Extent of Collective Bargaining in the Public Sector," in Aaron, Najita, and Stern, *Public Sector Bargaining*.

10. See, e.g., Lieberman, *The Teacher Unions*.

demands without losing business and employment to nonunion firms, and this too limits their ability to organize and bargain. As a general matter, competition breeds trouble for unions; and over the last few decades, due especially to the explosion of technology and the globalization of economic activity, the private sector has become much more competitive than in the past. This presumably has a lot to do with why unions have been losing ground in the private economy.

The governmental environment is very different. Public agencies usually have no competition and are not threatened by loss of business if their costs go up, while workers and unions know they are not putting their agencies or jobs at risk by pressuring for all they can get. Governmental decisions on labor matters, moreover, are not driven by efficiency concerns, as they are in the private sector, but by political considerations, and thus by power and constituency. In jurisdictions where unions have achieved a measure of political power, therefore, many public officials—especially Democrats, given their longtime political alliances with unions—have incentives to promote collective bargaining and submit to union demands, even if they know full well the result will be higher costs and inefficiencies.

Government is not always a union-friendly environment, of course. Some public officials, especially Republicans, respond to antiunion constituencies and may exercise great power. And in some governmental settings, officials of both parties are forced to deal with hard budget constraints that (particularly in bad economic times) heighten their concern for costs, make them more resistant to unionization, and prompt them to pursue strategies (like the contracting-out of public services) that unions abhor. These counterforces, in fact, may explain why unionization in the public sector has reached an equilibrium at slightly more than a third of the public workforce, rather than shooting up to much higher levels.

Even in government, then, the unions have opponents, and costs do matter. But the bottom line is that, given the lack of competition, and given the dominance of politics over efficiency, unions simply find it much easier to organize and prosper in the modern public sector than in the competitive, efficiency-conscious world of the private sector. It is no accident that the modern American labor movement has increasingly been driven (and kept afloat) by the resources, numbers, and leadership of the public sector unions—and that the largest, most powerful union in the country is not the Teamsters or the United Auto Workers, but the National Education Association.

## COLLECTIVE BARGAINING

Now let's take a closer look at the teachers unions, and at the fundamentals that explain their nature and success as organizations. As is true for all unions, collective bargaining is their core function, and their base of economic and political power. It is through collective bargaining that they attract and hold their members, get most of their resources (which come mainly from dues), wrest benefits and control from "management" (school boards)—and have the capacity, both organizational and financial, to take effective political action.

Collective bargaining is now the norm in American education as a whole, but it is not established in every district, and its incidence varies by region. As of 1994 (a year for which we have good data), almost all districts in the Northeast—98 percent—had collective bargaining. The comparable figures were 74 percent in the Midwest, 68 percent in the West, and just 12 percent in the South.[11] This variation across regions goes hand-in-hand with differences in state collective bargaining laws, which, as I suggested earlier, have played important causal roles in determining whether public sector unions will take root and prosper.

The vast majority of states, and all the states in the Northeast, have passed public sector bargaining laws that facilitate teacher union organization and collective bargaining. Seventeen states, however, have not passed such laws. Of this group, ten—Alabama, Arkansas, Colorado, Kentucky, Louisiana, Missouri, New Mexico, Utah, West Virginia, and Wyoming—allow collective bargain-

11. These figures are derived from the SASS data set for 1993–94.

ing to occur if the local school boards agree to it. The other seven—Arizona, Georgia, Mississippi, North Carolina, South Carolina, Texas, and Virginia—not only have no public sector bargaining statute for teachers, but make collective bargaining by teachers illegal.[12] The pattern is obvious and fits nicely with the regional figures on collective bargaining. Teachers unions face the least favorable legal environments in the South and in a few border and western states, and these are the places where they have had a hard time making progress. In the rest of the country, the laws work to their advantage, and collective bargaining by teachers has become firmly established.[13]

In districts with collective bargaining, the standard arrangement (called "exclusive representation") is that one union represents all the teachers in the district, including those who are not members of the union. Teachers cannot be legally required to join. But in four states—New York, Minnesota, Hawaii, and California—nonmembers are required to pay "agency fees" to the union if they prefer not to join. And in another fifteen states, almost all of them in the Northeast and Midwest, unions are allowed to negotiate for agency fees at the local level.[14] The rationale for these fees, as union supporters see it, is that nonmembers are represented by the union and benefiting from the contract and they should pay their "fair share." The upshot, however, is that agency fees are almost always set at a level very close to member dues, giving nonmembers strong incentives to go ahead and join the union anyway. When agency fee arrangements are in place, then, the unions gain additional revenues that may be substantial, and virtually all teachers tend to join.

12. Lieberman, *The Teacher Unions*.
13. It is worth reiterating that a state's laws are also a reflection of its political environment more generally—its conservative or liberal tilt, the relative power of business and labor, etc.—and these factors may have independent effects on how successfully unions are able to organize workers and bargain collectively. The South is different from the rest of the country not simply because it has right-to-work laws, but because its political environment is more conservative and more favorable to business than that of other regions.
14. Lieberman, *The Teacher Unions*. California has long been in the latter category, but new legislation passed in 2000 makes agency fees mandatory starting in 2001.

Unions bargain with school boards, which play the role of management. But school boards, like public managers generally, cannot be expected to behave like the managers of private firms in resisting union demands. The logic is just as I outlined in the previous section. In the first place, school boards face little or no competition and needn't worry that they will lose "business" by agreeing to union demands that raise costs, promote inefficiencies, or lower school performance. The kids and the tax money will still be there. In the second place, school boards are composed of elected officials, whose incentives are explicitly political and less tied to efficiency and costs than those of private managers. Moreover, the unions, by participating in local elections (see below), are thus in a position to determine who the "management" will be, and to give "management" incentives to bargain sympathetically. This is a stunning advantage that, for private sector unions, would be a dream come true.

What aspects of the public schools—what subjects of collective bargaining—are open to union influence? In principle, the answer depends on state laws, which define some subjects as mandatory (meaning school boards must bargain over them), some as permissive (meaning the two sides can bargain over them if they want), and some as illegal (meaning they can't bargain over them at all). In practice, however, unions have been successful, both through legal argument and through pressure on the districts, at pulling almost all aspects of schooling into the collective bargaining process—even those, like curriculum, that were once thought to be "policy" issues beyond the scope of bargaining.[15]

Union influence usually takes the form of rules, which are em-

---

15. The discussion that follows includes an overview of basic features of collective bargaining within public education and the kinds of rules and contracts that result. For more detail, see, e.g., Lieberman, *The Teacher Unions*; Lorraine M. McDonnell and Anthony Pascal, "Organized Teachers in American Schools" (Santa Monica: Rand Corp., 1979); McDonnell and Pascal, "Teacher Unions and Educational Reform" (Santa Monica: Rand Corp., 1988); Charles Taylor Kerchner and Julia E. Koppich, *A Union of Professionals: Labor Relations and Educational Reform* (New York: Teachers College Press, 1993); Randall W. Eberts and Joe A. Stone, *Unions and Public Schools: The Effect of Collective Bargaining on American Education* (Lexington, Mass.: Lexington Books, 1984).

bedded in the collective bargaining contract and specify, often in excruciating detail, what must or must not be done. In a typical union contract, there are so many rules about so many subjects, and the rules themselves can be so complicated, that it may take more than a hundred pages to spell them all out. (In many urban districts, where the teachers unions are strongest, contracts may run to two or three hundred pages or longer.)

There are rules, of course, about pay and fringe benefits. But there are also rules about hiring, firing, layoffs, and promotion. Rules about how teachers are to be evaluated, and how the evaluations can be used. Rules about the assignment of teachers to classrooms, and their (non)assignment to yard duty, lunch duty, hall duty, and after-school activities. Rules about how much time teachers can be required to work, and how much time they must get to prepare for class. Rules about class schedules. Rules about how students are to be disciplined. Rules about homework. Rules about class size. Rules about the numbers and uses of teacher aides. Rules about the school calendar. Rules about the role of teachers in school policy decisions. Rules about how grievances are to be handled. Rules about staff development and time off for professional meetings. Rules about who has to join the union. Rules about whether their dues will be automatically deducted from their paychecks. Rules about union use of school facilities. And more.

Union demands on these scores are not random or frivolous. There is a logic to them. The unions have certain fundamental interests that motivate their behavior and determine the kinds of rules they find desirable and worth fighting for. These interests arise from the primordial fact that, in order to survive and prosper as organizations, the unions need to attract members and money. Most of what they do can be understood in terms of these simple goals—which entail, among other things, securing benefits and protections for their members, increasing the demand for teachers, supporting higher taxes, regularizing the flow of resources into union coffers, minimizing competition, and seeking political power.[16]

16. See especially Lieberman, *The Teacher Unions.*

Note that these interests, and the sorts of behaviors they ultimately require of unions, need have nothing to do with what is best for children, schools, or the public interest, and may sometimes come into conflict with them. For this reason, collective bargaining often leads to contracts that make little sense as blueprints for effective organization. They make perfect sense, however, as expressions of union interests.[17]

Here, by way of illustration, are some of the common themes that govern the unions' approach to particular issues and give form and substance to the typical contract:

1. Unions are dedicated to protecting the jobs of all their members. The rules they insist upon, as a result, make it virtually impossible for schools to get rid of even the most poorly performing teachers, not to mention those that are merely mediocre.

2. Unions don't want basic personnel decisions—about pay, promotions, transfers—made on the basis of teacher performance. They oppose merit pay, for example. More fundamentally, they resist efforts to even measure teacher performance—through tests of teacher competence, for instance, or through assessments of classroom effectiveness (including how much students are learning). In the eyes of unions, performance evaluations create uncertainty for their members, force members to compete with one another, and put too much discretion in the hands of principals. The unions want personnel decisions to be made on the basis of seniority, formal education, and other objective criteria that are not matters of discretion, are within reach of all teachers, and are unrelated to performance in the classroom.

3. Unions seek to create, expand, and guarantee teacher rights by severely restricting the discretion available to principals and other administrators. For principals and district officials, discretion means the ability to lead and manage. But for unions, it means that administrators are able to make

17. For the basic facts on all these counts, see the works referred to in note 15.

decisions about where, when, and how teachers will do their work and how their incentives will be structured—and this flies in the face of everything the unions are trying to achieve. Discretion is to be driven out, replaced by rules that define realms of teacher control and autonomy.

4. Unions tend to oppose anything that induces competition or differentiation among teachers. This applies to performance-based assessments, of course. But it also applies to many other policies. They are opposed, for example, to differential pay in response to market conditions—which might mean paying math and science teachers a premium in order to attract and hold them. Unions want teachers to have the same interests, because this encourages them to act with solidarity on union issues. The notion that some teachers are better than others, or worth more than others, is stridently resisted.

5. Unions tend to oppose anything that induces competition among schools. Most fundamentally, they try to ensure that all schools in a district are uniformly covered by the same collective bargaining agreement, because the schools not covered (and thus free of the costs and rigidities it imposes) would have an advantage. This is especially true if the non-covered schools were allowed to be different in other ways too, and if parents were free to choose where to send their kids, for then the noncovered schools might attract kids, jobs, and resources away from the union schools. The union ideal is that all schools be regulated the same, and that all be guaranteed their "fair share" of students and resources.

6. Unions tend to oppose any contracting-out of educational functions that involves a shift of jobs and resources from the public to the private sector. This is true even if privatization may provide services at lower cost or more effectively. The goal is to keep public employment and public budgets as high as possible.

7. Unions want contract provisions that, so far as legally possible, induce all teachers to become members and force any nonmembers to pay agency fees. They also want dues and fees automatically deducted from teacher paychecks; this

guarantees the unions a regular flow of money and allows them to shift the administrative costs onto the districts.

The unions put the best public face on the positions they take in collective bargaining, arguing that what is good for teachers is good for kids, and that they are just fighting for quality public schools. Some scholars portray the unions as a positive force as well, arguing, among other things, that union-imposed standardization actually works well for the average student, and that unions promote professionalization, expertise, and productivity.[18]

Whatever the validity of these arguments—and I would argue that they are questionable, at best—it is pretty obvious that many aspects of union influence (not all) have negative consequences for kids and schools. How can it be socially beneficial that schools can't get rid of bad teachers? Or that teachers can't be tested for competence? Or that teachers can't be evaluated on the basis of how much their students learn? Or that principals are so heavily constrained that they can't exercise leadership of their own schools?

It is also clear that the aggregate effect of all the union-generated rules adds tremendously to the bureaucratization of the public schools. The unions are thus responsible for making the system much more formal, complex, and impersonal than it would otherwise be—and these are characteristics that tend to undermine school performance. Schools tend to do best when they are able to function in an informal, cooperative, flexible, and nurturing way: which is precisely the opposite of bureaucracy.[19]

Little research specifically links teachers unions to school per-

18. See, e.g., Randall W. Eberts and Joe A. Stone, "Teachers Unions and the Productivity of Public Schools," *Industrial and Labor Relations Review* 40, 1986: 355–63; and Charles Taylor Kerchner, Julia E. Koppich, and Joseph G. Weeres, *United Mind Workers: Unions and Teaching in the Knowledge Society* (San Francisco: Jossey-Bass).

19. See, e.g., Anthony Bryk, Valerie E. Lee, and Peter B. Holland, *Catholic Schools for the Common Good* (Cambridge: Harvard University Press, 1993), and Michael A. Zigarelli, "An Empirical Test of Conclusions from Effective Schools Research," *Journal of Educational Research*, Vol. 90, no. 2 (November/December, 1996): 103–110.

formance, so it is impossible to make an ironclad, empirically documented case about the direction of union effects. The few existing studies have led to mixed results, some showing negative effects and some showing positive effects.[20] But much of this is probably spurious, arising because the data are very poor and hard to get, and because the methodological difficulties in carrying out the analysis are formidable (mainly due to problems of mutual causality). The only confident conclusion that can be drawn from these studies is that unions clearly increase the costs of education, apparently by an average of 8 to 15 percent—and without (so far as can be determined) a correspondingly large increase, or any increase at all, in school quality. This tends to support the argument that, for a given level of expenditure, unions make the production of quality education more difficult. Future research will tell us more.

## Local Politics

Collective bargaining is the bread-and-butter activity of teachers unions, and the foundation of their survival and prosperity as organizations. It is not, however, the sum total of what unions do, nor does it fully explain why the unions are such important influences on our nation's schools. The key to the unions' preeminence in American education is that they are able to *combine* collective bargaining and politics into an integrated strategy for promoting union objectives.

Teachers unions are active in politics at all levels: local, state, and national. Not surprisingly, a division of labor prevails within both the NEA and the AFT. The local affiliates are almost entirely responsible for influencing policy and elections at the local level,

20. These studies are reviewed in Joe A. Stone, "Collective Bargaining and Public Schools," in Tom Loveless, ed., *Conflicting Missions: Teachers Unions and Educational Reform* (Washington, D.C.: Brookings Institution, 2000). Among them are Eberts and Stone, "Teachers Unions and the Productivity of Public Schools"; Eberts and Stone, *Unions and Public Schools*; Caroline Minter Hoxby, "How Teachers Unions Affect Education Production," *Quarterly Journal of Economics*, 111, 1996: 671–718; Sam Peltzman, "The Political Economy of the Decline of American Public Education," *Journal of Law and Economics* 36, 1993: 331–70.

the state affiliates are responsible for these things at the state level, and the national organizations take charge at the national level.

At the heart of local politics is the astounding fact that teachers unions are in a position to determine who sits on local school boards, and thus who they will be bargaining with. Assuming they can wield enough political power, they can actually choose the "management" teams that make decisions on behalf of the districts. Needless to say, they have strong incentives to mobilize their members and resources for political purposes, to participate actively in electoral campaigns, and to identify and recruit sympathetic candidates. These incentives are all the stronger, given that districts (and sometimes their electorates, through direct votes) make decisions on a wide range of policy, taxing, and funding issues of great relevance to union interests.

The details of local politics can vary considerably across districts, as a reflection of their individual histories, demographics, and problems. But there are certain characteristics that are common to most of them, that structure their politics—and that give the teachers unions great advantages in the struggle for influence:[21]

1. School board elections tend to occur in off years or times, and as a result tend to attract low turnout, often in the range of 10 to 20 percent.[22] Any group capable of mobilizing even small numbers of voters can tip the balance and influence the outcome. The unions are clearly in a good position to do this.
2. These elections are typically nonpartisan, meaning that candidates run as individuals and are not identified by party affiliation. Voters are thus denied the crucial information

21. For discussions of the basic features of education politics at the local level, see Frederick M. Wirt and Michael W. Kirst, *The Political Dynamics of American Education* (Berkeley, Calif.: McCutchan, 1997). For discussion of union resources and political strategies, see Lieberman, *The Teacher Unions*.

22. Here is a sobering example. In the school board election held in Los Angeles in April of 1999, there was actually a high profile battle—a rarity—between the unions and a coalition led by Mayor Riordan. Even so, turnout was just 17 percent of the registered voters, and a still smaller percentage of all possible voters. (Data were obtained directly from Los Angeles County records.)

that party normally conveys—about ideology, issue positions, and the like—and guarantees that, in a context of low
information and low interest (which is characteristic of
school board elections), the teachers unions will be in a better position to control how candidates are perceived and to
get their own candidates elected. In general, nonpartisanship
creates an informational void that works to the advantage of
powerful groups that can fill it.

3. Local politics is not very pluralistic. Typically, the teachers
unions have a far greater stake in these elections than any
other groups in their communities, and they have stronger
incentives to invest in political action. They overshadow
business and civic groups in this respect. They also overshadow parents, who are not organized as an interest group
(outside the PTA, which has long been under union control
in politics) and who vote in low numbers. In short: the
unions have few serious competitors for power.

4. Teachers unions are flush with political resources. They have
money for campaign contributions. But even more important, they control an army of political workers (teachers)
who are educated, well informed, have a direct stake in the
issues, and can readily be organized for political action: to
vote, make phone calls, ring door bells, distribute literature,
serve as campaign staff, and so on. No other community
group can come close to matching them in manpower and
political organization.

5. Most candidates running for school board are running on a
shoestring. This being so, candidates endorsed by the unions
and boosted by their money, manpower, and organization
cannot help but have advantages over their opponents.

The teachers unions can't always have what they want, of
course. In some districts, especially in the South, unions are weak
or nonexistent. And even where unions are strong, there may
sometimes be other groups—the religious right or business or
mayor-led reformists—that are also strong and take the unions on.
In addition, there may be salient issues, particularly bond issues or

property tax issues, that hit people's pocketbooks and generate higher levels of community participation, making union control more difficult. And in some communities, notably those that are socially advantaged, relatively high participation in local politics may be the norm, and the unions may find it harder to exercise power overall. So union influence will not be constant. It will vary as these sorts of conditions vary.

There is little systematic research on this, and much more needs to be done before we can be confident about exactly what the unions are doing in local politics and with what effects. What evidence there is, however, augmented by information regularly reported in the media, makes it clear that unions do tend to be formidable powers in local politics and often (but not always) get their way. The upshot is that, when school boards make official decisions about policy or money, or about the myriad rules that govern the operation of schools, their decisions tend to give heavy weight to the interests of unions—and may often depart, as a result, from what is best for children and effective education.

## STATE AND NATIONAL POLITICS

By law and tradition, the prime authorities in the field of public education are the state governments. The school districts are creatures of the states, and virtually everything about them—their boundaries, their governmental structures, their funding mechanisms, their policies, their very existence as political units—is subject to state authority. From the late 1800s until the mid-1900s, the states chose to delegate a good deal of this authority to the districts, and most aspects of public education were locally controlled. But this has changed over the last half-century, as the states have asserted their authority over educational policy, and as pressures for funding equalization (and court decisions requiring it) have produced shifts away from local property taxes toward more centralized mechanisms of educational finance. During this same period, the national government has become increasingly active in educational policy and funding, mainly though redistributive programs that funnel billions of dollars through the states and down to the schools. Federal money now represents about 8 percent of total school funding.[23]

Although the power of the teachers unions is rooted in their local districts, then, they have good reason to look beyond the districts when it comes to bringing their power to bear in politics. Increasingly, the big decisions on the big educational issues are being taken by state and (to a lesser extent) national governments, and many of these decisions have a direct bearing on the fundamental interests of unions. Active involvement in state and national politics is more than an attractive option for them. It is a necessity and, next to organizing and collective bargaining, their top priority.

The great value of higher-level politics is underlined by two major advantages that victory in these realms can convey. The first is that state governments, especially, are in a position to adopt virtually *any* restrictions, requirements, programs, and funding arrangements they want for the public schools. Whatever policies they adopt, moreover, are typically applied to *all* the districts and schools in their jurisdictions. When unions employ their political power at these higher levels, then, they can achieve many objectives they might be unable to achieve through local collective bargaining—from bigger education budgets to smaller classes to stricter credentialing requirements—and they can automatically achieve them for entire populations of districts and schools. One political victory can often accomplish what hundreds of decentralized negotiations cannot.

The second is that government policies at these higher levels can be designed to provide a favorable *structure* for local collective bargaining, and thus to create a context in which it is easier for unions to organize teachers, gain bargaining rights, and win concessions in negotiations. In most states, the unions long ago were able to mobilize sufficient power to achieve statewide bargaining frameworks. But the battles continue. They seek bargaining laws in the remaining states that don't have them, and they are con-

23. See John E. Chubb, "The System," this volume. See also Wirt and Kirst, *The Political Dynamics of American Education.*

stantly pushing to upgrade the frameworks in the states that do—
e.g., by getting agency fee requirements, or by expanding the scope
of bargaining. Moreover, they would dearly love to see the national government adopt a single bargaining framework that
would apply uniformly to every state in the country.[24] In general,
the more power they can wield in state and national politics, the
better able they are to promote their own collective bargaining
activities at the local level and to solidify and strengthen their organizational foundations.

Over the last few decades, the NEA and AFT have acted aggressively on these incentives, and they have emerged as extraordi-
narily powerful players in both state and national politics. A recent
academic study of interest-group politics at the state level, for instance, asked experts to rank interest groups according to their
influence on public policy—and the teachers unions came out
*number one* on the list, outdistancing general business organizations, the trial lawyers, doctors, insurance companies, utilities,
bankers, environmentalists, and even the state AFL-CIO affiliates.
Their influence was regarded as high, moreover, in virtually every
single state outside the South: a measure of the remarkable breadth
and uniformity of their political power.[25]

Part of the reason for their political success is that they spend
tremendous amounts of money on political campaigns and lobby-
ing. When compared to other interest groups, they regularly rank
among the top spenders at both the state and national levels, and
in many states are ranked number one. Probably the key to their
political firepower, however, is that they literally have millions of
members, and these members are a looming presence in *every* electoral district in the country. Candidates for major office are keenly
aware that the unions invest heavily in mobilizing their local activists, that they do so with great effectiveness, and that they have

24. On union efforts to secure more favorable bargaining laws, see., e.g.,
Lieberman, *The Teacher Unions*.
25. Clive S. Thomas and Ronald J. Hrebnar, "Interest Groups in the States,"
in Virginia Gray and Herbert Jacob, eds., *Politics in the American States*, 6th ed.
(Washington, D.C.: Congressional Quarterly Press, 1996).

considerable clout in seeing to it that their friends are elected and their enemies defeated.

Almost all of this firepower is employed to the benefit of Democrats, whose constituencies already incline them (usually) to favor policies that the teachers unions want—more public spending, higher taxes, higher public employment, more regulations, more job protections, more restrictions on competition, more collective bargaining—and who, with union backing and pressure, can be counted on to support many of the unions' specific demands on education policy and reform. Their alliance with the Democrats is perhaps best illustrated by where their money goes. In 1998, for example, the NEA was one of the nation's top contributors to congressional campaigns, and 95 percent of its money went to Democrats. The AFT, also a top contributor, gave 98 percent of its money to Democrats. Both unions also gave money to the parties directly (called "soft money"), rather than to candidates. Of these contributions, the NEA gave 98 percent to the Democrats, the AFT 100 percent.[26]

The most visible indicator of their alliance with the Democrats comes every four years, during the national presidential campaigns. Since 1976, when the NEA first became seriously active in presidential politics, the teachers unions have mobilized their activists to participate in the Democratic nomination process, and they have essentially colonized the Democratic national conventions. Although estimates vary, it appears the two unions together have regularly accounted for more than 10 percent of the total convention delegates, far more than any other special interest group.[27] Their leaders, meantime, have played central roles in shaping the Democratic presidential agenda on education. The stage was set the first year out, in 1976, when the NEA got Jimmy Carter to commit to its top political priority: the creation of a national department of education. In the years since, Democratic

26. These figures are derived from Federal Election Commission filings, and can be found on the internet through FECInfo, which is located at www.tray.com.

27. See, e.g., Lieberman, *The Teacher Unions*; Murphy, *Blackboard Unions*; Taylor E. Dark, *The Unions and the Democrats* (Ithaca: Cornell University Press, 1999).

nominees—and Democratic presidents—have never strayed far from what the teachers unions find desirable or acceptable.[28]

The teachers unions are prime movers in the Democratic Party, but they are also key players in the liberal coalition more generally. The members of this coalition—civil rights groups, antipoverty groups, women's groups, environmentalists, peace groups, gay-rights groups, and pro-abortion groups, among others—tend to support Democrats and make up much of the organized support base for the party. But the coalition also transcends the party. All these liberal interest groups are independent actors with specialized interests of their own, and the great benefit of a coalition is that they can work together—by supporting one another's causes—in order to maximize their influence and see that their own, individual objectives are separately achieved. The teachers unions, as leading members of this coalition, are beneficiaries of the support these other groups can give for union causes. By reciprocation, though, the unions are also engaged in political campaigns to achieve a whole array of liberal policy objectives that have nothing to do with teachers, collective bargaining, or even the public schools.

Here is just a smattering of the political causes the teachers unions have taken positions on in recent years. The NEA has adopted resolutions on universal health care, statehood for Washington, D.C., nuclear testing, abortion, environmental regulation, Native American remains, women's rights, minority-owned businesses, and mail-order brides. The AFT has taken stands on the war in Kosovo, peace in Northern Ireland, democracy in Burma, child labor in foreign nations, and fast-track procedures on international trade.[29]

The requirements of coalitional politics are not the only reasons teachers unions pursue these sorts of noneducational objectives.

28. See, e.g., Beryl A. Radin and Willis D. Hawley, *The Politics of Federal Reorganization: Creating the U.S. Department of Education* (New York: Pergamon Books, 1988).

29. Formal resolutions adopted by the NEA and the AFT at their annual conventions are summarized on each union's web site. See *www.nea.org* and *www.aft.org*, respectively.

The fact is, the activists and leaders within the teachers unions tend to be personally quite liberal, and, as they promote the broader liberal agenda, they are supporting policies that they are enthusiastic about anyway. If there is a disconnect between what the unions do in politics and what union members want, it emerges from the great mass of teachers who are not activists. The NEA's own polls have shown that most of its rank-and-file members are not Democrats and that most of them do not classify themselves as liberals. It appears that the liberal politics of the NEA simply does not represent their views.[30]

How do the teachers unions, as ostensibly democratic organizations, manage to carry this off? The answer comes in two parts. First, union democracy is a pale reflection of the ideal. Most members are poorly informed, don't participate in union decision-making, and leave control to (liberal) activists and leaders.[31] Second, rank-and-file members are tied into their unions for economic reasons, or simply because state laws or bargaining contracts effectively require them to join, and they will continue to belong and pay dues even if they are discontented with the liberal thrust of union politics.[32] These two democratic weaknesses—the weakness of "voice" via the lack of member influence, and the weakness of "exit" via the inability of members to quit on political grounds—essentially free the leadership to go its own way without fear of losing members or resources.[33]

The teachers unions can be active participants in the liberal coalition, then, and an outlet for the liberalism of its leaders and activists, without paying a price for failing to represent their mem-

30. See National Education Association, *The NEA Teacher Member, 1995–96* (Washington, D.C.: NEA). For supporting evidence, see also Emily C. Feistritzer, *Profile of Teachers in the US* (Washington, D.C.: National Center for Education Information, 1996).

31. See Lieberman, *The Teacher Unions.*

32. The theoretical basis for this phenomenon is developed in Mancur Olson's classic book, *The Logic of Collective Action* (Cambridge: Harvard University Press, 1965). See also Terry M. Moe, *The Organization of Interests* (Chicago: University of Chicago Press, 1980).

33. On the roles of exit and voice in making organizations responsive to their clienteles, see A. O. Hirschman, *Exit, Voice, and Loyalty* (Cambridge: Harvard University Press, 1970).

bers. This is one of the keys to understanding their politics, and their involvement in issues that have nothing to do with education. It would be a mistake, however, to think that pursuit of these extraneous issues as at the heart of their political agenda. In terms of money, activity, and the sheer exercise of power, it isn't. The teachers unions are driven by their fundamental interests—which are not rooted in the principles of liberal ideology, but rather in collective bargaining, the structure of public education, and the public taxing and spending that support it. These are the issues that animate their most serious political involvement.

In the electoral process, as we've seen, the teachers unions pursue their interests by investing heavily in the election of sympathetic candidates to public office. But the real goal, of course, is to gain influence over public policy, and thus to make sure that they get the laws, programs, regulations, and funding arrangements they want—and prevent the adoption of those they don't want. They go about this in various ways.

Most obviously, they are aggressive, omnipresent lobbyists in Congress and state legislatures. This is often true even in right-to-work states. They monitor and try to put their stamp on all relevant pieces of legislation, propose their own bills, carry out background research on the issues, attend committee hearings, keep scorecards on legislators—and bring their formidable power to bear in seeing to it that legislators vote their way. On education issues, the teachers unions are the 500-pound gorillas of legislative politics, and, especially in legislatures where the Democrats are in control, they are in a better position than any other interest group to get what they want from government.[34]

On occasion, they also attempt to put new laws in place through the initiative process, by designing their own bills and putting

34. There is very little serious research on how the teachers unions go about wielding their political influence, although accounts can be read with great frequency in the media, and particularly in *Education Week*, which tracks developments in American education. For critical but informative attempts to describe how the teachers unions transact their political business, see, e.g., Lieberman, *The Teachers Unions*; G. Gregory Moo, *Power Grab* (Washington, D.C.: Regnery Publishing, 1999); and Berube, *Teacher Politics*.

them on the ballot for a direct popular vote. Here, they can use their financial resources to bankroll the necessary signature gathering and to pay for the general campaign, and they can unleash an army of volunteers to do the legwork so crucial to electoral success. No other organizations are so well suited to initiative campaigns, and the unions have used them to their advantage when legislatures have failed to give them what they want. A good example is California's Proposition 98, which was heavily and successfully promoted by the California Teachers Association in 1989, and since then has required the state to spend at least 40 percent of its annual budget on the public schools.[35]

The teachers unions also pursue their interests with great success through active involvement in administrative arenas—which, to the uninitiated, may seem to be nonpolitical, but are actually realms in which important policy decisions are made and influenced. The national and state departments of education, in particular, administer countless educational programs, distribute billions of dollars, and have a great deal of discretion in deciding what the rules and goals of educational policy will be and exactly how the money will be spent. Within these departments, the unions are regular, quasi-official participants. Administrators regard them as key "stakeholders" who have legitimate, ongoing roles to play in shaping public decisions. The opportunities for union influence are everywhere, and virtually unobservable to outsiders unfamiliar with the byzantine world of government bureaucracy.

Often, the unions pursue their policy objectives by combining their legislative and administrative power. An important example can be found in their recent drive for teacher "professionalism," which is bound up (through no coincidence) with the larger national concern for higher standards in public education. In the abstract, these are goals with obvious political appeal. Who could be

35. There is no systematic research on this, although there are plenty of media accounts. For a detailed look at how the unions used their clout in initiative politics to soundly defeat the 1993 California voucher initiative, see Terry M. Moe, *Schools, Vouchers, and the American Public* (Washington, D.C.: Brookings Institution, 2001).

against professionalism and higher standards? The reality, however, is that the teachers unions are active on these issues because
their fundamental interests are at stake. Through professional self-
regulation, they are able to control entry into their field, and thus
to limit supply and put upward pressure on salaries. This is a classic political strategy that other occupations—from doctors and
lawyers to cosmetologists and plumbers—have long employed
with great success. The teachers unions just want to do the same.[36]

Specifically, the unions want stricter licensing and credentialing
requirements for teachers, and they want the process overseen and
enforced by state administrative boards that are controlled by
teachers—and thus, in practice, by the unions themselves. They
also want teachers to get a national certification, presumably as a
way of promoting uniformly high standards; and this certification
process is controlled by the National Board for Professional Teaching Standards, which in turn is controlled by the unions. In addition, they argue that teachers should get their training at education
schools that are accredited by the National Council for Accreditation of Teacher Education, in which the unions have heavy influence. Major progress along these lines calls for new legislation,
and the unions are currently active in state legislatures across the
country trying to create the new requirements. To the extent they
are successful, the key decisions—and the key union involvement—will take place in administrative bodies far from the public
eye, where the unions can exercise influence on a routine basis.[37]

When it comes to the pursuit of new public policies, the unions
are the most powerful of all education groups. But they cannot
always, or even usually, get the policies they want. Nor can anyone
else. The reason is that the American political system is built
around checks and balances. New legislation must run a gauntlet
of subcommittees, committees, and floor votes in each of two legislative houses, and survive filibusters, holds, and executive vetoes.
Proponents must overcome each and every veto point in order to

36. See Dale Ballou and Michael Podgursky, "Gaining Control of Professional Licensing and Advancement," in Tom Loveless, ed., *Conflicting Missions*.
37. Ballou and Podgursky, "Gaining Control . . . ."

get their ideas into law, while opponents need to succeed only once, at any veto point along the way, in order to block. The system is built to make new legislation very difficult to achieve—and to make blocking very easy.

Much of what the teachers unions do in politics, accordingly, is not about trying to put new policies in place. It is about blocking policies to which they are opposed. And it is here that they are especially well positioned to get their way. In particular, they are usually powerful enough to stop the enactment of reforms that they consider a threat to their interests, and thus to protect a status quo—the existing system of collective bargaining, extensive regulation, and top-down governance—that works to their great advantage. In a time of educational ferment, in which there is widespread pressure for change and improvement in the public education system, *this* is the way the teachers unions put their power to most effective use. They use it to prevent change.

The best illustration is in the teachers unions' response to the movement for school choice, which, over the last decade, has been the most far-reaching movement for change in American education.[38] Proponents see choice-based reforms—most prominently, vouchers, charter schools, and privatization (district contracting with private firms)—as means of putting more power in the hands of parents, giving parents and kids more choices, and giving schools stronger incentives to perform. But from the unions' standpoint, it is largely irrelevant whether these arguments are correct or not. For the overriding fact is that choice-based reforms naturally generate changes that are threatening to the fundamental interests of unions—and the unions, quite predictably, are opposed. Much of their political activity over the last decade has been dedicated to the simple goal of blocking school choice.

The unions see vouchers as a survival issue. Vouchers would allow money and children to flow out of the public sector into the

38. See, e.g., Paul Peterson, "Choice in American Education," this volume; Bruce Fuller, Richard Elmore, and Gary Orfield, eds., *Who Chooses? Who Loses? Culture, Institutions, and the Unequal Effects of School Choice* (New York: Teachers College Press, 1996); Mark Schneider, Paul Teske, and Melissa Marschall, *Choosing Schools* (Princeton: Princeton University Press, 2000).

private sector: threatening a sharp drop in public employment, and thus in union membership and resources; dispersing teachers to private schools where they are much harder for unions to organize; promoting competition among schools, which puts union schools at a disadvantage; and creating a more decentralized, less-regulated system in which the unions will have less power and control. Small wonder, then, that the teachers unions have done everything they can to defeat vouchers. This has been true even when vouchers are proposed solely for the poorest and neediest of children, and in public school systems that are clearly failing.

So far, thanks to the combination of their formidable power and the blocking advantage inherent in American politics, the unions have succeeded in blocking vouchers almost every time they have been proposed. Three programs have been adopted over their vigorous opposition—programs for low-income kids in Milwaukee and Cleveland, and a program for kids in "failing" schools in Florida. But even these programs remain under assault, as the unions use whatever avenues they can—judicial, legislative, administrative, electoral—to bring them down.[39]

The teachers unions are also involved in a continuing battle to block the advance of charter schools. Charter schools are public schools of choice that are largely independent of district control, and offer parents alternatives to the regular public schools. Charters do not take money or teachers out of the public system, and so are not as threatening as vouchers. But they are threatening on other grounds. They need not be unionized, and, as schools of choice, they attract students and money away from the regular public schools where union members teach; indeed, charters actually have a competitive advantage, because they can be more flexible in their programs, and are not burdened by the costs and regulations imposed through unionization (and district governance). The more charter schools there are, then, the greater the threat to the size and financial well-being of the unions. Moreover, as charters spread, the districts and unions simply have less control

---

39. For a more extensive discussion of teachers unions and the voucher issue, see Moe, *Schools, Vouchers, and the American Public.*

over public education, and less power over the things that matter to them.

There can be little surprise, therefore, that the teachers unions have fought against charters. On occasion, they "support" charter proposals, but these are strategic political moves designed to head off something much worse—vouchers. When they "support" charter proposals, moreover, they do what they can to put strict ceilings on the number of new charters, require that the new schools be unionized, and give the districts and the unions as much control over them as possible. Charter schools are on the rise nationwide: there are now some two thousand of them, attended by some four hundred thousand children, and the numbers are growing rapidly. But for now, most are constrained by charter laws that have been heavily influenced by the unions and that sharply restrict how much real choice and competition the new schools can bring.[40]

The teachers unions have also been engaged in an ongoing battle against privatization. In the 1990s, there emerged new, for-profit companies that sought contracts to run entire schools (or even entire districts), typically those regarded as failing. From the unions' standpoint, the problem was not that the privatized schools would be nonunion; for in reality, they would actually remain unionized—and quite public—schools that would simply be run by a contractor under terms set by the district. The problem was that the union would have less control over the contractor than over the district itself, that its new practices and procedures could disrupt (and outperform) those existing within the regular schools—and, most troubling of all, that any movement along this path could lead to far greater privatization in the future, and to a flow of jobs, money, and control from the public to the private sector. The last thing the unions want is a demonstration that private firms can do a better job of educating children than the regular, unionized schools can do.

40. On the charter movement and its politics, see Chester E. Finn, Bruno V. Manno, and Gregg Vanourek, *Charter Schools in Action* (Princeton: Princeton University Press, 2000).

The pioneer in this field, Education Alternatives, managed during the early 1990s to enter into contracts with a few struggling districts over vehement union opposition. But continuing trench warfare by the unions ultimately pressured district authorities to back out, and they sent the company packing (and into near bankruptcy). A second generation of private firms, led by Edison Schools, has learned from the political misfortunes of Education Alternatives and is making greater progress, particularly in districts that are hard-pressed to improve and where unions are weak or under pressure to acquiesce. Because of union opposition, however, their inroads into the public school system will be limited for the foreseeable future. Moreover, what progress they do make will usually involve them in contracts that are bogged down in district-imposed (and union-influenced) rules and regulations that make it difficult for these firms to take full advantage of their privateness, and of the efficiencies that markets can normally be expected to provide. If the unions can't block privatization entirely, their goal is to make sure that the contractor-operated schools look as much like regular public schools as possible—and thus that real reform is minimal.[41]

The bottom line, then, is that the teachers unions' greatest power is not the ability to get what they want, but rather the ability to block what they don't want—and thus to stifle all education reforms that are somehow threatening to their interests. School choice is not the only reform they oppose. Union interests are deeply rooted in the status quo, and most changes of any consequence are likely to create problems for them and to be opposed as well. The result is that, as our nation has struggled to improve its public school system, the teachers unions have emerged as the fiercest, most powerful defenders of the status quo, and as the single greatest obstacle to the reform of American education.

41. For a more detailed discussion of how unions have opposed privatization, with special attention to their successful attack on Education Alternatives, see Terry M. Moe, "Democracy and the Challenge of Education Reform," in Gary D. Libecap, ed., *Advances in the Study of Entrepreneurship, Innovation, and Economic Growth* (Greenwich, Conn.: JAI Press, 1997)

## Conclusion

The system that the teachers unions devote so much of their time and resources to protecting is very different from the one that prevailed during the first half of this century. During that period, the basic structure of public education looked very much as it does now, with schools subject to the authority of school boards, superintendents, state legislatures, and other arms of democratic government. Since then, the locus of effective authority has partially shifted from the local level to the state and national levels—and this, in many standard accounts, is what is significantly different about today's system. There has been another shift, however, virtually parallel in time, that is at least as significant. During the early period, unions and collective bargaining had almost no role in American education. The spectacular growth of teachers unions during the 1960s and 1970s changed that, and generated what deserves to be recognized as a new educational regime—a regime dominated by union power, suffused by union interests, and, after some thirty years, deeply entrenched.

Within the new regime, the teachers unions have profound influence on America's public schools. They shape the schools from the bottom up, through a collective bargaining process that touches virtually every aspect of school organization and activity. They also shape them from the top down, through a political process that determines each school's—and the entire system's—policies, programs, regulations, and financial resources, as well as which education reforms will and (more important) will not be adopted.

As the teachers unions put their stamp on the nation's schools, the objectives they pursue are reflections of their fundamental interests, which derive from their core functions of collective bargaining and organizational maintenance. These interests have no necessary connection to what is best for children, schools, or society, and are sometimes clearly in conflict with the greater good—as, for example, when they lead unions to protect the jobs of incompetent teachers, oppose performance-based evaluations, or burden schools with excessive bureaucracy.

It seems reasonable to suggest that, if our nation is to improve its public schools, and if it does not want to be locked into only those reform strategies the unions find acceptable, then the unions must be regarded as part of the problem—and targets of reform. In recent years, certain scholars and even a few union leaders have argued the need for "reform unionism," and claimed that, with enough prodding and enlightened thinking, the unions can dedicate themselves to the kinds of reforms that are actually good for kids, schools, and society. But this is a fanciful notion, based on a fatal misconception: that the unions can be counted upon to forgo their fundamental interests. Any reform premised on such an assumption is bound to fail.

For reform to succeed, something concrete must be done to remove the education system from the unions' grip. This, however, will surely not be easy, precisely because the unions can (and regularly do) use their power to "persuade" would-be reformers to turn their sights elsewhere. Most Democrats, in particular, would be committing political suicide by trying to alter the unions' current role in public education, and they will resist any efforts to do so. In a political system of checks and balances, this alone will be enough to block most reform proposals most of the time.

If the foreseeable future holds a solution to the problem of union power, it will probably develop as a by-product of the school choice movement. The best bet is that, despite union opposition, school choice in various forms will gradually spread—for it is being pushed by proponents in all fifty states and in thousands of districts, and the unions cannot win every battle. As choice spreads, the unions will be faced with an increasingly competitive environment. Children and resources will begin to flow to non-union schools, and unions will find themselves with fewer members, less money, and with a growing number of schools and teachers that are outside the traditional system and difficult to organize. Just as in the private sector, competition spells trouble for unions. It undermines their organizational strength—and in so doing, it undermines their political power.

Whether choice and competition will ultimately win out remains to be seen. In the meantime, the teachers unions will remain the preeminent power in American education. And they will continue to shape the public schools in their own image.

# CHAPTER 8

# Curriculum and Competence

## *E. D. Hirsch Jr.*

### DEFINING ACADEMIC COMPETENCE

In a democracy, a minimal aim of schooling is to bring every child who is not mentally retarded to competence. Recently, in the new economy, even dictatorships have attempted for economic reasons to foster universal education. But long before the information age, indeed ever since the American and French Revolutions, the aim of universal competence—universal literacy and numeracy among the people—has been an avowed educational goal of democracies, where the people rule. Such competence means at a minimum the ability to understand written and oral materials addressed to a general audience; the ability to communicate in speech and writing; and the ability to do math up to prealgebra.

This chapter makes the straightforward claim that it is impossible to bring all children to competence without conveying needed knowledge to them through a coherent, cumulative curriculum in the early grades. Literacy, for example, depends at a minimum on having a wide enough vocabulary to understand newspapers, talk shows, teachers, and vocational training manuals. Having this broad vocabulary depends on having the broad knowledge represented by the words, and broad knowledge cannot be conveyed to everyone through schooling without schools' offering a an effective, cumulative curriculum free of huge gaps and boring repetitions. The failure of our public schools to deliver such a curriculum is the chief reason for the U. S. failure to bring all children to competence.

Several of the distinguished authors of this book favor structural changes to improve school performance, especially changes that impose upon our ill-performing monopoly the element of competition and other free market principles. I also favor the principle of competition in schooling. But efficient markets depend on the free flow of accurate information. We know enough about what works and what does not work to intervene in the educational market in order to prevent malpractice and misinformation from having a distorting influence on the competitive environment—just as false and deceptive advertising does. That is why three of the authors, Ravitch, Walberg, and I, have focused as much on content and pedagogy as on market-style structural change—which is to say we have focused on some of the historical, cultural, and scientific foundations of effective versus ineffective schooling. My task in this chapter is to discuss why it is the case that each and every school in order to be effective needs a specific, coherent, and well-conceived curriculum, plus sound tests that indicate how well that curriculum has been taught and learned.

The immediate policy implications of this thesis lie in its relevance to the state standards movements. Forty-nine of the fifty states have imposed curricular standards exhibiting varying degrees of prudence and effectiveness. It has been argued that some of the existing standards and some of the tests by which they are enforced have actually diminished educational effectiveness and are failing in their avowed purpose of bringing all children to competence. To the extent that these defects exist, they should be remedied. But the criticisms should be met, not be allowed to halt the progress of the standards movement. The standards movement says in essence that every school should deliver a coherent, well-conceived curriculum and should give sound tests that indicate how well the curriculum has been taught and learned.

My chief complaint about the state standards movement is its failure to achieve this fundamental aim. The so-called content standards are often vague to the point of nullity. Moreover, there is a needless lack of fit between the various content standards among the various states and localities. If all the states agree that young children need to learn about ancient Egypt and the river Nile, then, given the constant movement of children from one state to another, it is pointless and harmful that Egypt should be assigned to grade one in one state and to grade three in another.

Needless to say, a national curriculum—so labeled—is not on the policy table. But state and local curricular guidelines are to be found everywhere. Once a state decides that children should learn certain skills and contents, then the sequence in which they are taught should be subject to negotiation with other states that have decided on similar goals. This would lessen the harmful effects of student mobility and make textbooks more effective. Textbooks would then compete for their effectiveness in delivering a curriculum, not in the pointless novelty of a new sequence for the curriculum. A sequence is not a curriculum. To the extent that state guidelines share similar cognitive goals, there should be a convergence of state standards toward an agreed-upon sequencing of those goals. That is the first policy proposal of this chapter. The second policy proposal is that the high-stakes tests that measure whether the standards have been met should be improved.

## THE MYTH OF THE EXISTING CURRICULUM

The curricular chaos of the American elementary school is a feature of our public education that few people have been even remotely aware of, and the growth of that awareness has been one of the origins of the standards movement. We know there is no national curriculum, but we assumed, quite reasonably, that agreement had been reached in the district or school regarding what shall be taught to children at each grade level. The stated reason for preserving the principle of local control of education has been that the localities ought to determine what our children shall learn. But the idea that there exists a coherent plan for teaching content within the local district, or even within the individual school, has been a gravely misleading myth.

That the idea is a myth is not a darkly kept secret. Rather, the idea that there is a local curriculum is accepted as truth by experts within the school system. Recently, a district superintendent told me that for twenty years he had mistakenly assumed that each of his schools was determining what would be taught to children at each grade level but was shocked to find that the assumption was entirely false. He discovered that no principal in his district could tell him what minimal content each child in a grade was expected to learn. He was not surprised when I told him I had received a letter from a distraught mother of identical twins in which she complained that her children had been placed in different classes at the same school and were learning totally different things.

Local districts have produced thick documents that call themselves "curriculum guides" but which, for all their thickness, do not answer the simple question "What specific content are children at a grade level required to learn?" This same defect applies to most of the new state standards. If challenged on this point, an administrator at the state or local level might respond that each teacher at a grade level is encouraged to use a certain textbook. But using specific textbooks does not assure teaching minimal content any more than a thick pile of guidelines. Consider the following research regarding textbook-use in American schools:

> Daunted by the length of most textbooks and knowing that the children's future teachers will be likely to return to the material, American teachers often omit some topics. Different topics are omitted by different teachers, thereby making it impossible for the children's later teachers to know what has been covered at earlier grades—they cannot be sure what their students know and do not know.[1]

## GAPS AND REPETITIONS

It might be wondered how it is possible for states and localities to produce lengthy curricular guides that, for all their bulk, fail to define specific knowledge for specific grade levels. Here are some typical instructions. They pertain to first-grade social studies.

1. H. Stevenson and J. Stigler, *The Learning Gap: Why Our Schools Are Failing and What We Can Learn from Japanese and Chinese Education* (New York: Summit Books, 1992), p. 140.

> The child shall be able to identify and explain the significance of national symbols, major holidays, historical figures and events. Identify beliefs and value systems of specific groups. Recognize the effects of science and technology on yesterday's and today's societies.

These words disclose a characteristic reluctance of official guides to impinge on the teacher's prerogatives by stating which national symbols, major holidays, historical figures, and historical events the local curriculum makers have in view. But, in the absence of specifics, is there any reason to believe that different teachers will respond to these directions in similar ways? When children from first-grade classes enter second grade, what shared knowledge can the second-grade teacher take for granted among them? What are the "specific" groups that the students became acquainted with in studying the "beliefs and value systems of specific groups"? The word *specific* in such a context carries an unintended irony. Some states have moved toward greater specificity, a hopeful sign.

A few district curricula are more specific but exhibit grave unevenness in thoughtfulness and coherence. Take, for example, the subject of plants and seeds in the best local science curriculum I could find.

- Grade one: "Describe seeds and grow plants from seeds. State three requirements for seed germination and plant growth."

- Grade two: "Arrange illustrations of plants in various stages of development in order from seed to adult."

- Grade four: "Plant seeds and identify and determine the environmental factors responsible for the success and failure of plant development."

- Grade five: "Identify and plot the growth of the seed parts and infer that the cotyledon is food for the living embryo."

The theory behind this sort of repetition is that of deepening through "spiraling." But it is universally experienced by students as boring repetition, as in the oft-heard complaint from students who have been made to read *Charlotte's Web* three times in six grades.

If repetition and boredom are dangers in the "strand" approach to curriculum, an equal danger is the creation of gaps that open up in the spaces between the strands. Frequent repetitions and gaps are the besetting weaknesses of American curricula, and they are made inevitable when the strand approach is compounded with vagueness. Huge gaps are bound to arise. There was no indication even in this topflight local curriculum as to when children were to be introduced to photosynthesis, or that they were to be made aware of simple tools and how they work, or that they would know how to measure physical things in inches, feet, pounds, kilograms, grams, quarts, pints, or cubic centimenters. It might be assumed that the individual teacher would fill in these gaps. But experience has shown this to be an unwarranted assumption. Major gaps in the local guidelines become major gaps in students' minds—especially among students for whom the school is the only source of academic knowedge.

## STANDARDS FROM PROFESIONAL ORGANIZATIONS

To rectify these problems, national organizations were recently commissioned to supply national standards in the different subjects, with notoriously uneven results. The standards for language and literature were rejected by the Department of Education as being entirely vague. The standards in history were denounced by a vote in the U. S. Senate. The curriculum standards in math have become a subject of fierce debate within the mathematics community. And there are three national science standards at odds with one another. Quite apart from these ongoing debates at the national level, the states and districts that have accepted the national standards still face the task of translating them into curricula that overcome the defects of the vague guidelines they are supposed to replace.

How did we achieve this degree of curricular ineptitude, unique in the developed world? As Diane Ravitch has shown in detail, beginning in the 1930s as part of the advance of progessive education in the public schools and colleges of education, there were curriculum revision movements across the land. Over the past six decades such vague, gap-ridden "conceptual" curricula were developed as a reaction to earlier content-oriented approaches to forming a curriculum. The new curricula have attempted to get beyond the "rote learning" of "mere facts" and to gain unity and conceptual depth by following broad and deep instructional aims. Even the best local and state guides of this type have fundamental weaknesses.

The first inherent weakness is the arbitrariness of the conceptual schemes and classifications that make up all broad curricular "strands" or "objectives." Such schemes may appear to be deep and comprehensive, but most are quite arbitrary. The large conceptual objectives in each state and district tend to be different from one another, with each state and district preferring its own. Equally striking is the arbitrariness of the different conceptual schemes that curricular experts recently produced for the American Association for the Advancement of Science, the National Council of Teachers of Science, and the National Academy of Sciences, each with its own conceptual scheme.

There is another inherent shortcoming in an overreliance on abstract large-scale objectives (as opposed to "mere" content) as a means of determining a curriculum. These general objectives do not compel either a definite or a coherent sequence of instruction. That is because the large conceptual scheme and the concrete expressions of the scheme through particular contents have a very tenuous and uncertain relationship to each other. A big scheme is just too general to guide the teacher in the selection of particulars. For instance, one multigrade science objective in our superior local district states: "Understand interactions of matter and energy." This is operationally equivalent to saying "Understand physics, chemistry, and biology." The teachers who must decide what to include under such "objectives" are given little practical help.

Adequately detailed guidelines help teachers by discriminating between knowledge that is required and knowledge that is merely desirable. The selection of particular important "facts" reduces the total number of facts that a teacher needs to consider essential. Without specifics, disadvantaged students and their teachers play a Kafkaesque game whose rules are never clearly defined. Soon the

unlucky are consigned to slow tracks and never enter the mainstream of learning and society.

## The Problem of Mobility

A systemic failure to teach all children the knowledge they need in
order to understand what the next grade has to offer is the major
source of avoidable injustice in our schools. It is impossible for a
teacher to reach all children when some of them lack the necessary
building blocks of learning. Under these circumstances, the most
important single task of an individual school is to ensure that all
children within that school gain the prior knowledge they will
need at the next grade level. Because our system currently leaves
that supremely important task to the vagaries of individual classrooms, the result is a systemically imposed unfairness even for students who remain in the same school. That inherent unfairness is
greatly exacerbated for children who must change schools, sometimes in the middle of the year.

Add to these academic handicaps the emotional devastation of
not understanding what other children are understanding, and add
to avoidable academic problems the unavoidable ones of adjusting
to a new group, and it is not hard to understand why newcomers
fail to flourish in American schools. Then add to all of these draw-
backs the fact that the social group with the greatest percentage of
school-changers are low-income families who move for economic
reasons, and one understands more fully why disadvantaged children suffer disproportionately from the curricular incoherence of
the American educational system.

It is often said that we are a nation of immigrants. We are also
a people that continues to migrate within the nation's borders.
According to the United States General Accounting Office, about
one-fifth of all Americans relocate every year.

The United States has one of the highest mobility rates of all
developed countries; annually, about one-fifth of all Americans
move. Elementary school children who move frequently face disruption to their lives, including their schooling.[2]

2. General Accounting Office (GAO), "Elementary School Children: Many
Change School Frequently, Harming Their Education," GAO/HEHS-94-45, Feb.
1994, p. 1.

In a typical community, the average rate at which students transfer in and out of schools during the school year is nearly one-third: The average rate for Milwaukee public elementary schools is around 30 percent. And among the parents who move, it is those in the lowest income brackets who move most frequently—much more often than middle- and high-income families. This high mobility among low-income parents guarantees that disadvantaged children who will be most severely affected by the educational handicaps of changing schools are the very ones who move most often. In a typical inner-city school, only about half the students who start in September are still there in May. The myth of the local curriculum can be matched by the myth of the local school—if one means by the term *local school* not just a building and a staff but also the students who attend it during the year.[3]

Student mobility is rarely mentioned in discussions of school reform. That says more about the self-imposed restrictions on our educational thinking than about the urgencies of our educational problems. Any challenge to the principle of an autonomous local curriculum is considered taboo. Hence all the problems that are exacerbated by that taboo, including the deleterious effects of student mobility, receive far less public attention than they deserve.

The term of art for the percentages of transferred students is "mobility rate." The average mobility rates for the inner city lie routinely between 45 and 80 percent, with many suburban rates between 25 and 40 percent. Some inner-city schools in New York City and elsewhere have mobility rates of over 100 percent. That is to say, the total number of students moving in and out during the year exceeds the total number of students attending the school. "In some of the nation's most transient districts where some slots turn over several times, schools have mobility rates of more than 100 percent." The adverse effects of these moves on educational achievement contribute significantly to the low achievement of our

3. Deborah Cohen, "Moving Images," *Education Week*, August 3, 1994, pp. 32–39. David Wood, Neal Halfon, and Debra Scarlata, "Impact of Family Relocation on Children's Growth, Development, School Function, and Behavior," *Journal of the American Medical Association* 270, no. 1334–8 (September 15, 1993).

system as a whole. The General Accounting Office found that many more migrating third-graders were reading below grade level, as compared those who had not yet changed schools. Given the curricular incoherence of schooling even for those who stay at the same school, the fragmentation and incoherence of the education provided to frequently-moving students approaches the unthinkable.[4]

The deleterious effects of mobility should be placed in a particular historical, cultural, and educational context, rather than conceived of as timeless and inevitable. There is strong evidence that the adverse effects of student mobility are much greater in the United States than in countries that use a core curriculum. In a summary of research, Herbert Walberg, citing the work of Bruce C. Straits, states that "common learning goals, curriculum, and assessment within states (or within an entire nation), moreover, also alleviate the grave learning disabilities faced by children, especially poorly achieving children who move from one district to another with different curricula, assessment, and goals."[5]

Even those who hold strongly to the principle of local control of curriculum might well concede the need for a voluntary agreement about a common sequence in the curriculum—at least in those areas like math and science and basic facts of history and geography that, unlike sex education, are not or should not be subjects of controversy. Other things equal, the principle of the local curriculum is desirable in a democracy. But things are not now equal or effective or fair. Against the principle of local autonomy must be weighed the principles of educational excellence and social fairness. Democratic principles sometimes conflict with one another; none is absolute.

## TESTS: THE ROLE OF THE STATES

Statewide content standards are beginning to spawn high-stakes tests that have evoked furious opposition—not without cause.

4. GAO, "Elementary School Children," p. 6.
5. H. J. Walberg, "Improving Local Control and Learning," Preprint 1994. Walberg cites B. C. Straits, "Residence, Migration, and School Progress," *Sociology of Education,* 1987, 60, 34–43.

Under present circumstances, the backlash against curriculum-based tests has been warranted. The policymakers who have instituted these high-stakes tests have made two strategic mistakes. First, they introduced content standards and tests before providing teachers and students with detailed outlines and teaching materials that define what the content standards really are. They have put in place no adequate system for training teachers in the subject matters identified by the content standards. They have failed to do the hard work of deciding which aspects of the content are the most essential to be included in textbooks, teacher seminars, and tests—a lack of specificity and selectivity that has made at least some of the tests less reasonable and fair than they should be. Despite these flaws, the curriculum-based tests (where the state standards are beginning to be specific enough to generate a curriculum, as in California, Virginia, and Massachusetts) are the most promising educational development in half a century.

How these curriculum-based tests should be phased in as criteria for student promotion and graduation is a practical and political question to be decided in a democracy by the representatives of the people. I want to shed light on a technical issue that can be useful in helping to make such policy decisions better informed—that is, the differences and the connections between competency-based tests and curriculum-based tests.

Competency-based tests sample knowledge from a broad range of domains, which enables the tests to exhibit a reliably high correlation between test scores and real-world competencies. Curriculum-based tests are narrower. They try to determine how well specific content standards in a particular domain for a particular age group have been learned. Whereas competency tests indicate overall achieved ability, curriculum tests indicate whether specific knowledge has been gained. The astute reader will perhaps see where I am going—that a well-devised curriculum, monitored by good curriculum-based tests should, over time, extend the breadth of a student's knowledge and thus raise scores on broad-gauged competency-based tests.

Because an indispensable aim of schooling is to increase student competency, the public has a right to demand that results on the two kinds of test should in due course show a positive correlation. I shall try to explain why good curriculum-based tests, based on good content standards, are the surest and most democratic means of raising scores on competency-based tests and achieving real-world competencies.

## COMPETENCY TESTS

An excellent example of competency-based tests would be standardized reading tests such as the verbal portions of the Stanford 9, the ITBS, CTBS, the Nelson-Denny reading test, and so on. Although these are norm-referenced instruments that rank students against one another in percentiles, they can also be scored to indicate a student's grade level of reading comprehension. A score of 5.2 would mean that the student is reading at the level the average student has reached by the second month of grade five. These grade-level calibrations (which have been criticized on various grounds) could be also translated into absolute scores that can be equated over many decades. All the well-established reading tests are valid, reliable, and highly correlated with one another.[6] What sorts of questions are asked on a standardized reading test that cause it to indicate so reliably academic achievement and readiness? In the earliest-grade versions, there are of course questions about sounds and letters. Later versions include questions about vocabulary, the meanings of individual sentences, and the implications of passages from literature, the natural sciences, the social sciences, practical affairs, and several other domains. How could

6. The intercorrelation of reading tests with one another forms part of the technical literature accompanying the tests. Different tests published by a large company are often "equated" to the other reading tests or test components sold by the company. Researchers have found strong intercorrelations between reading scores on the Armed Services Vocational Aptitude Battery (ASVAB) and the Armed Forces Qualification Test (AFQT) and the various standardized reading tests such as Gates-Maginitie, Nelson-Denny, and the Stanford Tests of Academic Skills. The intercorrelations determined for reading-related skills range between .99 and .87—at the very limits of the reliability of the tests! See B. K. Waters, J. D. Barnes, P. Foley, S. Steinhaus, and D. C. Brown, *Estimating the Reading Skills of Military Applicants: Development of an ASVAB to RLG Conversion Table* (Alexandria, Va.: Human Resources Research Organization, 1988).

such a test, disconnected from any specific curriculum, so reliably calibrate academic achievement, learning readiness, and even real-world competency? One needs to offer not just the ample evidence that this claim is true but to provide a credible theory that explains the strong correlation between reading and general competency.

So I think it will be useful to state some of the theoretical principles that explain why good competency tests in reading turn out to be powerfully indicative of achieved abilities that go far beyond reading. Such a theory has the additional benefit of explaining the potency of curriculum-based tests and illustrating the bond of necessity between curriculum and competence.

1. Reading has been shown to be a process of mentally rephonicizing language, rather than being a separate linguistic process. The interpretation of the written word is a reenactment of the interpretation of the spoken word. Many of the conventions used in written language are used in speaking and listening. This mental reenactment of speech explains why reading ability is correlated with general communicative competence—the ability to understand and make oneself understood in oral as well as written speech.[7]

2. Such general communicative competence is required for effective social intercourse in modern society, and is especially critical in schooling, where it forms the basis for understanding the oral and written communications of other people, including teachers.

3. The level of one's reading ability (as reflected in the vocabulary items and passage types on a reading test) predicts the level of one's ability to learn new things. A person learns

---

7. R. Conrad and A. J. Hull, "Information, Acoustic Confusion and Memory Span," *British Journal of Psychology* 55 (1964): 429–32; D. L. Hintzman, "Articulatory Coding in Short-Term Memory," *Journal of Verbal Learning and Verbal Behavior* 6 (1967): 312–16; M. Naveh-Benjamin and J. T. Ayres, "Digit Span, Reading Rate, and Linguistic Relativity," *Quarterly Journal of Experimental Psychology* 38, 379–51. A general discussion of the underlying "phonological loop" is to be found in A. Baddeley, *Human Memory: Theory and Practice* (Needham, Mass.: Allyn & Bacon, 1998), pp. 52–70 and passim.

new things by associating them with things already known. Scoring high on a reading test requires a broad vocabulary that represents broad knowledge that offers multiple points of association for gaining further knowledge. The more you know, the easier it is to learn still more—a principle well established in cognitive psychology.

This is the critical element of the theory. Breadth of knowledge is the single factor within human control that contributes most to academic achievement and general cognitive competence. Breadth of knowledge is a far greater factor, for instance, than socioeconomic status. The positive correlation between achieved ability and socioeconomic status is .422, whereas the correlation between achieved ability and general information is .811. This little-known and momentous fact means that imparting broad knowledge to all children is the single most effective means of narrowing the competence gap through schooling.[8]

4. A score on a test of reading ability shows the degree to which this broad knowledge is readily deployable. A merely passive vocabulary that cannot be marshaled and used critically for reading comprehension is inert knowledge. Psychologists use terms like *accessibility* and *availability* to describe such actively usable knowledge. Accessibility of knowledge is attested to by a person's ability to bring that knowledge to bear in comprehending and analyzing the diverse passages in the test.[9]

8. For these precise correlations see D. Lubinski and L. G. Humphreys, "Incorporating General Intelligence into Epidemiology and the Social Sciences, *Intelligence* 24, no. 1, 159–201. In cognitive science the knowledge-competence principle has become so foundational that it has branched off into different specialties such as schema theory and expert-novice studies. Experts learn new things faster than novices do because of the high accessibility of multiple points of reference and analogy. See, for instance, J. Larkin et al., "Models of Competence in Solving Physics Problems," *Cognitive Science* 4 (1980): 317–48. General discussions may be found in any textbook on cognitive psychology. See, for instance, A. Baddeley, *Human Memory: Theory and Practice* (Needham, Mass.: Allyn & Bacon, 1998), pp. 125–43.

9. See, for instance, E. Tulving, "The Effects of Presentation and Recall of Material in Free-Recall Learning," *Journal of Verbal Learning and Verbal Behavior* 5, 193–97. Baddeley, *Human Memory*, pp. 193–94.

In sum, theory predicts that a good reading test will indicate students' level of communicative competence, their breadth of knowledge, and their ability actively to apply that knowledge to learning new things. Theory further predicts that these competencies will correlate well with job performance and the capacity to be an active citizen because communicative competence and the ability to learn new things are highly important skills in meeting the duties and responsibilities of the modern world.

These predictions are confirmed by massive evidence.

1. Scores in early reading tests predict scores in later reading tests. The more one reads, the more automated becomes the process, and, through reading itself, the broader becomes one's knowledge and vocabulary, and consequently the more readily one understands ever more difficult matter.[10]
2. Scores on reading tests predict grades in school. There is a positive correlation between reading scores and academic achievement.[11]
3. Scores on reading tests predict job performance. Obviously, reading scores do not predict whether somebody can fix your car's engine. But, according to studies conducted by the armed services, reading scores do predict how readily and well a person will learn to fix your car's engine.[12]

10. Anne E. Cunningham and Keith E. Stanovich, "Early Reading Acquisition and Its Relation to Reading Experience and Ability 10 Years Later," *Developmental Psychology* 33, no. 6 (November 1997): 934–45.

11. Sari Lindblom-Ylanne et al., "Selecting Students for Medical School: What Predicts Success during Basic Science Studies? A Cognitive Approach," *Higher Education* 31, no. 4 (June 1996): 507–27. Boris Blai Jr., "The Nelson-Denny Reading Test and Harcum-Earned Academic Averages," Harcum Junior College, Bryn Mawr, Pa., June 1971. Sirkka Gudan, "The Nelson-Denny Reading Test as a Predictor of Academic Success in Selected Classes in a Specific Community College," Schoolcraft College, Livonia, Michigan, January 1983.

12. B. L. S. Scribner, D. A. Smith, R. H. Baldwin, and R. L. Phillips, "Are Smart Tankers Better? AFQT and Military Productivity," *Armed Forces and Society* 12 (1986): 193–206; D. Horne, "The Impact of Soldier Quality on Army Performance," *Armed Forces and Society* 13 (1987): 443–45; J. C. Fernandez, "Soldier Quality and Job Performance in Team Tasks," *Social Science Quarterly* 73 (1992): 253–65; C. Jencks and M. Phillips, eds., *The Black-White Test Score Gap* (Washington, D.C.: Brookings, 1998), pp. 14–15, 75–76.

4. Scores in reading tests predict income. Given the causal connections between communicative ability, learning ability,
and job performance, it is not surprising that superior job
skill should be rewarded, on average, with superior pay.[13]

## THE NEED FOR CURRICULUM-BASED TESTS

The scores on a reading test or other competency test may sometimes be relatively independent of the quality of schooling. One's
reading score is better predicted by one's family environment and
the amount of reading one has done than by the school one attends. This is a version of the finding by Coleman that influences
outside the school are more determinative of academic achievement than influences inside the school. This is not an inevitable
sociological law but rather a persistent feature of current American schooling, and it does not hold with the same force in France
or Sweden. The gap-closing educational results in these countries
remind us that an important purpose of democratic schooling is to
help able people overcome accidents of birth and circumstance. I
believe that educational policy in a democracy should aim to create a system of schooling in which scores on reading tests depend
much more on school influences than they recently have in the
United States.[14]

Schools can accomplish this egalitarian purpose by making students better readers, that is, causing them to score higher on competency tests, whether or not they come from educated homes.
This goal can be reached only by an effective, cumulative curriculum that gradually builds up the knowledge and vocabulary that
is being sampled in a reading test. This seems to me a criterion
that should be met by state curriculum standards: Will teaching

13. Jencks and Phillips, *The Black-White Test Score Gap,* pp. 445, 489–94
passim; C. Richard Hofstetter, Thomas G. Sticht, and Carolyn Huie Hofstetter,
"Knowledge Literacy, and Power," *Communication Research* 26 (February
1999): 58–80.
14. R. Erikson and J. Jonsson, eds., *Can Education Be Equalized? The Swed-
ish Case in Comparative Perspective,* (Boulder, Colo.: Westview Press, 1996).
For translated articles on France and data see *www.coreknowledge.org,* link to
preschool, link to "French Studies."

this content provide children with high communicative competence and the ability to learn new things, no matter what their home disadvantages may be?

This democratic criterion means putting in place the very policies that have created the current backlash—setting forth grade-by-grade knowledge standards and monitoring whether that knowledge is being gained, an aim that has won strong support in low-income districts that recognize the democratic effect of this reform.

John Bishop of Cornell has shown that educational systems that require definite content standards and that use curriculum-based tests to determine whether the curriculum has been learned greatly improve achievement for all students, including those from less-advantaged backgrounds. Additional evidence in support of curriculum-based testing comes from the recent finding that gains in reading are directly proportional to the completeness with which a school implements a coherent, content-rich curriculum. Put starkly, a system of coherent standards, coupled with curriculum-based tests, will in fact cause achievement on noncurriculum-based tests to rise. It will result in higher achievement overall and a narrowing of the academic gap between rich and poor.[15]

But this change must be instituted wisely, and the critical policy decisions must not be left to technical test makers. Testing companies are very good at creating instruments that have good "psychometric properties," that is, which rank-order students in a smooth, normal curve. Curriculum-based tests should not exhibit those statistical properties, at least not at first. The tests should mainly dis-

15. John Bishop, *Do Curriculum-Based External Exit Exam Systems Enhance Student Achievement?* (Philadelphia, Pa.: Consortium for Policy Research in Education, 1998). John H. Bishop, "The Effect of Curriculum-Based External Exit Systems on Student Achievement," *Journal of Economic Education* 29, no. 2 (spring 1998): 171–82. John H. Bishop, "Impacts of School Organization and Signalling on Incentives to Learn in France, the Netherlands, England, Scotland and the United States, Working Paper 93-21, National Center on the Educational Quality of the Workforce, Philadelphia, Pa., November 9, 1993. John Bishop, "The Power of External Standards," *American Educator* 19, no. 3 (fall 1995): 10–14, 17–18, 42–43. See the three-year Johns Hopkins study excerpted with graphs at *www.coreknowledge.org*. Level of curricular implementation predicts level of reading gain over three years at multiple sites.

criminate between the students who have gained essential knowledge and those who haven't, with maybe one further category for students who give an abundance of right answers. The earliest versions of the new tests shouldn't rank-order students beyond those three categories—fail, pass, superior. Later on, in a mature, content-based system, such as those Bishop studied, more refined scores might be appropriate.

To grasp the distinction between fancy test items, which aren't appropriate, and plain ones, which are, consider the following examples:

The Civil War ended in

    a.  1864
    b.  1865
    c.  1866
    d.  1867

The Civil War ended in

    a.  1812
    b.  1830
    c.  1865
    d.  1880

Few will doubt that the first question will do a better job of inducing incorrect answers. By including plenty of hard items, test makers can ensure refined, neat rank orderings among students. But it should not be left up to test makers, or even to ad hoc advisory committees, to decide whether students at a particular grade level should have such exactitude of knowledge. That decision should be made and announced in advance by those officials who create the standards and the supporting materials. Curriculum-based exams best serve their purpose, at least at first, by being straightforward and unpedantic.

These considerations lead me to suggest that state education officials should

1. Recognize that we are in a transition period after half a century of content-meager schooling and that state departments

of education must provide the means for teaching and learning the required content standards before too much weight is placed on them. Low stakes before high stakes. Given the historical context, that's only fair.

2. Make public in a very clear and detailed fashion the important aspects of the content standards that are to be emphasized in teacher training, textbooks, and curriculum-based tests.
3. Use the tests as devices to focus effort on productive and important learning that yields centrally useful knowledge and high competence.
4. Grade the straightforward tests generously on a pass-fail basis (with perhaps a "superior" for answering a very high number of straightforward questions) during the transition period while teachers are being trained and appropriate textbooks are being created.
5. Offer, apart from the official, secure tests, informal, no-stakes, year-by-year diagnostic tests that will enable schools to detect knowledge deficits and monitor student progress.
6. Resist any call for a complete test moratorium and give no ground on the basic principle of curriculum-based tests, which are in theory and, as Bishop has shown, also in fact the best route to improved quality and equity.
7. Keep at least a few competency tests in reading, writing, and math. They should carry high stakes (but not unreasonably exalted cut-off points) so long as society agrees that our citizens need these competencies. Well-verified competency-based tests are like those little birds who tell us whether the air in the mine is safe. They reflect the reality principle in education by showing whether competence is truly being achieved.

In short, those states brave enough to have started down this path should continue and improve the policy of using curriculum-based tests, with the stakes gradually getting higher. This is the only known way of achieving the democratic ideal of making the school as effective educationally as the home. That is the appropriate

norm by which content standards and tests should be measured in
a democracy.

Those state tests, on the other hand, that are based on no specific content standards mainly increase anxiety without increasing
learning. They are no better than commercially available competency tests; in fact they are generally less fair and accurate. For
profound theoretical reasons, these skills-tests cannot help schools
narrow the achievement gap between groups.[16]

In states where good curriculum-based tests are built upon
good, specific-content standards, the following can be predicted
for current kindergartners and first-graders. By grade seven or
eight, when the content-based curriculum has "diffused knowledge" (to use Jefferson's phrase) and has done much of its compensatory work, academic achievement will have risen for all groups.
Higher scores on curriculum-based tests will be well correlated
with higher scores on competency-based tests, which will show a
significant narrowing of the competency gap between groups. At
that point, we shall have moved closer to the ideal of a truly democratic system of education.

16. Besides encouraging time-wasting skills practice on narrow themes, state
skills tests offer no theoretical improvement whatever over ordinary competency-
based tests, which is what they essentially are. Although they do encourage everyone to work harder in a narrow range, they waste time on empty exercises that
cause small gains in general competence and less in equity. They preserve the test-
score gap between groups instead of narrowing it because the biggest factor in
the competency gap is a gap in general information, which can be narrowed only
by a long-range, coherent focus on content. This is another illustration of the
importance of basing policy on strong evidence and sound theory.

CHAPTER 9

# Standards and Accountability

*Williamson M. Evers*

The idea seems simple enough. Set standards for what students should be learning, and then hold them and their teachers accountable for seeing that the learning actually takes place. So why, then, after years of various benchmarks and commissions and legislative agendas, are the standards and accountability programs in this country all too often mediocre and ineffective? Because they are the product of politics. Standards and accountability, like most of the contentious issues concerning public schools today, are caught between powerful and conflicting political forces—forces that hold sway even in the face of a clear and widespread desire to improve the public education that 89 percent of this nation's children receive.

In the specific case of standards and accountability, two forces in particular are at play: resistance from the teachers' unions and the rest of the education establishment (which includes school boards,

The author wishes to thank Mychele Brickner, Beth Ann Bryan, Paul Clopton, Ralph Cohen, Maureen DiMarco, Michelle Easton, Eric Hanushek, David Klein, Bill Lucia, Doug McRae, Stan Metzenberg, James Milgram, Terry Moe, Janet Nicholas, Sandra Stotsky, Abigail Thernstrom, Kate Walsh, Darv Winick, and Ze'ev Wurman for reading earlier drafts of this paper, in whole or in part, and offering valuable suggestions. He also wishes to thank Kate Feinstein for her help with research and editing and Peggy Dooley for extensive help with editing and revising.

superintendents, and principals) who often want to avoid being evaluated when it comes to whether their students are learning; and struggles between the progressive and traditionalist schools of thought as to what educational standards should look like, and, indeed, whether there should be any standards at all.

These conflicts, how they came to be, and how they have manifested themselves in states across the country, go a long way toward explaining why the current crop of standards-and-accountability programs have yielded such divergent programs and disappointing levels of progress so far. The modern standards-and-accountability movement can succeed only if it can move beyond these conflicts to practical ways of measuring student learning and using those measurements to reward and sanction students, teachers, and administrators.

## A NATION AT RISK

This movement got its start in April of 1983, when a hard-hitting report entitled *A Nation at Risk* was released by a national education commission. This report showed that other countries were not only matching but exceeding America's level of educational achievement, and that, as a result, these countries were overcoming America's competitive edge in business, science, and engineering. "A rising tide of mediocrity" was eroding the quality of American schools and colleges, according to the report, and this mediocrity had come to prevail because Americans had lowered their expectations about their schools' performance.[1]

To remedy these low expectations, *A Nation at Risk* proposed establishing academic standards for America's schools as an important part of improving student performance.[2] As one prominent critic of standards and accountability has written, this "galvanized the fledgling accountability movement," giving it national prominence and momentum. "The impact of *A Nation at*

1. National Commission on Excellence in Education, *A Nation at Risk: The Imperative for Educational Reform* (Washington, D.C.: U.S. Government Printing Office, 1983), pp. 5–7.
2. See Recommendation B, *A Nation at Risk*, pp. 27–29.

*Risk*, even twenty years later, on the politics of American schools can't be overstated."[3]

It is interesting to note that from the vantage point of 1983 and *A Nation at Risk*, many Americans undoubtedly believed that the public school system had once performed well and then had declined. Many a Baby Boomer probably felt that the public schools would be all right if they only returned to the way schools had been when they were young in the 1950s. The truth is, the early 1950s were the heyday of the most academically weak fad ever to sweep American education—"life adjustment," which filled the school curriculum with courses like "How to Get Along on a Date." In 1953, Fred M. Hechinger, the education reporter for the *New York Times*, said that in teachers' colleges across America, "too much stress on methods and the omission of real knowledge of subject matter are both an indication of shallowness and a boost to the trend of anti-intellectualism."[4]

"Life adjustment" went out of fashion, but omission of subject matter continued. In 1958, Arthur Bestor said that over half of the high schools in the United States offered no physics courses, and approximately a quarter offered neither physics nor chemistry. Similarly, no geometry was offered in about a quarter of the high schools. He cited U.S. Office of Education figures reporting that in 1900 close to 84 percent of high school students were taking science courses, whereas only 54 percent were doing so in 1958. In mathematics, the drop had been from 86 to 55 percent.[5] The 1950s were clearly not a Golden Age of school performance.

In fact, we need to go all the way back to the beginning of the last century to find one of the few periods in our history that might qualify as a Golden Age of standards (even though they were not explicitly cataloged in formal documents), because it is one of the few extended periods of time when expectations for student learn-

3. Peter Sacks, *Standardized Minds: The High Price of America's Testing Culture and What We Can Do to Change It* (Cambridge, Mass." Perseus Books, 1999), p. 77.

4. "The Fate of Pedagoguese," *Saturday Review*, Dec. 12, 1953.

5. Arthur Bestor, "We Are Less Educated Than 50 Years Ago," *U.S. News & World Report*, Nov. 30, 1958.

ing were high—a time when so few people went on to college that high school diplomas were highly prized and taken seriously by local school districts.[6] Textbooks of the time were few in number, similar in content, and demanding in their lessons. Even the colleges of the time came together to demand that the curriculum of American public schools remain rigorous.

In 1892, the National Education Association (then a professional organization, not a labor union) named a panel whose members proposed that both college-bound and non-college-bound K–12 students alike receive the same college-preparatory liberal education. This "Committee of Ten" was headed by Charles William Eliot, then president of Harvard University, and included the U.S. Commissioner of Education, college presidents, professors and high school principals.[7] Their work led to the creation in 1900 of the College Entrance Examination Board, which published lists of recommended reading (including Shakespeare and Longfellow) for college-bound high school students and developed America's first subject-matter content exams (which began in 1901). These privately produced exams set high-school achievement standards and encouraged similar academic preparation in high schools across the country.

Unfortunately, this idea of a liberal arts education for all slowly fell out of fashion after the first two decades of the twentieth century as the pervasive influence of "progressive" education began

6. Schooling for blacks and rural whites was often inadequate in this period. During much of following period of the twentieth century, the numbers who were educated and the time they spent in school expanded. But, at the same time, progressive ideology tended to reduce the quality of the curriculum.

7. This account of turn-of-the-century developments is based on Richard Hofstader, *Anti-Intellectualism in American Life* (New York: Knopf, 1963), pp. 329–32; Diane Ravitch, *Left Back: A Century of Failed School Reforms* (New York: Simon & Schuster, 2000), pp. 41–50; Ravitch, *National Standards in American Education: A Citizen's Guide* (Washington, D.C.: Brookings Institution, 1995), pp. 33–41; Paul Gagnon, "What Should Children Learn?" *Atlantic Monthly*, vol. 276, no. 6 (Dec. 1995), pp. 65–78; I. L. Kandel, *American Education in the Twentieth Century* (Cambridge, Mass.: Harvard University Press, 1957), pp. 141, 179; Lawrence A. Uzzell, "Contradictions of Centralized Education," *Wall Street Journal*, Jan. 4, 1985. See also National Education Association, *Report of the Committee of Ten on Secondary School Studies; with the Reports of Conferences Arranged by the Committee* (New York: American Book Co., 1894).

to take hold. Since then, the story of American public schools has largely been the story of content-light education, with a couple of episodes of academic rigor here and there: most notably in the 1950s to the mid-1960s after the collapse of the "life adjustment" fad and in response to the launching of Sputnik; and another brief back-to-basics movement in the 1970s after the collapse of the progressive open-classrooms experiment.[8] Aside from these interludes, twentieth-century American education was dominated until *A Nation at Risk* by the anti-intellectual strain of progressive education that has generally neglected solid academic subject matter. In terms of what students have learned, the gaps and deficiencies revealed in the 1938 Carnegie Foundation report *The Student and His Knowledge* are just as troubling as those revealed in *What Do Our 17-Year-Olds Know?* almost fifty years later.[9]

## POLITICS AND PLAYERS: ROADBLOCKS TO STANDARDS AND ACCOUNTABILITY

In the wake of *A Nation at Risk*, reformers sought to improve schools—as they had in the past—by varying and increasing the inputs: Spending was increased, textbooks and other teaching materials were revised, the number of academic class offerings was expanded, and graduation requirements were tightened.[10] But by the end of the 1980s, tinkering with inputs was still producing

8. On these events, see Ravitch, *Left Back*, pp. 361 (collapse of life adjustment), 399–402 (collapse of open classrooms), and 361–2 (launching of Sputnik).

9. William S. Learned and Ben D. Wood, *The Student and His Knowledge: A Report to the Carnegie Foundation on the Results of the High School and College Examinations of 1928, 1930, and 1932* (New York: Carnegie Foundation for the Advancement of Teaching, 1938); Diane Ravitch and Chester E. Finn Jr., *What Do Our 17-Year-Olds Know? A Report on the First National Assessment of History and Literature* (New York: Harper & Row, 1987).

10. For a similar list, see Chester E. Finn Jr., "Who's Afraid of the Big, Bad Test?," in Diane Ravitch, ed., *Debating the Future of American Education: Do We Need National Standards and Assessments?* (Washington, D.C.: Brookings Institution, 1995), p. 124. See also *The Nation Responds: Recent Efforts to Improve Education* (Washington, D.C.: U.S. Department of Education, May 1984), pp. 15–16; Michael W. Kirst, *Who Controls Our Schools? American Values in Conflict* (Stanford, Calif.: Stanford Alumni Association, 1984), pp. 126–7.

lackluster school performance, at which point many school reformers reached the conclusion that wholesale systemic reform
was necessary.

Some of them turned to vouchers, with the belief that replacing
the existing public-school monopoly with a system of competing
schools would lead to more effective schools. Others turned to
accountability, which would require a testing system to measure
student mastery of explicit curriculum standards—something state
governments in America had never had before.

With rising public awareness of low-performing schools, both
of these reform movements slowly started to gain public support
and momentum—and it was this growing public sense that something was wrong with our schools, and a willingness to do something about it, that finally caught the attention of the teachers'
unions and the rest of the education establishment. They began
to acknowledge that perhaps there were public schools that were
unsafe, where test scores were persistently low, where many students left school without graduating, and where many of those
who did graduate could scarcely read or write. Vouchers, though,
were anathema to the education potentates, as anything that took
money out of the public schools' coffers naturally would be. Ele-
vating educational standards, though, seemed to be something
they could accept.

With the important players now accepting the principle that
standards and accountability were needed, momentum continued
to grow. By the early 1990s, many states had started taking steps
to put statewide educational standards and testing into place. But
this seemingly straightforward enterprise of setting standards and
holding students and educators accountable for meeting them
quickly ran into political difficulties that have continued to affect
and shape the issue ever since, the two most significant being the
strength of the education interest groups who resist accountability,
and the dominance of the progressives' child-centered teaching
ideology that is fundamentally opposed to the very idea of standards and accountability.

Before we discuss these competing interest groups and ideologies, though, it is important to point out one other key factor that

has stood in the way of effective standards and accountability efforts: the structure of our American system of public education.

## Structure

Public schools in this country are controlled at the local level. They are managed by a district superintendent, this superintendent answers to a locally elected board, and this board is elected by the minority of local voters who turn out for school board elections.[11] A public school's power base, in other words, rests at the local level, so there has been little inclination on its part to hand any control over to state or national authorities. This would include control over the academic subject matter being taught. Add to that the fact that schools receive most of their funding simply for having students in attendance, that their customers (parents) don't pay the full costs of operation, and the owners (citizen-taxpayers) cannot exercise ownership rights, and you see that—prior to the current accountability efforts—public schools faced few consequences if they failed in the job of educating their students.

We must also remember that educating their students has not been the sole focus of these schools. Like any public bureaucracy, local school systems have a tendency to look for ways not only to hold on to their existing budget and range of activities, but to expand them as well.[12] Schools are therefore endeavoring to provide sports and recreation, solve various public health problems, make peace in the battle of the sexes, reconcile the races, and eliminate adult illiteracy—as well as teach academic subject matter to children.[13] They are, in other words, spreading

11. Chaira R. Nappi, "Local Illusions," *Wilson Quarterly*, vol. 23, no. 4 (Autumn 1999), p. 46.

12. Anthony Downs, *Inside Bureaucracy* (Boston: Little, Brown, 1967).

13. Compare Peter Schrag: "Americans have asked the schools to acculturate our great waves of immigrants; teach practical skills to the boys who were destined for the local work force; train competent homemakers to marry them and make good citizens of them all; train safe drivers and combat the evils of drugs, alcohol and obesity; teach tolerance and warn about the dangers of AIDS and VD. We have given high schools the task of entertaining communities with Friday-night football games in the fall and with basketball games all winter long; we have made them the centers of adolescent social life, and, for lack of better

themselves thin, with academic content getting lost in the process.[14]

Finally, the structure and funding of the public school system has provided no incentives for local authorities to adopt any accountability program that would compare their district with others—unless, of course, they thought their district was one of the few at the top. Comparisons hold too much potential for bad news, and bad news might result in political trouble or loss of control. It has therefore been in their interest to make sure there are no hard criteria by which it could be shown that their students were failing to learn, or that their teachers were failing to teach. Some districts have been willing to adopt diagnostic tests to help them with teaching, but most are reluctant to adopt tests that would clearly show comparative results.[15]

---

alternatives, delivery points for meals, healthcare and other social services."
Schrag, "The Education of Diane Ravitch," *The Nation*, vol. 271, no. 9 (Oct. 2, 2000), p. 34. Compare also John Bishop, "The Power of External Standards," *American Educator*, Fall 1995, p. 14; Harold W. Stevenson and James W. Stigler, *The Learning Gap: Why Our Schools Are Failing and What We Can Learn from Japanese and Chinese Education* (New York : Simon & Schuster, 1992), p. 203; Kirst, *Who Controls?*, pp. 3, 153; Melville J. Homfled, "Schools for Everything," *Atlantic Monthly*, vol. 203, no. 3 (March 1959), pp. 62–64; Kandel, *American Education in the Twentieth Century*, p. 22.

A *Nation at Risk* speaks of the "multitude of often conflicting demands" placed on America's schools and colleges. They are regularly asked to solve "personal, social, and political problems" that the home and other institutions have been unable to solve. Such demands on America's schools and colleges "exact an educational cost as well as a financial one." p. 6.

For a social science analysis of the multiple missions of government agencies, see Peter H. Aranson, *American Government: Strategy and Choice* (Cambridge, Mass.: Winthrop Publishers, 1981), pp. 456–457.

14. Diane Ravitch, a prominent advocate of standards, for example, argues that schools should concentrate on their most basic mission: the transmission of knowledge. Ravitch, *Left Back*, pp. 465–7. See also Kirst, *Who Controls?*, p. 17.

15. It is human nature to want to look as if you are doing a good job. Testing specialists have long been aware of the "Lake Wobegon Effect," in which school officials juggle the figures (especially by making use of old norms) to make their district look "above average." See John J. Cannell, "Nationally Normed Elementary Achievement Testing in America's Public Schools: How All 50 States Are Above the National Average," *Educational Measurement: Issues and Practice*, vol. 7, no. 2 (Summer 1988), pp. 5–9. Officials tend to consider accountability

So, until the late 1980s, America's 15,000 local school districts held almost all of the responsibility for academic standards, and next to no accountability systems were in place either to set those standards or to see that they were achieved. This started to change for two reasons: the accountability movement continued to gain momentum and acceptance; and the relationship between states and local school districts started to change. Local school districts are now supporting themselves less and less off their own local tax base as states across the country have enacted expensive and wide-ranging educational programs—many of them in response to a growing demand for improved schools from their own constituents—while upping the state contribution to education funding at the same time. This means that in many states, the bulk of operating funds and most of the taxing and spending decisions pertaining to K–12 education now rests increasingly in the hands of state officials[16]—and these state officials, spurred on by taxpaying voters, are increasingly looking for more accountability from local schools and districts.

## Interest Groups

This, then, is the landscape where the struggle over standards and accountability is taking place. We must never forget that it is a political landscape: public schools are run by government, and government by necessity operates in the political world. In this world, school district officials, principals, and especially teachers are among the best organized and most influential groups in American politics. Accountability advocates, on the other hand, are a more diffuse group, including parent organizations, business groups, think tanks, and pro-reform legislators and governors.

---

systems friendly that make them look good and unfriendly those that make them look bad.

16. Over 15 years ago, Michael W. Kirst wrote: "The most striking feature of state/local relations in the last 20 years has been the growth of state control over education." In Kirst, "The Changing Balance in State and Local Power to Control Education," *Phi Delta Kappan*, vol. 66, no. 3 (Nov. 1984), p. 190. See also Lawrence A. Uzzell, "Contradictions of Centralized Education," *Wall Street Journal*, Jan. 4, 1985.

This motley assortment has nevertheless been able to give the education establishment a run for the money when it comes to gaining public and legislative acceptance for setting academic standards and measuring achievement. The tug-of-war between the interest groups on both sides has and will continue to play a major role in what standards and accountability look like in our nation's public schools.

When it comes to government bureaucracies, "what gets measured, gets done," which is why accountability interest groups have insisted upon establishing high academic standards and measuring achievement against those standards. In this way, the standards movement hopes that accountability systems can do for the public schools at least some of what profit and loss does for commercial businesses, by rewarding what works and those who are productive, and sorting out what doesn't work and those who are not productive.

The powerful education establishment, of course, has little interest in being looked at or evaluated in this way, and they have developed various arguments about the appropriateness, form, and use of accountability benchmarks. These arguments have proved to be a potent tool for leaders of education interest groups as they maintain their professed support for standards while resisting effective accountability measures at almost every turn.[17]

One of these arguments is that it is wrong, in principle, to hold teachers accountable, that once teachers are credentialed, they should not have to worry about being scrutinized as to their effectiveness.[18] Progressive educator and accountability critic Susan Ohanian argues that no one should have the authority to tell an individual teacher what to do on curricular matters, that this re-

17. In 1988, North Carolina adopted a Testing Code of Ethics that said "test scores should never be used in formal teacher or principal evaluations." Sacks, p. 123.

18. During the nineteenth-century debate in America over public education, welfare-state advocate and sociologist Lester Frank Ward advocated governmental provision of schooling because it would shield teachers from accountability to parents:

> The secret of the superiority of state over private education lies in the fact that in the former the teacher is responsible solely to society. As in private, so also in public education, the calling of a teacher is a profession, and his personal

sults in "deskilling" teachers and insinuating that they are "incapable" of making their own decisions.[19] Yet Ohanian leaves out one important consideration: many teachers are not content specialists, especially in elementary school, and in secondary school many of them teach outside of their fields. The upshot of Ohanian's position would be a pedagogic sinecure at taxpayers' expense. Certainly everybody would like a job in which you could do whatever you want, nobody could tell you what to do, and you have job tenure so no one could fire you—but it is unlikely that people in such jobs would be as effective and productive as they could be. Nor is it obvious that the important task of educating children should be organized this way.

Of course, when arguments fail, you can always fall back on raw political muscle, which education interest groups have done all too often in standards-and-accountability dust-ups. It is important to remember that the teachers unions devote most of their resources and energy to straightforward issues of pay, working conditions, and job security. That is where their constituents' interests reside. So, while the teachers unions and other interest groups may say friendly and supportive things about standards and accountability, their actions deserve quite careful scrutiny.[20]

---

success must depend upon his success in accomplishing the result which his employers desire accomplished. But the result desired by the state is a wholly different one from that desired by parents, guardians, and pupils. Of the latter he is happily independent.

*Dynamic Sociology*, 2nd ed. (New York: Appleton, 1897), vol. 2, pp. 589–90.

19. Susan Ohanian, *One Size Fits Few: The Folly of Educational Standards* (Portsmouth, N.H.: Heinemann, 1999), p. 99. See also p. 140: "The proliferation of standards documents results in the deskilling and the deprofessionalization of teachers. How else are teachers to feel except helpless in the face of being told to *deliver* a curriculum that is invented by external authorities?" Actually, standards are only outlines of what, at least, should be in a curriculum. Teachers and others flesh out the full curriculum. In any case, actors are professionals and do not feel demeaned when asked to deliver material that is created by playwrights. (I am indebted to Ze'ev Wurman for this analogy.)

20. Sometimes representatives of teachers' interests complain that standards are more difficult than they actually are. Bob Chase, the president of the NEA, told the delegates to his union's annual meeting that some state standards are so high as to be "absurd," claiming (wrongly) that California expects fifth-graders

For instance, the two largest teachers unions, the National Education Association (NEA) and the American Federation of Teachers (AFT), have both taken positions in favor of standards and accountability, yet they have focused their publicity efforts and political might on issues such as supporting the national certification of teachers and raising the standards for admission into the teaching profession.[21] The unions do this in the name of improving the quality of teaching, but their critics point out that it also has the effect of restricting entry into the profession and strengthening the unions' monopoly power—power they can therefore use, for example, to protect incompetent current teachers from ever getting fired. And the stronger the unions are, the better equipped they will be to continue opposing any teacher-accountability measures that have teeth.

The AFT, in fact, has gone out of its way in support of standards and accountability, consistently producing excellent material in support of both effective teaching practices and standards for student learning. But for all its promotion of high standards, the union has viewed accountability as something directed at the performance of students. Teachers weren't to be considered responsible if students weren't doing well. The late Albert Shanker, longtime president of the AFT, wrote the following passages about holding students accountable:

> School reformers who are working to solve the problem of students' low achievement levels have come up with all sorts of new and creative things, but as long as students are given no reason to work, it is hard to see how any reform, however ingenious or creative, will achieve what is needed. The absence of stakes makes the whole system trivial. . . .
>
> Stakes for kids go right to the heart of what motivates them to work

---

to memorize the periodic table of the elements. Ann Bradley, "Union Heads Issue Standards Warnings," *Education Week*, July 12, 2000.

21. The certification process of the National Board for Professional Teaching Standards uses no objective tests and is focused on the pedagogic practices of teachers, rather than the achievement of their students or the teachers' knowledge of the subject matter they teach. See Danielle Dunne Wilcox, "The National Board for Professional Teaching Standards: Can It Live Up to Its Promise?" in Marci Kanstoroom and Chester E. Finn Jr., eds., *Better Teachers, Better Schools*

and learn. If you want someone to behave in a certain way, you connect that behavior with something the person wants. . . . [T]he last great experiment with a system [Soviet socialism] that dismissed incentives—and relied instead on the goodness of people's instinct and motives—went down in flames. . . . And for most kids, unless they have to do it, they will not.[22]

The question that quickly comes to mind after reading this is: if this is true for students, why is it not also true for teachers and principals and school systems?

The answer, of course, is that it is. If students are to be held accountable for learning specific material, it only makes sense to hold those responsible for teaching them accountable as well.[23] And yet teacher accountability has been the sticking point time and again as states have attempted to establish valid standards and accountability frameworks, and regrettably this aspect of accountability has been watered down time and again in an effort to get the teachers and the rest of the education establishment on board. The teachers' unions will accept or even promote high standards for student learning, testing of students, and rewards and sanctions for students based on test results. They do not, however, accept the same for their members. It is hardly surprising, then, that student achievement—which is crucially dependent on teacher effectiveness—continues to fall short across the country.

### Rival Ideologies: Progressives versus Traditionalists

Of course, the question of what those standards should be—or if there should be standards at all—has been no less contentious, batted around for the most part between proponents of the two principal approaches to teaching in this country: the progressives

(Washington, D.C.: Thomas B. Fordham Foundation, July 1999), pp. 163–97. I am indebted to Janet Nicholas for this reference.

22. Albert Shanker, "The Case for High Stakes and Real Consequences," in Ravitch, *Debating the Future*, pp. 147, 149. Compare the AFT treatment of merit pay on the AFT web site: *http://www.aft.org/issues/meritpay/turmoil.html*; and AFT Resolution on Redesigning Low-Performing Schools, adopted July 1998, *http://www.aft.org/edissues/rsa/guide/resolution.htm*.

23. Compare Tyce Palmaffy, "Are High School Exit Exams Fair?" *Investor's Business Daily*, Jan. 20, 2000.

and the traditionalists.[24] Between these two ideologies lies a chasm of disagreement as to whether students should be tested, how often they should be tested, and what they should be tested on.

Progressives can trace their ideological genealogy back to Jean-Jacques Rousseau in the eighteenth century. Today, they dominate the education establishment: the faculties of the schools of education at American universities, the early childhood groups, and the professional associations of subject-matter specialists. Given the political and bureaucratic milieu of public education, it is not altogether surprising that progressive education has thrived. The historian and Shakespearean scholar A. L. Rowse describes the flavor of progressive education as "kindly, humane, fussy, bureaucratic, flat, insipid, like a minor civil servant's dream, without energy or power, hazard or enterprise, the standards set by people who cannot write English, who have no poetry or vision or daring, without the capacity to love or hate."[25]

Progressives believe in *discovery learning*. They contend that students truly learn only when they have "discovered" and applied knowledge and skills to solve problems.[26] Most progressives take a child-centered approach to discovery learning,[27] meaning that teachers should help their students, but the students' interests

24. I am presenting "ideal types" of progressive and traditionalist teaching. I have, therefore, described them as systematic and coherent approaches to teaching. This helps to bring out the different implications of each for policy on standards and accountability. Actual teachers do not rely on one or the other exclusively and may combine elements from each.

25. Quoted in Robert Schuettinger, "Modern Education vs. Democracy," *New Individualist Review* (University of Chicago chapter, Intercollegiate Society of Individualists), vol. 1, no. 1 (April 1961), p. 23.

26. Compare Marc S. Tucker and Judy B. Codding, *Standards for Our Schools* (San Francisco: Jossey-Bass, 1998), p. 78. See also Williamson M. Evers, "From Progressive Education to Discovery Learning," in Evers, ed., *What's Gone Wrong in America's Classrooms* (Stanford, Calif.: Hoover Institution, 1998).

27. Throughout the history of progressive education, the child-centered progressives have been more numerous than the intellectualist progressives. The intellectualist minority calls for discovery learning, but also believes that there is a culturally established body of knowledge that students need to learn. See Ravitch, *Left Back*, pp. 16, 190, 463; Evers.

should guide the content and direction of schoolwork.[28] Child-centered progressives do not believe there is a culturally established body of knowledge that students need to learn; therefore they oppose the idea of standards and accountability.

Susan Ohanian succinctly conveys the attitude of her fellow child-centered progressives toward standards-based instruction in this passage about her teaching practices:

> The concept of kids and teachers "messing about" [has] transformed my teacherliness more radically than any other pedagogical idea I've encountered. That's what I do: Mess about. [Advocates of standards] seem intent on cramming the day so neither teachers nor children have thirty-three seconds left over for thinking, never mind messing about.[29]

Ohanian also finds it outrageous that sixth-graders who take a nationally normed, commercially published achievement test are expected to be able to locate Idaho and Utah on a U.S. map, or know about Eli Whitney, or the Holocaust.[30] This is because progressives also believe in the doctrine of *developmental appropriateness*, which holds that each individual child goes at his or her own natural pace through a set of discrete learning stages.[31] These discrete stages are supposedly biological, internally hard-wired into children: there is the stage of sensory awareness (birth to age 2); a stage which prepares for awareness of concrete things (age 2 to age 7); a stage of concrete awareness (age 7 to age 11); and,

28. This approach was advocated by progressive educator William Heard Kilpatrick. For a criticism of child-centered progressive education, see Albert Lynd, *Quackery in the Public Schools* (Boston: Little, Brown, 1953), chap. 9, "The World of Professor Kilpatrick," pp. 212–54.

29. Ohanian, *One Size*, p. 76.

30. Susan Ohanian, "News from the Test Resistance Trail," *Phi Delta Kappan*, vol. 82, no. 5 (January 2001), see *http://www.pdkintl.org/kappan/koha0101.htm*.

31. See Evers, pp. 15–17; J. E. Stone, "Developmentalism: An Obscure but Pervasive Restriction on Educational Improvement," Education Policy Analysis Archives, vol. 4, no. 8 (Apr. 21, 1996), *http://olam.ed.asu.edu/epaa/v4n8.html*; and E. D. Hirsch Jr., *The Schools We Need and Why We Don't Have Them* (New York: Doubleday, 1996), pp. 79–91.

finally, a stage for logical thinking (age 11 and older). In addition, children can only learn a limited amount at these various stages.

As is the case with child-centeredness, this idea of developmental appropriateness has serious consequences when it comes to setting academic standards. If every child learns at his or her own pace, how can you then set standards for a "typical" sixth-grader, or third-grader, or first-grader? If you are a progressive educator, the obvious answer is that you cannot. They will look at any proposed set of elementary-grade standards and say, "This is too much, too high, and too early." According to Ohanian, the "hallmark" of standards advocates is "cramming ever more sophisticated information into ever younger children, whether they are ready or not."[32]

The alternative to progressive education is traditional education, as modified by modern research findings. Adherents of this approach trace its lineage back to Aristotle and other ancient Greeks. Today, traditionalists are few and far between in the command posts of American primary and secondary education. The traditionalists are also not as well organized as the progressives, but there is an abundance of them among parents, state legislators, business leaders, and college professors who teach outside of schools of education.[33]

Traditionalists believe in systematic and sequential teacher-led instruction. Traditionalists point out that the progressives have no evidence proving that reliance on the discovery method boosts students' achievement.[34] Indeed, the existing evidence supports the

32. Ohanian, *One Size*, p. 72. See also pp. 90 (where the author maintains that fourth-graders are innately unfit to learn longitude and latitude), 94 (where the author maintains that twelfth-graders are likewise unfit to gain an in-depth understanding of the institutions of American government—"the people writing [the California State] history standards . . . gave no consideration at all to developmental appropriateness").

33. On support for traditional instruction among members of the general public, see Jean Johnson and John Immerwahr, *First Things First: What Americans Expect from the Public Schools* (New York: Public Agenda, 1994).

34. John R. Anderson, Lynne M. Reder, and Herbert A. Simon, "Radical Constructivism and Cognitive Psychology," in Diane Ravitch, ed., *Brookings Papers on Educational Policy, 1998* (Washington, D.C.: Brookings Institution, 1998), p. 240.

efficacy of content-focused explicit teaching.[35] Traditionalists believe that there is a culturally established body of knowledge that
students should learn; they believe that successful instruction involves lectures and book learning; and they believe that memorization, drills, and practice are effective learning tools.[36] Furthermore,
traditionalists do not accept the doctrine of developmental appropriateness. They point to psychological research that shows that
learning develops along a continuum over the years of a student's
life, not in discrete stages. In fact, the research finds this idea of
stages or stair steps of learning—this idea so beloved of progressives—empirically unsound.[37]

Accepting or rejecting the tenets of "child centeredness" and
"developmental appropriateness" has enormous consequences
when it comes to standards and accountability. If a student indeed
follows his or her own path of learning, it is impossible to set
grade-level academic standards—which is one of the arguments
used by progressive educators who are opposed to standards. If a
child cannot learn something until he or she is developmentally
"ready" to learn it, how can you hold the child responsible for
knowing the material—indeed, how can you hold a teacher accountable for having taught it effectively? Again, the argument
from the progressive side is that you cannot. Traditionalists, on
the other hand, believe that there is body of knowledge and set of
skills that children should learn and that they can learn if they put

35. See Jeanne S. Chall, *The Academic Achievement Challenge: What Really
Works in the Classroom* (New York: Guildford Press, 2000); *Effective School
Practices* (Association for Direct Instruction), vol. 15, no. 1 (Winter 1995–6,
"Project Follow Through" special issue); Hirsch.

36. See, in the case of mathematics instruction, David C. Geary, *Children's
Mathematical Development* (Washington, D.C.: American Psychological Associ-
ation, 1994), pp. 74, 125, 269–70; Anderson et al., pp. 241, 249–50; Hung-
Hsi Wu, "Basic Skills Versus Conceptual Understanding: A Bogus Dichotomy in
Mathematics Education," *American Educator*, vol. 23, no. 3 (Fall 1999).

37. Charles J. Brainerd, "The Stage Question in Cognitive-Developmental
Theory," *The Behavioral and Brain Sciences*, vol. 1, no. 2 (June 1978), pp. 173–
82, with commentaries by Thomas J. Berndt, pp. 183–84; John H. Flavell, p. 187;
Annette Karmiloff-Smith, pp. 188–90; also Robert S. Siegler, *Children's Think-
ing*, 3rd ed. (Upper Saddle River, N.J., Prentice Hall, 1998), pp. 5–7, 55–58;
Anderson et al., pp. 235, 251.

in the effort and are taught well. Hence, traditionalists believe that you can and should test each child to evaluate whether the child has learned the material and the teacher has taught it effectively.

These, then, are the two major battles shaping the standards and accountability debate in this country: (1) traditionalists who support standards versus progressives who do not; and (2) accountability advocates who want to hold both students and educators responsible for meeting academic standards versus powerful education interest groups who resist accountability measures that could adversely affect their members. Politics, of course, is not always this straightforward, and there have probably been as many variations on this political breakdown as there are states that have instituted standards and accountability. Two things, though, have remained consistent. Whenever accountability has come under consideration, the politically powerful interest groups (like teachers' unions or associations of school administrators) have weighed in. And whenever standards and testing have been considered, ideological groups have dominated the controversy.

## In the States

In most states, standards and accountability remain a work-in-progress, so to get a better picture of how politics is affecting their implementation, let's take a look at four states: Massachusetts, where education interest groups are particularly strong; Virginia, where reaction against progressive education practices led to some of the toughest standards in the country; and Maryland and Texas, two states where political consensus on the issue has led to decidedly different results.[38]

### Massachusetts

Massachusetts is a strong union state with a large contingent of progressive educators, so it should come as no surprise that there

---

38. Except as indicated, the information in the following state profiles comes from *Education Week*, Jan. 11, 2001 ("Quality Counts" special report) or from the author's personal knowledge.

are heated battles taking place in that state's standards-and-accountability effort between accountability advocates (including the Republican governor, pro-accountability state legislators, the governor-appointed State Board of Education, and pro-accountability elements in the inner-city education community) and a vocal anti-testing coalition. The issues? The high-stakes state tests given to students, state testing of prospective teachers, and check-ups on already hired teachers.

In 1993, Massachusetts passed an extensive education package that included a dramatic increase in funding for K–12 public education in exchange for a promise from the teachers unions to support accountability measures. The state set up the Massachusetts Comprehensive Assessment System (MCAS), which tests students in grades 4, 8, and 10 in English and math. Starting in 2003, students have to pass the 10th-grade test in order to graduate from high school. As that 2003 deadline approaches, however, the state's NEA affiliate has decided that "no single test should be used to make these kinds of high-stakes decisions"[39]—though test defenders point out that students have five chances to pass the graduation test. The union does not like the fact that the accountability system does not employ teacher-graded measures of student performance, such as homework and class performance.[40] In 2000, the union ran a three-week $600,000 ad campaign opposing the very test-based accountability system it had agreed to support in 1993. "Now that they have all the money," Governor Paul Cellucci has said, "they are trying to renege on the agreement."

In addition to the ad campaign, about 200 protesters—including students, teachers and other accountability critics—protested in Boston against the 10th-grade tests that are the

39. Frank Phillips, "Cellucci Blasts Teachers on Tests," *Boston Globe*, Nov. 9, 2000; John Gehring, "Mass. Teachers Blast State Tests in New TV Ads," *Education Week*, Nov. 22, 2000; "Blaming the Test," editorial, *Wall Street Journal*, Nov. 24, 2000.

40. Teachers often grade their own students more favorably than external examiners do. Tucker and Codding (pp. 25–29) describe the difference between what their previous teachers said incoming high school students in Pasadena were ready to do in mathematics and what external examinations said they were ready to do.

linchpin of the state's accountability system. The union and the protesters are part of an anti-testing coalition that includes self-satisfied suburban school districts and progressive educators who oppose what they perceive as a deluge of testing that stifles teachers' creativity. [41]

The 1993 law also set forth plans for standards and accountability for prospective teachers. Starting in 1998, prospective teachers in Massachusetts faced reading, writing, and subject-matter exams. When the tests were first administered in April of that year, 59 percent of those who took them failed. The test included a dictation exercise to assess spelling skills, and it asked prospective teachers to define words like "abolish," "preposition," and "democracy."[42] In describing how test-takers did, the *Boston Globe* said: "Some of the . . . student answers shown to reporters yesterday illustrated a strikingly poor grasp of English grammar. Some sentences were missing verbs; in others, common words were misspelled or incorrectly defined."[43] The dismal results produced a national outcry and provided fodder for television-show comedians.

In the spring of 2000, the State Board of Education moved to test all math teachers from districts where a high percentage of students failed the math portion of the MCAS exam.[44] Both unions (the NEA and AFT affiliates) responded to this with a lawsuit, which is still pending. When the governor had earlier floated a plan for testing all current teachers, the unions responded with rallies in opposition to teacher-testing, and in support of smaller class sizes (i.e., more teachers), increasing base salaries for new teachers (i.e., more money for teachers), and devolving administrative decision making to principals and teachers (i.e., more

41. On the anti-MCAS alliance, see Georgia N. Alexakis, "Test Prep: What Bush Can Learn from a Tryout of School Reform in Massachusetts," *Washington Monthly*, March 2001.

42. Rachel Smolkin, "In Search of Competency, States Test Their Teachers," Scripps-Howard News Service, Mar. 28, 1999.

43. Quoted in William Raspberry, "A Problem with Would-Be Teachers," *Washington Post*, July 3, 1998.

44. Heidi B. Perlman, "Math Teachers Vow to Refuse to Take Pilot Test," Associated Press, July 6, 2000.

power for teachers).[45] "A proposal that engenders so much hostility [in] our teachers has some inherent problems," said one state Democratic legislator.[46]

True, but are those problems with the tests or with the teachers' implacable resistance to being subjected to them? The education interest groups in Massachusetts agreed to accountability measures in 1993. True to form, some of them have been resisting ever since.

*Virginia*

Virginia has one of the most rigorous sets of standards in the country, standards that clearly and specifically spell out what children should learn in each grade.[47] These standards are as strong as they are and have a deliberate focus on content (specific learning expectations for children in specific grades) in large part because grass-roots activists rejected the progressive and content-light education practices that dominated Virginia education in the early 1990s. This traditionalist backlash came to a head during the state's 1993 governor's race, to such an extent that the outgoing Democrat, Governor Doug Wilder (who was not a candidate), pulled the plug on a progressive state standards document (called the Common Core of Learning) that was being developed at the time. The Republican who won the governor's race, George Allen, disavowed progressive education during the campaign, and one of his first acts as governor was to appoint a commission to start laying the groundwork for academic standards and testing in four core subjects.[48]

The commission's recommendations had to be approved by the State Board of Education, which at the time included six Democrats (who usually align themselves with their staunch political

45. Darrell S. Pressley, "Educators Set to Rally Today as Cellucci Stands By Tests," *Boston Herald*, June 16, 1999.
46. Pressley, "Educators Set to Rally."
47. The author is indebted to Michelle Easton and Lil Tuttle for their insights on the Virginia situation.
48. "History of SOLs," Parents and Students Supporting SOLs, *http://www.-pass.sol.org/history/*.

supporters, the education interest groups) and three Republicans (who usually find their political support on the accountability side). But such was the strength of the accountability movement in Virginia at the time that conventional alignments took a back seat, and the Board adopted state tests in English, mathematics, science, and history. Virginia students today are tested in grades 3, 5, and 8. Results will be a factor (together with grades and other tests) in determining whether they are promoted to the next grade. Beginning in 2004, high school students will have to take tests in English, math, science, and history, and the results will determine whether they get a diploma. In 2007, schools where less than 70 percent of the students pass the exams risk losing their state accreditation. Students who fail the tests are able to retake them several times during the year.

Because content-light progressive education has been the fashion in Virginia, as it has throughout the country, and because schools did not teach the material listed in the standards, nearly every school in the state failed the tests in 1998 and 1999—the first two years they were given. And while the number of schools meeting state standards rose dramatically in 2000, that has failed to quell a new burgeoning opposition, this time from the teachers' unions and other education interest groups who complain the tests are too rigorous and too demanding. School principals in particular are protesting the tests, saying their schools' accreditation status shouldn't rely on student scores, and taking up the progressive argument that the state standards are too fact-driven and too reliant on memorization at the expense of critical thinking skills.

Virginia's educational standards emphasize content and facts, so it was perhaps inevitable that progressive forces would eventually call Virginia's state standards into question. Progressives, remember, emphasize child-directed schoolwork and discovery learning rather than academic subject matter. Perhaps just as inevitable should be the subsequent call for relaxing the state's tough accountability standards. As one former State Board member explains, "As 2004 comes closer [and high schoolers must pass tests to receive their diplomas], there will be lots of nervous politicians," on both sides of the aisle.[49]

And so the backsliding begins. There have been recent efforts in the Virginia state legislature to make the accountability system more flexible (or less rigorous, depending how you want to look at it). Union-allied legislators have proposed allowing high school students who fail the state tests to graduate, as long as they come close to passing the tests or as long as their school grades are acceptable. Other proposals would dilute the 2007 requirements to revoke a school's accreditation if less than 70 percent of the school's students pass the test. And instead of making student academic performance the fundamental basis of accreditation, proposed legislation would mix in other factors such as dropout rates, school attendance, and teacher training. Roger Gray, the president of the Richmond, Virginia, teachers' union, has an even more radical solution, one that is popular with teachers throughout the state: keep the standards but throw out the graduation test.

So we see that even in a state where accountability advocates had a strong hand going in, the education interest groups and dogmatic progressives continue to try to chip away at what they see as overly rigorous standards-and-accountability requirements.

## Maryland and Texas

Unlike Massachusetts and Virginia, where intense political disagreements continue concerning both standards and accountability, Maryland and Texas have managed to achieve relative consensus on both. However, this consensus has affected education in each state quite differently.

Maryland, according to its state schools superintendent, has a "somewhat narrower . . . mainstream political spectrum" than many other states, which is her way of explaining why Maryland state policy on education has not changed all that much over the last decade.[50] The narrow spectrum may well have reduced the

49. Interview with Lil Tuttle.
50. Nancy S. Grasmick, "Looking Back at a Decade of Reform: The Maryland Standards Story," in Terri Duggan and Madelyn Holmes, eds., *Closing the Gap* (Washington, D.C.: Council on Basic Education, 2000), pp. 51–52.

opportunities for political challenges to policy and allowed the state educational bureaucracy to have a carte blanche on testing. Maryland has one of the oldest statewide testing systems in the country, created back in 1991 when progressive project-based tests were quite trendy. The test has no multiple-choice questions. Students must instead answer almost every question with a short or long written response that the test designers hope will show the students' skills in more than one subject area.[51] Grading is "holistic," which critics consider too subjective, and graders have the discretion to discount spelling and grammar errors. Maryland's "narrow political spectrum" has left this test in place for a decade. The test did come under scrutiny in 2000, when a research team sponsored by the Baltimore-based Abell Foundation criticized it for a myriad of factual errors, deficient coverage of academic content, and basing student scores more on writing style than on demonstrated knowledge of content.[52]

In truth, Maryland's test has never been strong, whereas its accountability system is: Maryland is one of the few states to replace teachers and principals in persistently failing schools, and it has contracted out the management of failing schools to private firms. Maryland provides an interesting twist on the states we have looked at so far, where we've usually had the proponents of comprehensive and detailed standards and tough accountability facing off against the progressive educators and those attempting to weaken accountability systems. In Maryland, the progressives were in charge of the standards and tests from the beginning and have controlled the tests for the duration—this may have made accepting accountability based on those progressive measures more palatable to the education establishment.

This twist may in fact owe much to the "somewhat narrow political spectrum" described above, which reduces controversy about education policy. This political consensus of leaders has easily deflected any efforts to revisit the state's standards and testing

51. Mike Bowler, "MSPAP Is Imperfect but Gets Passing Grade," *Baltimore Sun*, Nov. 19, 2000.
52. The author was the head of this research team.

program. This consensus may also have exacted a price, in that Maryland students' achievement levels on the National Assessment of Educational Progress (NAEP) have hovered at or below the national average during the last decade, although the state has a comparatively high average income.[53] The state recently upgraded its standards (though not to the level found in the top-performing countries), prompting some familiar reactions from both sides of the standards-and-accountability debate. Worried that students are ill-prepared, the Maryland state school board voted last summer to delay using new graduation tests as a prerequisite for a diploma until 2007. The scores, however, will appear on student transcripts starting in 2002, which has business groups applauding and the state's largest teachers union complaining that publicizing individual scores will only discourage students facing too-high expectations.

Texas, like Maryland, experienced a rare political consensus when it came to implementing its state standards-and-accountability measures, but unlike Maryland this consensus was borne of a unique set of circumstances rather than a narrow spectrum of opinion. At the outset of Texas's reform effort, educational interest groups (with the exception of the Texas affiliate of the AFT) strenuously opposed accountability. For several years, these experienced groups had the capacity to hamstring accountability in the legislature and to control the legislative agenda on the issue. The school-quality lobby, made up primarily of business interests, hung on and gradually won over public opinion. With backing of the general public came political support in the legislature. The accountability movement was successful because the state's influential business community organized a permanent, well-funded lobby and established public communications groups. Members of the business community took their concerns about the quality of Texas's workforce and their desire for more accountability in the schools to politicians and parents and turned public opinion into such a political juggernaut that change seemed inevitable. Not

53. There has been a recent improvement in the state's reading score for fourth-graders.

only did momentum for reform build, but opposition from the education establishment faded, perhaps because the state is unusual in having four rivalrous teachers unions. The state's AFT affiliate allied with the business community from the beginning in the quest for accountability.[54]

Since the business community was the driving force behind standards and accountability in Texas, it should come as no surprise that the state based its reforms on a basic lesson from the business world: teachers and schools will find effective ways to succeed if they are allowed to try new ways to do their job and are held accountable for their performance. During the 1990s, legislators delegated ever-increasing authority to the local level, while at the same time establishing state standards and tests to measure student performance. With these three key pieces in place, the state then started to rate schools based on their test results. In the words of Laurence Toenjes, an economist at the University of Houston, "the school districts and schools that historically haven't done too well are now getting exposed."[55]

It is this stringent rating and accountability system that has marked Texas's success so far—so much so that other states are now adding tests, creating or toughening school rating systems, and breaking down testing data by racial and ethnic subgroups, in the hope of seeing similar success in their own schools. In 1996, Texas fourth-graders finished in the top ten for math on the NAEP test, black fourth-graders scored higher in math on average in Texas than in any other state, and while wide racial disparities still exist in Texas, the gap is clearly narrowing.

Texas's accountability system will get even tougher in the next two years, when the state begins introducing new and more difficult tests that, starting with the class of 2005, students will be required to pass in order to graduate. Texas is also one of the few

54. Tyce Palmaffy, "The Gold Star State: How Texas Jumped to the Head of the Class in Elementary School Achievement," *Policy Review* (Heritage Foundation), no. 88 (March–April 1998).

55. Claudia Kolker, "Texas Offers Hard Lessons on School Accountability," *Los Angeles Times*, Apr. 14, 1999.

states where, as of 2003, students will have to pass tests to be promoted in certain grades.

The unique consensus in Texas does not mean there haven't been critics. Lawyers from the Mexican American Legal Defense and Educational Fund filed a lawsuit in 1997 that argued the state's testing requirements were discriminatory, a suit that was subsequently dismissed. Other critics contend that the state's strict testing and rating system is narrowing teacher creativity in the classroom, a contention which is open to debate, and driving up the dropout rate, which is false.[56] For the time being, though, the state's educational establishment seems reconciled to—even supportive of—accountability. It remains to be seen whether tougher tests and tougher accountability measures will evoke resistance. For now at least, Texas—unlike Maryland—is not backing away from its tough accountability benchmarks, and it is seeing impressive improvements in student achievement as a result.[57]

## THE CALIFORNIA STORY

In these four states, the political and ideological forces interested in standards and accountability produced four different results: Massachusetts, where the education interest groups remain powerful and are vigorously resisting accountability measures; Virginia, where a powerful coalition created some of the toughest standards in the nation but where accountability measures are now under siege from their opponents; Maryland, where political consensus has led to sluggish student achievement; and Texas, where political momentum and an active business community have led to an effective accountability system and higher student achievement, but where the advent of tougher testing could open

56. Lawrence A. Toenjes and A. Gary Dworkin, "Are Increasing Test Scores in Texas Really a Myth, or Is Haney's Myth a Myth?" University of Houston, unpublished MS, March 2001.

57. David Grissmer and Ann Flanagan, *Exploring Rapid Achievement Gains in North Carolina and Texas* (National Education Goals Panel, 1998); David Grissmer et al., *Improving Student Achievement: What NAEP Scores Tell Us* (Santa Monica, Calif.: RAND, 2000).

the door to political and ideological battles in the future. While all four states have seen some measures of success—Texas in particular, with its improved test scores—none of them can yet claim to have a system of standards and accountability that is firmly in place and no longer in need of important improvements.

California, on the other hand, is one state that is widely viewed as having one of the most promising standards-and-accountability systems in the nation. How did this happen in a state filled with progressive educators? Especially a state with extremely powerful interest groups and teachers' unions? And is the system really as solid as everyone seems to think it is?

To answer these questions, and to see how the different interest and ideological groups interacted, we are going to take a closer look at two specific education-policy battles in California and how they played out: the conflict over the current state mathematics standards and the conflict over the state accountability measures.

Before we can understand what happened in these two instances, though, it is important to understand what had taken place in California public education in the preceding years, primarily the fallout from the debacle of progressive education in the 1980s and early 1990s. The backlash inspired by this—and the backlash in California was even stronger than the one we have already described that took place in Virginia—has had an enormous effect on subsequent education reform efforts in the state, and on standards-and-accountability measures in particular.

"Debacle" may seem to be a rather strong word, but it is one that has been used repeatedly to describe what happened to California public schools under the influence of progressive educational philosophies such as "higher-order thinking" and "teaching the child, not the subject."

The early 1980s was a good time for public education in California: A well-respected state superintendent, who wanted all schoolchildren to have a thorough liberal-arts education, was in office,[58] and student test scores were on the rise—which led to the

---

58. Bill Honig, State Superintendent of Public Instruction: "I ran on a platform of traditional education that anticipated most of [*A Nation at Risk*]'s eventual recommendations. . . . [T]here is a core of knowledge in the arts and sciences

state's being hailed as a pathfinder for the nation. And yet despite this success, by the late 1980s state education officials moved to embrace progressive-education nostrums.[59] In short, traditional learning was shunted aside for progressive education, and four years of solid academic improvement in the schools quickly reverted to falling or stagnant student achievement.

Under new state laws and curriculum guidelines, psychological empowerment and student self-esteem became core elements of teacher training and classroom teaching in California. Math teachers were informed their job was to facilitate discussion and guide exploration, not to teach math facts or how to get a correct, precise answer to a problem.[60] The new project-based test (the California Learning Assessment System or CLAS), in the words of Governor Pete Wilson's education secretary, "gave no individual scores, tested no basic skills, was related to a scale no one could explain, and never used the expertise of professional measurement experts."[61] Perhaps the most drastic shift was the adoption of "whole language" reading instruction in place of the traditional phonics method. Whole language is a philosophy whose adherents believe that children should learn to read "naturally" by guessing based on cues (like story-book illustrations) rather than by sounding out words, and also believe that not teaching or cor-

---

that every member of society is entitled to encounter." Honig, *Last Chance for Our Children: How You Can Help to Save Our Schools* (Reading, Mass.: Addison-Wesley, 1985), pp. 4, 7.

Honig also criticized two progressive methods: child-centered instruction and the "open classroom." At the time, he considered himself something of a sadder-but-wiser progressive and had by no means rejected many aspects of progressivism. For example, he concurred with progressives in opposing drill and practice.

59. Ben Boychuk, "The Decline of Academic Standards in California Education: The Story Behind the Student Testing Fiasco," *California Politics Briefings* (Claremont Institute), no. 1996–49 (March 15, 1996), p. 2, *http://www.claremont.org/gsp/gsp49.htm.*

60. John Agonida, "The New, New Math," *The Report Card* (Center for the Study of Popular Culture), July/August 1995, cited in Boychuk, p. 10.

61. Maureen DiMarco, "Measurement and Reform," in Evers, *What's Gone Wrong?* p. 158. For more on CLAS, see Boychuk; Michael W. Kirst and Christopher Mazzeo, "The Rise, Fall, and Rise of State Assessment in California: 1993–1996," *Phi Delta Kappan*, vol. 78, no. 4 (1996), pp. 319–323; Peter Schrag, "The Days of School Daze," *Orange County Register*, Oct. 4, 1994.

recting spelling helps encourage children to become "natural" writers.[62]

After eight years of these progressive-education experiments, NAEP test results showed that the state's fourth-graders were tied for last place with Louisiana in reading. In 1994, Governor Pete Wilson vetoed continued funding for the progressive, largely project-based CLAS tests, saying they were unreliable and could not give individual scores to students.

1995 marked a new beginning for the standards movement in California, one that would be heavily influenced by the debacle of progressive education and the outrage it inspired in a broad coalition of parents, business leaders, education reformers, and even many of the educators themselves. It is in this milieu—amid the detritus of failed progressive-education theories—that our two stories begin.

### The Struggle over Mathematics Standards: Progressives versus Traditionalists

Mathematics content had been woefully watered down along with other academic subject matter during California's years (1987 to 1995) of experimental progressive education. California bought heavily into the "new-new" math in the early 1990s, and by 1992 had released new state curriculum guidelines, expanding upon the so-called "bible" of new-new math, the National Council of Teachers of Mathematics (NCTM) standards.[63]

California's progressive guidelines set out to make sure students felt good about math, that they felt "mathematically empowered."[64] This sense of empowerment would come from letting their

62. Charles Sykes, *Dumbing Down Our Kids: Why American Children Feel Good About Themselves But Can't Read, Write, or Add* (New York: St. Martin's Press, 1995), p. 93, quoted in Boychuk, p. 3.

63. Leah Vukmir, "2 + 2 = 5: Fuzzy Math Invades Wisconsin Schools," *Wisconsin Interest*, vol. 10, no. 1 (Winter 2001), pp. 9–12.

64. *Mathematics Framework for California Schools* (Sacramento: California Department of Education, 1992). The progressives endeavored to make mathematics less challenging and hence make it easier for the bottom 20 percent of mathematics students. However, experience in top-performing countries shows that virtually all such students can learn challenging subjects like algebra.

natural curiosity guide them, by tackling real-world problems, and by inventing their own ideas about how to solve problems. It would not come from traditional means, like memorizing the multiplication tables, learning how to do long division, or mastering the quadratic formula. Teachers were encouraged to reinvent themselves as facilitators of learning on topics that students chose or uncovered in their discovery-learning projects.

Eventually groups of California parents—many of them from scientific backgrounds—started to take note of this new math, and they started to worry that their own children would never be able to succeed in professions like theirs with the anemic math skills they were acquiring in school. These parents started to organize, and they became a powerful voice when the state moved to revise state math standards in the mid-1990s.[65]

The debate over these new math standards pitted the hard-core progressive educators who still fervently believed in new-new math against those who believed in the more traditional methods of mathematics instruction. Those on the progressive side—who had written and backed the existing state curriculum guidelines and were determined to see progressive methods maintained— were found in many of the usual places: in the state mathematics teachers' organizations, the state Department of Education, the state schools of education, and on the state commission drafting the new standards.[66] The coalition on the traditionalist side, on the other hand, had some new blood, including a large contingent of university mathematics professors, and members of various parents' groups who came from all parts of the political spectrum. Of the four founding members of the largest of these groups—a parents' group called "Mathematically Correct"—three describe

---

65. For two excellent accounts of the controversy over the California mathematics standards, see Hung-His Wu, "The 1997 Mathematics Standards War in California," in Sandra Stotsky, ed., *What's at Stake in the K-12 Standards Wars* (New York: Peter Lang, 2000), pp. 3–31; David Klein, "Big Business, Race, and Gender in Mathematics Reform," in Steven G. Krantz, *How to Teach Mathematics*, 2nd ed. (Providence, R.I.: American Mathematical Society, 1999), pp. 221–32.

66. The author was a member of the commission (the California State Commission for the Establishment of Academic Content and Performance Standards) that wrote the initial draft of the standards.

themselves as liberal Democrats, only one as a conservative Republican. One of the most actively involved mathematics professors is a member of the Green Party and voted for Ralph Nader in 2000, and he says "California's mathematics policies [since 1997] and its direction are not motivated by conservative politics . . . [T]hey are motivated by a recognition that the policies of the past decade were deeply flawed from the point of view of mathematics itself."[67]

So there was some crossing of political lines going on as California tackled the issue of new mathematics standards. Such crossing of lines was also evident in the state legislature in which Democrats and Republicans united to call for internationally competitive standards for the state's public schools and to restore phonics-based reading instruction in the schools. It is in this context that one must consider the actions of perhaps the key player in this debate: the California State Board of Education, which by state law sets the policy for the state's schools. Board members are appointed by the governor, who at that time was Republican Pete Wilson, the same governor who discontinued the ineffectual and largely project-based CLAS tests in 1994. Board members are also confirmed by the State Senate, which was controlled by the Democrats at the time. The State Board, then, had a membership with support from across the political spectrum, and at the outset of the mathematics-standards debate, a majority of the board supported the state's 1992 progressive math-curriculum guidelines and undoubtedly looked forward to having new math standards that would be similar.

However, a few members of the State Board were convinced early in the process that the state had tilted too far in the progressive or new-new math direction. They had been convinced, in part, by the diverse assortment of professors, parents, and other grass-roots organizers who effectively expressed their disgust at the condition of mathematics instruction in the state. Another spur to change also came in the form of the 1996 NAEP math test, which

67. David Klein, Professor of Mathematics, California State University–Northridge.

showed that more than half of California's fourth-graders scored below the basic proficiency level, and close to half of the eighth-graders had "below basic" math understanding. Overall, California fourth-graders ranked fourth-worst in the nation, tying with Mississippi, Guam, and the District of Columbia.[68]

In the end, the State Board of Education definitely moved away from the policy, prevalent in the late 1980s and early 1990s, of prescribing progressive teaching practices. It declined to endorse any particular school of thought on teaching practices. At the same time, the Board kept certain reasonable components of progressive education (like attention to conceptual understanding), while restoring the content knowledge that traditionalists had been calling for. A look at the debate surrounding some of the specific issues helps to clarify how this happened.

*Natural learning.* Those on the progressive side wanted to imbed in the state's new mathematics standards their idea that children should always learn things "naturally." For example, the progressive school of thought says that students should come to an understanding of quantity and develop their number sense naturally, not through explicit instruction, in which the teacher explains things directly to the students. The progressives also insist that students must discover their own techniques for mental mathematics, instead of being taught the simplest and most reliable ways to solve a problem. The State Board took account of the fact there are alternative methods of teaching, but edited the mathematics standards to remove the proposed sections that mandated the use of the progressive method of learning through discovery. The Board wanted to be clear about what students should know, but did not want to dictate how they should be taught. In their final form, the California mathematics standards are neutral about teaching methods. Teachers may use discovery learning, direct instruction, or other methods.

This neutrality on teaching methods may at first glance seem to be evasion on the part of the Board. But it is a reasonable resolution, in that it preserves local control and teacher flexibility, while

68. Vukmir, "$2 + 2 = 5$."

at the same time another part of the state reform effort—the state-wide testing and accountability program—is providing evidence as to which textbooks and teaching methods are the most effective.

*Problem-solving skills.* The proponents of progressivism wanted the state mathematics standards to specify exclusive reliance on problem-solving as the way to teach mathematics, and to say that students should learn generalized "problem-solving skills" in the abstract. This is because the progressive school of thought believes that teachers can develop and test a student's capacity for critical thinking and problem solving that is detached from his or her knowledge of subject matter, e.g., they can "discover" how to solve a math problem without knowing the standard techniques for procedures like long division or dividing one fraction by another. The fact of the matter is students can think critically and solve problems only if they are operating from a base of acquired knowledge. A consensus of research psychologists holds that it is not possible to teach problem solving or develop critical thinking in a vacuum.[69] After edits from the State Board, the official California standards again are pedagogically neutral: They do not compel teachers to use only problem solving as an instruction method (which is the method the progressives wanted to be required), nor do they assume that students can learn generalized "problem-solving skills" without acquiring a knowledge of the subject matter (an assumption that is in line with the progressive way of thinking).[70]

*Traditional courses.* Progressives are uncomfortable with traditional courses in mathematics such as algebra and geometry. They would prefer that mathematics were presented as a series of problems and puzzles, to be grouped perhaps by themes, such as

69. Hirsch, p. 135–43. See also Anderson, pp. 251–52; Geary, chaps. 2–3.
70. Mathematicians have their own way of thinking about problem solving. To them, problem solving cannot be detached from content knowledge: (1) Analyzing the situation to see if it can be solved using mathematics; (2) Setting up a mathematical problem; (3) Solving the problem; and (4) Interpreting the solution. I am indebted to Paul J. Sally Jr. for this point. See also Geary, pp. 116–27; Wu, "Basic Skills."

all problems having to do with automobile mechanics or all problems about cooking recipes.[71] So to get away from these traditional courses, the progressives in California proposed that the state mathematics standards direct schools to mix algebra and geometry together in an integrated curriculum.[72] The State Board disagreed. The official standards—again, pedagogically neutral—allow integrated courses or the standard course sequence of Algebra I, geometry, and Algebra II. Whichever sequence a school chooses to adopt, it must eventually cover the same topics. Allowing these options adds expensive complexity to the California testing system, yet it also gives flexibility to local school districts and preserves local control while retaining accountability.

*Calculators.* The progressive school of thought believes that students can come to true mathematical knowledge only via problem solving, not through memorization of multiplication tables or learning how to do long division. Progressives want to provide students with a simulated "real world" situation in which they feel empowered to solve problems, so it only makes sense that because some people in the real world use calculators, students should too when they are doing their schoolwork. Many influential progressives go so far as to insist that students should always be able to use calculators for their homework, classwork, and exams.[73] The California progressives proposed allowing students to use calculators on the statewide standards-based mathematics test. The traditionalists argued that reliance on calculators in elementary school reduces fluency with math facts and pointed out that students in

71. See, for example, Rick Billstein and Jim Williamson, Middle School *Math Thematics* series (Evanston, Ill.: McDougal Littell, 1999). I am indebted to Paul Clopton for this reference.

72. In addition, some people—progressives and traditionalists alike—have said they want to imitate the integrated courses in Japan and other top-performing countries. But California teachers are not prepared to teach the demanding mathematics courses found in Japan. At the time of the California mathematics-standards controversy, there were several existing and proposed programs that integrated some of the content of algebra and geometry, but that did not have the full content or rigor of the instructional programs in Japan.

73. See, for example, *California Mathematics Framework* (1992), p. 199.

the top-performing East Asian countries do not use calculators for schoolwork.[74] The Board of Education decided that no mathematics standard will be tested at the state level or at any grade using calculators, and they organized the standards so that students do not need calculators to master content material prior to the sixth grade. The Board's decision leaves discretionary power in the hands of districts and elementary school teachers.[75] It is up to them whether to allow students to use calculators for classroom work and homework, but districts and teachers know that if students are overly dependent on calculators, they are likely to perform poorly on the statewide nationally normed and standards-based tests, where calculator use is not allowed.

*Math facts and algorithms.* Progressive educators believe that memorizing math facts (like the multiplication tables) and learning reliable problem-solving techniques (standard algorithms) in advance robs students of the discovery experience. Therefore, the progressives in California did not want memorization of those facts and knowledge of certain standard algorithms traditionally taught in the United States (in particular, long division by multiple-digit divisors) included in the state mathematics standards.[76] The traditionalists argued that students need near-automaticity with math facts and algorithms in order to have the tools for basic

74. The U.S. government's report on the TIMSS data on fourth-grade mathematics states: "In six of the seven nations that outscore the U.S. in mathematics, teachers of 85 percent or more of the students report that students never use calculators in class." National Center for Education Statistics, U.S. Department of Education, *Pursuing Excellence: A Study of U.S. Fourth-Grade Mathematics and Science Achievement in International Context* (Washington, D.C.: U.S. Government Printing Office, 1997), *http://nces.ed.gov/timss/report/97255–2a.html#i.*

75. The 1999 California Mathematics Framework recommends that calculators should not play a major role in mathematics curriculum and instruction until students have completed fifth grade or until they have mastered basic skills and concepts. *Mathematics Framework for California Schools* (Sacramento: California Department of Education, 1999), p. 225.

76. *Standard algorithms* should not be confused with *standards*. *Standard algorithms* are efficient, reliable operations for solving a certain sort of problem. *Content standards* catalog what students should know, and *performance standards* say how well they should know it. The issue is whether standard algorithms should be in state content standards.

mathematical understanding.[77] The official California mathematics standards, as edited by the State Board, do expect students to know the standard algorithms traditionally taught in the United States, including long division.[78]

*Final result.* During the drafting of the mathematics standards, the progressives tried to give privileged status to their favored discovery-learning techniques and to infuse the standards with their progressive doctrines. They failed in this endeavor. The California State Board of Education decided not to make progressive education the state's official way of teaching mathematics. The revised set of state mathematical standards that was adopted by the Board in December of 1997 is substantially neutral as to pedagogy, which allows different teaching methods to compete and to show their effectiveness in meeting the standards. It also clearly delineates the content students are expected to know and gives thorough coverage to math facts, algorithms, applications, mathematical reasoning, proof, and conceptual understanding.[79] While it opted for neutrality rather than outright rejection of progressive teaching doctrines, the Board did lay out a set of math standards that explicitly emphasizes the mastery of math facts and skills—an emphasis which traditionalists had sought as their highest priority for the state math standards. [80]

*The Struggle over Accountability:*
*Self-Protection versus Scrutiny*

California's early embrace of progressive education has loosened considerably after years of dismal student performance and test scores. The state's current academic standards reflect this change in opinion. As we have seen with the mathematics standards de-

77. Wu, "Basic Skills."

78. For an excellent report on the importance of the standard U.S. algorithms, see *Second Report* from the Mathematical Association of America Task Force on the NCTM Standards, June 17, 1997. *http://www.maa.org/past/maanctm3.html.*

79. From kindergarten through grade 7, the California mathematics standards are organized on a grade-by-grade basis. After grade 7, the document lists topics by subject, e.g. geometry, rather than grade level.

80. Vukmir, "2 + 2 = 5."

scribed above, California's state standards in all academic subject matters today are more focused on skills and content rather than teaching methods, and they are being hailed as models for the nation.

California's accountability measures were a longer time in coming, but they too are now lauded as being among the best. How did they come to be? What are the political factors influencing their implementation? And are they really as laudable as they are supposed to be?

Following his refusal to continue the CLAS tests in 1994, Governor Wilson proposed a new program in 1997 designed to test and hold students accountable for learning the new state academic standards. Called the Standardized Testing and Reporting (STAR) program, this program uses an off-the-shelf commercial test (the Stanford Achievement Test, 9th ed.) along with questions based completely on the state's current academic standards; students are tested every year in grades 2–11; and individual scores are provided for each student.[81] As can be expected for any testing system that aims at accountability, this one did not come into existence without controversy.

The statewide association of principals and superintendents, as well as top officials in the California Department of Education, initially opposed the STAR program, as they opposed the entire concept of accountability through testing. After this stance proved to be politically untenable, they proposed diagnostic testing instead, which would provide teachers with some information about student weaknesses but would not provide individual scores that could be used for accountability purposes. If the state insisted on any incentives, sanctions or rankings, though, they wanted a matrix-sample test.[82] (In such a test a large number of questions are

81. Scores are also posted on the WorldWide Web by grade, school, district, and county.

82. For the outline of this plan, see Delaine Eastin, State Superintendent of Public Instruction, letter to State Senator Quentin L. Kopp, Aug. 1, 1997. Compare Mony Neill's proposal of accountability via project-based tests given to a sample of students. Neill, "What Is the Purpose of Assessment?" in Kathy Swope and Barbara Miner, eds., *Failing Our Kids: Why the Testing Craze Won't Fix Our Schools* (Milwaukee, Wisc.: Rethinking Schools, 2000), p. 103.

divided into subsets, and test-takers are divided into groups. Each group of test-takers is given only one of the subsets of questions.) A matrix-sample test would detect performance weaknesses at the district or school level, but E. D. Hirsch Jr. calls such a test "pseudo-accountability" because it produces a "no-fault diagnosis" that cannot pinpoint the failings of individual students or teachers. Since matrix tests do not yield scores for individual students, they do not create incentives for either students or teachers to improve their performance.[83]

As we have seen, such a strategy is not unique to the education establishment in California. In states across the country, teachers and administrators actively resist effective accountability measures, and diagnostic-only testing is just another way of accomplishing this.[84] Education interests in California and elsewhere continue to push for tests that supposedly aid in teaching practices but shy away from measuring student mastery of content and skills—which, of course, means they don't measure the effectiveness of teachers either. As a group of California school officials put it—in the feel-good jargon of the education profession—they want to shift the focus of accountability from "judgment" to "continuous improvement" by establishing an accountability system that is "supportive, not punitive."[85]

In spite of vigorous resistance, the anti-accountability forces lost this battle, the proposed matrix-sample test was never created, and the state launched the STAR system in 1998. Standards and accountability at last? Not quite. The existing California testing law carried with it a legal provision backed by the teachers' unions

83. Hirsch, p. 193.

84. Rhea Borja, "From Diagnosis Then to Treatment Now; Standardized Tests Alter, Act as Catalyst," *Richmond Times-Dispatch*, Mar. 7, 1999. I am indebted to Doug McRae for his insights on this topic. See also Nancy S. Cole, "The Future of High-Stakes Testing," speech, Stanford School of Education, Oct. 19, 2000, audiotape (available from Stanford School of Education Office of Communications and Special Projects). Cole is the immediate past president of the Educational Testing Service.

85. Task Force on Student Performance and School Accountability, Association of California School Administrators, "Special Report on Continuous Improvement Accountability System," Nov. 1997, *http://222.acsa.org/publications/*.

that prohibits using results from standardized norm-referenced tests (like the Stanford-9 adopted in the STAR program) for decisions on hiring, firing, and promotion of teachers.[86] California still had no accountability measures in place.

Governor Gray Davis succeeded Governor Wilson in 1999, and armed with a nearly billion-dollar education package that includes monetary incentive rewards for schools and teachers, was finally able to get accountability components on the books and into the schools of California.[87] The package also includes provisions for student scholarships, peer review of teachers' performance, and voluntary state-subsidized improvement plans for low-performing schools. As currently constituted, California's system of standards, testing, and accountability is considered one of the best in the country.[88]

Yet the system has flaws worth noting. For instance, it can sometimes reward and sanction schools in ways that are not deserved. Low-performing California schools and high-performing schools alike have to meet the same goals of percentage growth in performance. This sounds fine in principle, but it means that a low-performing school that grows from a performance index rating of 300 to a rating of 325 (on a scale that ranges from a low of 200 to a high of 1000) is held up as exemplary, while a high-performing school that starts at 750 and shows no growth is seen as a poor example.[89] This system of targets and rewards tends to magnify gains by low-performing schools and to downplay how

86. Local districts in California must evaluate their teachers' performance as it contributes toward district-adopted content standards (as distinguished from the state content standards, which the district may, if it wishes, adopt as its own). Districts may, if they wish, evaluate teachers based on student results on the statewide standards-based tests. California Education Code, Sec. 44662. I am indebted to Bill Lucia for this reference.

87. The California Teachers Association opposed the accountability plan because it focused "too much" on test results. Kolker, "Texas Offers Hard Lessons."

88. Chester E. Finn Jr. and Michael J. Petrilli, eds., *The State of the Standards, 2000* (Washington, D.C.: Thomas B. Fordham Foundation), p. 3.

89. The state has set a performance target for all schools of 800. The yearly growth goal is 5 percent of the difference between a school's current performance and the target.

far these schools still need to go in boosting their students' achievement. Undoubtedly, it was politically attractive to policymakers for just this reason.[90]

Another flaw in this accountability system is that the state has defined "low performing" as everything from just a little below average to absolutely the worst—and as the program exists today, the just-below-average schools seem to be getting most of the money. Schools must volunteer for the program, so the slightly-below-average schools apply for the money and make some minor adjustments. State officials can then lay claim to having improved a troubled school. The worst-performing schools, on the other hand, have for the most part simply declined to take part in the program. This may mean they don't get the subsidies their students so desperately need, but it means they won't get sanctioned either.[91] So the program is not only missing its proclaimed target group (failing schools) and rewarding a different group (near-average schools), but it will be almost politically impossible to refocus the reward structure in the future because it will mean taking money away from numerous near-average schools with large numbers of parents and teachers and principals who want to hang on to that money, and giving it to failing schools which are fewer in number and have less political clout.

California's accountability system has other features that are simply too new to evaluate, such as peer review of teachers, the reconstitution of failing schools, and a high school exit exam.[92] The bottom line is that the state has implemented first-rate content standards, it tests students on the mastery of those standards, it pays attention to objective measures of student achievement, and it rewards improvement and sanctions persistent failure. That means it should have one of the better accountability systems as well, right?

90. I am indebted to Bill Lucia and Janet Nicholas for these points.

91. Lance T. Izumi, "What Accountability?" *Capital Ideas* (Pacific Research Institute), vol. 5, no. 40 (Oct. 5, 2000).

92. For a discussion of the weaknesses of peer-review systems, see Myron Lieberman, *Teachers Evaluating Teachers: Peer Review and the New Unionism* (New Brunswick, N.J.: Transaction Publishers, 1998) (Studies in Social Philosophy & Policy, No. 20).

The problem is that, so far, no one loses. Local school districts have the option of ignoring state content standards. Yes, they have to test their students and report how well they measure up, but they are forbidden to use student results from a nationally normed test (which is what all districts in the state are now using to test students) to evaluate teachers. Whether districts use the normed tests or the state standards-based tests to evaluate students is completely up to the districts. Whether they use the student results on the standards-based tests to evaluate teachers is likewise up to them. California's accountability system is indeed one of the best in the country but that isn't saying much. It is also an accountability system that has been cushioned to soften any real repercussions that might come to those (especially the adults) who are supposedly being evaluated by it. And this comes close to accountability in name only, the kind of accountability system that education interest groups across the country are trying to have adopted: an accountability system that doesn't hold them accountable.[93]

## CONCLUSION

Setting standards and accountability measures for public education would seem to be a simple and straightforward enterprise: You set academic standards, and you hold students and teachers and schools accountable for meeting those standards. And yet the enterprise seems to be one that is continually swimming upstream—getting systems in place, trying to make them work, then backsliding again and again.

Almost all states now have some kind of standards and tests in place, which means the urgency of the issue may have diminished in some peoples' opinion. This is a mistake. Standards and accountability remain political issues. The well-organized and well-funded education interest groups remain adamantly opposed to

93. Rather few incompetent teachers have been fired by states based on the performance of the teachers' students on accountability tests. See "Ultimate Sanctions," *Education Week*, Jan. 11, 2001 ("Quality Counts 2001" special report), p. 84; Kathleen Kennedy Manzo, "N.C. Teachers Battle State over Firings," *Education Week*, Dec. 9, 1998.

having their members evaluated, which means they remain stead-
fastly opposed to accountability measures that sanction teachers
and administrators. The progressive educators and their supporters continue to argue with traditionalists over what educational
standards should look like and whether there should be any standards at all. These disputes are not going to go away, in fact they
are likely to intensify in the years to come as student-performance
benchmarks start to approach and accountability opponents
renew their efforts to lower what constitutes a passing grade and
to postpone any day of reckoning.

Not only will standards and accountability remain politically
controversial, but they came into existence as products of the political process, which explains why their results around the country
have been so diverse and in many cases disappointing. What are
our children learning and how well are they learning it? This is
still the question uppermost in the minds of accountability advocates—and it looks as if it is a question we are going to have to
continue asking in the years to come.

# CHAPTER 10

# Choice in American Education

## *Paul E. Peterson*

Historically, most school boards in the United States assigned students to schools by drawing boundaries that established specific attendance areas. Where one lived determined the school one attended, if one chose to attend a public school. Families did not *seem* to have any choice at all—though the reality, as we shall see, was not quite this simple.

The situation has changed substantially in recent years. Today, a wide variety of school choice mechanisms are available to parents and students—vouchers, magnet schools, charter schools, interdistrict choice programs, home-schooling, tax credits and tax deductions for private tuition, and, above all, school choice through residential selection. Responding to the increasing demand by parents for greater choice among schools, states today provide a greater range of choices to parents than ever before. Approximately 63 percent of American families with school-age children are making a choice when sending their child to school. According to a 1993 Department of Education survey, 39 percent of all parents said that where they have chosen to live was influenced by the school their child would attend.[1] Another 11 percent

1. U.S. Department of Education, National Center for Education Statistics, "Findings from 'The Condition of Education 1997: Public and Private Schools:

of the population sends their children to private school.[2] And still another 13 percent of families have a choice of some kind of public school such as a magnet school, charter school, participation in an interdistrict choice program, or other choice program.[3] Currently, choice programs are rapidly expanding in size and number, and the topic has become a matter of significant public discussion and debate, with most public opinion studies finding increased demand for school choice, especially among citizens from low-income and minority backgrounds.[4]

In this essay I review the growth in the range of choices available in American education and examine in depth the way in which the most controversial of existing choice programs—school vouchers—has worked in practice in the few cities where vouchers have been tried.

## ORIGINS OF THE CHOICE CONCEPT IN EDUCATION

The extended and explicit practice of school choice in the United States came of age only in the late 1980s and early 1990s. But choice in education is an ancient concept, dating back to the days when Socrates and his fellow philosophers walked the Athenian agora, teaching for a fee.[5] The earliest forms of choice left education strictly to the private market. It was John Stuart Mill who first made a fully developed argument on behalf of school choice within the context of publicly funded, universal education: "Is it

How Do They Differ?' " (Washington, D.C.: GPO, 1997) <http://nces.ed.gov/pubs97/97983.htm>.

2. U.S. Department of Education, National Center for Education Statistics, Common Core of Data and "Fall Enrollment in Institutions of Higher Education" Surveys; Integrated Postsecondary Education Data System (IPEDS), Higher Education General Information Survey (HEGIS), "Fall Enrollment" Surveys, and Projections of Education Statistics to 2007 (Washington, D.C., 1997) <http://nces.ed.gov/pubs/digest97/d97t002.html>.

3. Lynn Schnaiberg, "More Students Taking Advantage of School Choice, Report Says," Education Week, September 22, 1999, p. 6.

4. Joint Center for Political and Economic Studies, 1997 National Opinion Poll (Washington D.C., 1997), table 7.

5. Andrew J. Coulson, Market Education: The Unknown History (New Brunswick, N.J.: Transaction, 1999), chap. 2.

not almost a self-evident axiom, that the State should require and compel the education . . . of every human being who is born its citizen?" he asks. He then goes on to point out that

> were the duty of enforcing universal education once admitted, there would be an end to the difficulties about what the State should teach, and how it should teach, which now convert the subject into a mere battlefield for sects and parties, causing the time and labor which should have been spent in educating, to be wasted in quarrelling about education. . . . It might leave to parents to obtain the education where and how they pleased, and content itself with helping to pay the school fees.[6]

In the United States school choice within a system of publicly funded, universal education was first seriously proposed by economist Milton Friedman, who in 1955 argued that a voucherlike arrangement where the government finances the education but families choose the school would lead to a more efficient educational system.[7] The idea gained considerable public currency in the 1970s, when the Office of Economic Opportunity helped fund a school choice experiment in the Alum Rock school district in California. When this experiment encountered strong opposition from teacher organizations and failed to be implemented effectively,[8] enthusiasm for school choice waned for about a decade, except for sporadic use of the magnet school concept as a tool for school desegregation.

Then, in the 1980s and early 1990s, a number of events helped give the school choice movement new impetus. First, a major study by a research team headed by James Coleman (discussed more fully below) reported that students in Catholic schools outperformed their public school peers. These findings were subsequently

6. John Stuart Mill, "On Liberty" in *Educational Vouchers: Concepts and Controversies,* ed. George R. La Noue (New York: Teachers College Press, 1972), pp. 3–4.

7. Milton Friedman, "The Role of Government in Education," in Robert Solo, ed., *Economics and the Public Interest* (New Brunswick, N.J.: Rutgers University Press, 1955), p. 127.

8. David K. Cohen and Eleanor Farrar, "Power to the Parents? The Story of Education Vouchers," *Public Interest*, Spring 1977, pp. 72–97.

supported by a second major study by the Brookings Institution
that, in addition, explained the original results by showing that
private schools had more autonomy and, as a result, were organized more effectively than public schools.[9] The authors, John
Chubb and Terry Moe, proposed school vouchers as the solution.
Although critics questioned both studies, their impact was reinforced by a Department of Education proposal to give compensatory education funds directly to low-income families to be used as
vouchers.[10] At the same time, experiments that gave families
greater choice of public school began to appear in Minnesota,
Massachusetts, Wisconsin, and East Harlem. When test score
gains were reported for East Harlem, public interest in the idea
grew rapidly, producing today a wide variety and ever-growing set
of school choice initiatives.[11] What had been the gleam in the eye
of a few intellectuals in 1970 had become, by the end of the century, a major political movement with a wide variety of actual
policies operating in many parts of the United States.

### Residential Location and School Choice

Although explicit school choice programs are quite recent, in fact
school choice by selection of one's place of residence is a deeply
entrenched part of American education. Self-conscious school
choice has long been exercised by many families when they rent or
purchase a house in a place where they think the school is good.
Because the quality of the school affects a family's residential decisions, housing prices vary with the quality of local schools. As a
result, many families indirectly pay for their children's education

9. John Chubb and Terry Moe, *Politics, Markets, and America's Schools*
(Washington, D.C.: Brookings, 1990).

10. Paul E. Peterson, "The New Politics of Choice" in Diane Ravitch and
Maris A. Vinovskis, eds., *Learning from the Past* (Baltimore: Johns Hopkins University Press, 1995).

11. Joseph P. Viteritti, *Choosing Equality: School Choice, the Constitution
and Civil Society* (Washington, D.C.: Brookings, 1999), pp. 60–62; Bruce Fuller
et al., *School Choice* (Berkeley and Stanford: Policy Analysis for California Education, University of California, Berkeley, and Stanford University, 1999).

by purchasing homes that cost more simply because the home is located in a neighborhood which is perceived to have a higher-quality school.[12]

School choice by residential selection is highly inegalitarian, especially when one considers that the purchase of a home requires a capital investment. As school quality drives up housing prices, access to the neighborhood school is determined by one's capacity to obtain a mortgage. Those with higher earning power and more capital resources are able to command access to the best schools.

School choice by residential selection, the most inegalitarian form of school choice, is becoming more widespread, simply because more families have more choice in selecting a neighborhood in which to live than ever before. A half-century ago, the attractiveness—and thus the average cost (per square foot)—of a residential location was strongly influenced by its proximity to workplaces, which were concentrated in specific parts of a metropolitan area, primarily the central city. But when highways replaced railroads and rapid transit systems as the primary mode of transport in metropolitan areas, employment opportunities diffused throughout the metropolitan area. Once jobs became widely distributed, the dominant factors affecting community housing prices became local amenities, such as the neighborhood school.[13] As a result, many families today consider the local school when selecting a place to live.[14]

The amount of school choice by residential selection varies across metropolitan areas. In the Miami metropolitan area, for example, this form of choice is restricted by the fact that one

12. H. S. Rosen and D. J. Fullerton, "A Note on Local Tax Rates, Public Benefit Levels, and Property Values," *Journal of Political Economy* 85 (1977): 433–40; G. R. Meadows, "Taxes, Spending, and Property Values: A Comment and Further Results," *Journal of Political Economy* 84 (1976): 869–80; M. Edel and E. Sclar, "Taxes, Spending, and Property Values: Supply Adjustment in a Tiebout-Oates Model," *Journal of Political Economy* 82 (1974): 941–54.

13. Paul E. Peterson, "Introduction: Technology, Race, and Urban Policy," in Paul E. Peterson, ed., *The New Urban Reality* (Washington, D.C.: Brookings, 1985), pp. 1–29.

14. National Center for Education Statistics, *Findings from the Condition of Education*, 1997.

school district is responsible for almost the entire metropolitan area, whereas the Boston metropolitan area is divided into more than one hundred school districts.

The quality of education is higher in metropolitan areas that give parents more choice by virtue of the fact that they have more school districts. Students take more academic courses, students spend more time on their homework, classes are more structured and disciplined, parents are more involved with schools, student test scores are higher, and sports programs are given less emphasis.[15]

It is difficult for low-income families to exercise choice through residential selection. Most do not have the earning power or access to financial markets to locate in neighborhoods with schools perceived to be of high quality. On the contrary, they often can afford a home or apartment only because it is located in a neighborhood where schools are perceived to be of low quality, a perception that depresses property values. In short, in a system of residentially determined school choice, such as exists in most metropolitan areas today, low-income families are very likely to be concentrated in areas where schools are thought to be of low quality. Conversely and ironically, once a neighborhood school serving a low-income community improves, local land values will rise, making it more difficult for additional poor families to gain access to the school.

It was precisely this link between school and residence that provoked one of the most turbulent periods in American educational history, the school busing controversy. Since school choice by residential selection gave better-off families access to better schools, many felt that racial segregation and inequality could be obtained only by forcefully breaking the link between school and residence

15. Caroline Minter Hoxby, "The Effects of School Choice on Curriculum and Atmosphere," in Susan B. Mayer and Paul E. Peterson, eds., *Earning and Learning: How Schools Matter* (Washington, D.C.: Brookings, 1999), pp. 281–316; Caroline B. Hoxby, "Does Competition among Schools Benefit Students and Taxpayers?" *American Economic Review*, forthcoming; Caroline M. Hoxby, "Analyzing School Choice Reforms That Use America's Traditional Forms of Parental Choice," in Paul E. Peterson and Bryan C. Hassel, eds., *Learning from School Choice* (Washington, D.C.: Brookings, 1998), pp. 133–51.

by compelling families to send their children by bus to schools distant from their place of residence.[16]

## Magnet Schools

So unpopular was compulsory busing with many Americans that the magnet school, exploiting the choice concept, was developed to replace it. Magnet schools sought to increase racial and ethnic integration of schools by enticing families to choose integrated schools by offering distinctive, improved education programs. The magnet idea was initially broached in the 1960s. But it was not until after 1984 that the magnet school concept, supported by federal funding under the Magnet Schools Assistance Program, began to have a national impact. "Between 1984 and 1994, 138 districts nationwide received a total of $955 million" in federal funds to implement this form of school choice.[17] As a consequence, the number of schools with magnet programs doubled between 1982 and 1991, while the number of students tripled.[18] In some school districts, parents can choose a magnet school only if their choice increases the level of racial integration within the magnet school. In other school districts, magnet school places are offered on a first-come, first-served basis. In still other school districts, schools that are highly magnetic must choose students by means of a lottery. Nationwide, in the early 1990s, more than 1.2 million students attend 2,400 magnet schools in more than two hundred school districts.[19]

Cleveland provides an illustrative example of the way in which

16. Gary Orfield, *Must We Bus? Segregated Schools and National Policy* (Washington, D.C.: Brookings, 1978).

17. Fuller et al., *School Choice*, p. 26.

18. Lauri Steel and Roger Levine, *Educational Innovation in Multicultural Contexts: The Growth of Magnet Schools in American Education* (Palo Alto, Calif.: American Institutes for Research, 1996).

19. Dennis P. Doyle and Marsha Levine, "Magnet Schools: Choice and Quality in Public Education," *Phi Delta Kappan* 66, no. 4 (1984): 265–70; Rolf K. Blank, Roger E. Levine, and Lauri Steel, "After 15 Years: Magnet Schools in Urban Education," in Bruce Fuller, Richard Elmore, and Gary Orfield, eds., *Who Chooses? Who Loses? Culture, Institutions and the Unequal Effects of School Choice* (New York: Teachers College Press, 1996), pp. 154–72.

school desegregation controversies led to the introduction of magnet schools. In 1981, the federal district court issued an order that
explicitly asked the Cleveland school district to establish magnet
schools. Gradually, a number of magnet schools were created, and
in 1994 the city of Cleveland and the state of Ohio agreed to a
plan that would "enlarge the capacity of its magnet schools from
6,800 seats in 1992–93 to approximately 12,800 seats by the
1994–95 school year."[20] In the 1999–2000 school year twenty-
three magnet schools were expected to enroll well more than ten
thousand students in kindergarten through eighth grade.

The magnet school concept, if taken to its logical conclusion,
opens all the public schools in a district to all families, allowing
them to select their preferred public school, subject to space constraints. Such programs, generally identified as open-enrollment
programs, can be found at the high school and middle school levels
in a few school districts.

Most studies of the effects of magnet schools and open-enrollment programs find positive effects on student learning.[21] Although some of these findings have been questioned on the
grounds that the apparent effects were simply a function of the
initial ability of the students selected to attend magnet schools,[22]
two studies that carefully addressed this issue still found positive
effects from attendance at a magnet school.[23]

20. *Reed v. Rhodes*, 934 F.Supp. 1533, 1575 (N.D. Ohio 1996).
21. R. Kenneth Godwin, Frank R. Kemerer, and Valerie J. Martinez, "Comparing Public Choice and Private Voucher Programs in San Antonio," in Paul E.
Peterson and Bryan C. Hassel, eds., *Learning from School Choice* (Washington,
D.C.: Brookings, 1998), pp. 275–306; Corrie M. Yu and William L. Talor, "Difficult Choices: Do Magnet Schools Serve Children in Need?" Citizens' Commission on Civil Rights, 1997, Washington, D.C.
22. California Department of Education, as cited in Fuller et al., *School
Choice*, 1999, pp. 30, 38–39; Carnegie Foundation for the Advancement of
Teaching, *School Choice: A Special Report* (Princeton, N.J.: Carnegie Foundation for the Advancement of Teaching, 1992).
23. Adam Gamoran, "Student Achievement in Public Magnet, Public Comprehensive, and Private City High Schools," *Educational Evaluation and Policy
Analysis* 18 (1996): 1–18; Robert L. Crain, Amy Heebner, and Yiu-Pong Si, *The
Effectiveness of New York City's Career Magnet Schools: An Evaluation of
Ninth-Grade Performance Using an Experimental Design* (Berkeley, Calif.: National Center for Research in Vocational Education, 1992).

In the East Harlem community school district within New York City, the magnet school was expanded so as to give most parents within the community a choice of schools. Test scores climbed both within the magnet schools and within traditional neighborhood schools competing with these magnet schools.[24]

## Interdistrict School Choice

If most magnet school programs limit parental choice to public schools within a particular school district, in a number of places school choice has been expanded to include access to public institutions outside the local school district. As early as 1985, Minnesota gave local school boards permission to allow students from outside their district to attend their school (but the program was restricted to students who would not adversely affect the racial integration of participating school districts).[25] By 1997, nearly twenty thousand students were participating.[26] In 1966, Massachusetts enacted a program that allowed minority students to exit the Boston schools and enter participating suburban schools, then in 1991 enacted a more general interdistrict choice program without regard to a student's ethnicity or a district's racial composition.[27] By 1995 nearly seven thousand students and more than three hundred school districts were participating in this program. By 1997 similar programs had been enacted in sixteen states.

Although many of these programs are too new to enable researchers to draw conclusions about their long-term effect, preliminary evidence from the Massachusetts program indicates that the students participating in the programs enacted in that state are ethnically representative of the student composition of the public

24. Mark Schneider, Paul Teske, and Milissa Marschall, *Choosing Schools: Consumer Choice and the Quality of American Schools* (Princeton, N.J.: Princeton University Press, 2000).

25. Viteritti, *Choosing Equality,* 1999, pp. 62–63.

26. Fuller et al., *School Choice,* p. 33.

27. David J. Armor and Brett M. Peiser, "Inter-district Choice in Massachusetts," in Peterson and Hassel, *Learning from School Choice,* pp. 157–86; David J. Armor and Brett M. Peiser, *Competition in Education: A Case Study in Interdistrict Choice* (Boston: Pioneer Institute, 1997).

schools more generally. Also, it appears that school districts losing students often make significant efforts to upgrade their curriculum in order to stanch the flow of students outside the district.[28]

## Charter Schools

Magnet schools and interdistrict enrollment programs limit parental choice to schools operated by school boards. Charter schools have enlarged choice opportunities so as to include government-financed schools operated by nongovernmental entities. By 1998 thirty-four states and the District of Columbia had enacted charter school legislation, and more than 1,199 charter schools were educating more than a quarter-million students.[29] At the beginning of the 1999 school year the number of charter schools had increased 40 percent, to 1,684—a notable increment by any criterion.[30] Although the percentage of students in charter schools nationwide is still a small fraction of all students, in some states charter schools are providing the school of choice for a significant fraction of the student population. For example, in 1997, 4.4 percent of the students in Arizona were attending charter schools.[31]

Charter school terminology varies by state, as does the legal framework under which these schools operate. The common characteristics of charter schools are twofold. First, the entity operating the school is ordinarily not a government agency, though it may receive most of its operating revenue from either the state or a local school board. Second, charter schools do not serve students within a specific attendance boundary; instead they recruit stu-

28. Armor and Peiser, "Inter-District Choice," 1998.
29. Bryan C. Hassel, *The Charter School Challenge* (Washington, D.C.: Brookings, 1999), p. 1.
30. "Operating Charter Schools, Fall 1999–2000," memorandum prepared by the Fordham Foundation, Washington, D.C., October 1999.
31. Robert Maranto, Scott Milliman, Frederick Hess, and April Gresham, "Real World School Choice: Arizona Charter Schools," in Robert Maranto, Scott Milliman, Frederick Hess, and April Gresham, eds., *School Choice in the Real World: Lessons from Arizona Charter Schools* (Boulder, Colo.: Westview, 1999), p. 7.

dents from a large catchment area that may be beyond the attendance boundaries of traditional public schools. As a result, they must persuade parents that their offerings are superior to those provided by traditional public schools in their vicinity.

Studies of charter schools find that, on average and taken as a whole, students attending charter schools are fairly representative of the school population more generally.[32] Most charter schools are popular with parents and substantially oversubscribed, though some charter schools have been closed because safety and education standards were subnormal. Charter schools are better able than traditional public schools to attract teachers who were educated at selective colleges and who have received higher education in mathematics and science.[33] Whether or not students learn more in charter schools than traditional public schools has yet to be ascertained by an independent research team.

### Tax Deductions/Credits for Private Education

Recently, two states—Minnesota and Arizona—have facilitated parental access to private schools by providing tax deductions or tax credits that can be used to help pay the cost of private education. In Minnesota, families earning less than $33,500 a year can claim a tax credit of up to $1,000 per child ($2,000 per family) for school-related expenses, including costs incurred in attending a private school such as the purchase of books and other educational materials—although a credit cannot be claimed for private school tuition. Any family can claim a tax deduction for educational expenses of up to $1,625 for students in kindergarten through sixth grade and $2,500 for students in seventh grade

32. U.S. Department of Education, Office of Educational Research and Improvement, *A Study of Charter Schools: First-Year Report* (Washington, D.C.: GPO, 1997); Gregg Vanourek, Bruno V. Mann, Chester E. Finn Jr., and Louann A. Bierlein, "Charter Schools as Seen by Students, Teachers, and Parents," in Peterson and Hassel, *Learning from School Choice*, pp. 187–212.

33. Caroline Minter Hoxby, "The Effects of Charter Schools on Teachers," Department of Economics, Harvard University, September 1999.

through high school. Private school tuition counts toward the deduction.[34] Demonstrating its popularity, 37,951 Minnesotans claimed the tax credit in 1998, averaging $371 per credit. (Information on the deduction is not available at this writing.)[35] In Arizona, any person may receive a tax credit of up to $500 if they contribute to a foundation that is providing scholarships to students attending private schools. Again, this program has proven popular, with 5,100 Arizonans claiming the credit.[36] If this practice should spread to other states, it is possible that the growth in the numbers of students attending private schools might increase in future years.

## Private Schools

Although research on the operations of these recently enacted tax credit programs is not yet available, other information about the place of private schools in the U.S educational system is extensive because the presence of private schools constitutes the oldest form of school choice—dating back to before the Constitution was ratified.

*Historical development of private education.* In colonial times, education was privately provided, mainly by schools that had a religious affiliation. Those who wanted to enhance educational opportunity sought to do so by means of voucherlike arrangements. For example, when the radical populist Thomas Paine proposed a more egalitarian system of education, he recommended a system of vouchers: government should provide monies to parents, he said, so that they could send their children "to school, to learn reading, writing and common arithmetic; the ministers of

34. Minnesota Department of Children, Families, and Learning, "Take Credit for Learning," 1997 <*http://www.children.state.mn.us/tax/credits.html*>.

35. John Haugen, Legal Services Division, Minnesota Department of Revenue, telephone interview, October 21, 1999.

36. Rob Robinson, senior tax analyst, Arizona Department of Revenue, telephone interview, October 21, 1999.

every parish, of every denomination to certify . . . that the duty is performed."[37]

State-operated schools were constructed in the United States only many decades later—largely in response to the migration of poor Catholics from Ireland and Germany into the large cities of the Northeast in the 1840s. In 1852 the Boston School Committee urged that "in our schools they [the foreign-born children] must receive moral and religious teaching, powerful enough if possible to keep them in the right path amid the moral darkness which is their daily and domestic walk." Horace Mann, the first secretary of education for the Commonwealth of Massachusetts, explained the need for public schools in the following terms: "How shall the rising generation be brought under purer moral influences" so that "when they become men, they will surpass their predecessors, both in the soundness of their speculations and in the rectitude of their practice?" When Mann established public schools in Massachusetts, the new institutions won praise from the Congregational journal *New Englander*, which excitedly exclaimed in language that anticipated the phrasing (if not quite the sentiments) of the Gettysburg Address: "these schools draw in the children of alien parentage . . . and assimilate them to the native born. . . . So they grow up with the state, of the state, and for the state."[38]

Over the ensuing decades, public schools grew rapidly, and the share of the population attending private schools shrunk substantially. In some states—most notably, Nebraska and Oregon—the state legislature attempted to consolidate state power over the education of children by closing private schools, but key Supreme Court decisions declared such actions unconstitutional.[39] Nonetheless, the share of the population educated in private schools

37. Thomas Paine, *Rights of Man* (1792), 1:245, as quoted in David Kirkpatrick, *Choice in Schooling: A Case for Tuition Vouchers* (Chicago: Loyola University Press, 1990), p. 34.

38. As quoted in Charles L. Glenn Jr., *The Myth of the Common School* (Amherst: University of Massachusetts Press, 1987), pp. 83–84.

39. *Meyers v. Nebraska* 401 U. S. 399; *Pierce v. Society of Sisters*, 268 U. S. 528.

dropped steadily throughout the late nineteenth and early twentieth century, until by 1959 the percentage of students attending
private school was but 12.8 percent and by 1969 as low as 9.3
percent.

After reaching this nadir, the place of the private school began
to stabilize and edge back upward. By 1980, 11.5 percent of students in kindergarten through twelfth grade were attending private
schools, a number that has stayed relatively constant since then.[40]
Families who could afford the cost of private education were increasingly reaching the conclusion that they needed an alternative
to what was being provided by the public sector.

*Private schools today.* The image of private education held by
some is of an expensive day school catering to well-to-do families
or an exclusive boarding school attended by college-bound "preppies." The reality is quite different. Most private schools have a
religious affiliation, modest tuition, and limited facilities. Nationwide, the average private school expenditures per pupil in
1993–94 were estimated at $3,116, considerably less than public
school expenditure per pupil, which was $6,653.[41]

It has been pointed out that private schools do not have the
same costs as public schools, so expenditure comparisons may be
comparing apples and oranges. In New York City, I was able to
conduct a more exact, apple-to-apple comparison of schooling
costs in the eighty-eight public and seventy-seven Catholic elementary and middle schools located in three New York boroughs, the
Bronx, Brooklyn, and Manhattan.

To make sure the comparison subtracted out from public school
expenditures amounts that covered activities not provided by
Catholic schools, we deducted from public school expenditures
the amounts for all items that did not clearly have a private school

40. U.S. Department of Education, National Center for Education Statistics,
Common Core of Data and "Fall Enrollment in Institutions of Higher Education" surveys; Integrated Post-secondary Education Data System (IPEDS), Higher
Education General Information Survey (HEGIS), Fall Enrollment: Surveys, and
Projections of Education Statistics to 2007 (Washington, D.C., 1997) <*http://
nces.ed.gov/pubs/digest97/d97t002.html*>.
41. Coulson, *Market Education*, p. 277.

counterpart. Among other things we deducted all monies spent on transportation, special education, school lunches, other ancillary services, and the cost of financing the far-flung public school bureaucracy that runs the citywide, boroughwide, and districtwide operations.

Taking all these deductions from public school expenditures subtracted out of the analysis nearly 40 percent of the cost of running the New York City public schools. But even after taking all these deductions, public schools were still spending more than $5,000 per pupil each year, more than twice the $2,400 spent on similar services in the Catholic schools in the three boroughs. In other words, private schools, on average, do in fact have fewer fiscal expenditures.

For many years it was generally believed that the education typically provided by private schools was, as a result of these more limited resources, inferior to the education provided by public schools. As a result, researchers and policymakers were surprised when a national study, funded by the U.S. Office of Education, undertaken by a research team headed by the well-known, reputable sociologist James Coleman (later elected president of the American Sociological Association), found that students attending Catholic schools outperformed public school students.[42] This result was obtained even after Coleman and his colleagues took into account family background characteristics, which also affect school performance.

Coleman's surprising and upsetting findings were subjected to careful scrutiny. Many methodological issues were raised, and numerous similar studies have subsequently been undertaken. Some scholars continue to find that students learn more in Catholic and other private schools; other scholars do not detect any differences.[43] Two conclusions may be drawn from the literature, taken

42. James S. Coleman, Thomas Hoffer, and Sally Kilgore, *High School Achievement* (New York: Basic Books, 1982).

43. Major studies finding positive educational benefits from attending private schools include Chubb and Moe, *Politics, Markets,* 1990; Derek Neal, "The Effects of Catholic Secondary Schooling on Educational Achievement," University of Chicago, Harris School of Public Policy and National Bureau for Economic

as a whole: (1) Students, on average, learn at least as much (or more) in Catholic schools. (2) Although it is not altogether clear whether middle-class students learn more in Catholic schools, low-income, minority students clearly do. For this segment of the population, there is a definite advantage that comes from attending a private school.[44]

Where access to private schools is more readily available, their presence seems to provide desirable competition that spurs a positive response from public schools: The test scores of public-school students are higher, the likelihood that public-school students will attend college increases, and the wages they earn later in life are higher.[45]

## Home-Schooling

Home-schooling constitutes one of the more rapidly growing segments of the American educational systems. Although home-schooling has an enviable historic reputation—Abraham Lincoln was home-schooled, and so were Theodore and Franklin Delano Roosevelt—as late as 1980 only three states explicitly sanctioned this practice. But between 1982 and 1992, thirty-two states changed their compulsory school attendance rules so as to specifically allow families, under certain conditions, to educate their chil-

Research, 1996. Critiques of Coleman's findings and other studies have been prepared by Arthur S. Goldberger and Glen G. Cain, "The Causal Analysis of Cognitive Outcomes in the Coleman, Hoffer, and Kilgore Report," *Sociology of Education*, 55 (April–July 1982): 103–22; Douglas J. Wilms, "Catholic School Effects on Academic Achievement: New Evidence from the High School and Beyond Follow-up Study," *Sociology of Education* 58 (1985): 98–114.

44. John F. Witte, "School Choice and Student Performance," in Helen F. Ladd, ed., *Holding Schools Accountable: Performance-Based Reform in Education* (Washington, D.C.: Brookings, 1996), p. 167.

45. Caroline Minter Hoxby, "The Effects of Private School Vouchers on Schools and Students," in Helen F. Ladd, ed., *Holding Schools Accountable: Performance-Based Reform in Education* (Washington, D.C.: Brookings, 1996), pp. 177–208; Caroline Minter Hoxby, "Do Private Schools Provide Competition for Public Schools?" working paper 4978, Cambridge, Mass.: National Bureau of Economic Research, 1994.

dren at home.[46] But in recent years it has grown rapidly. The full size and extent of home-schooling is unknown; estimates of the number of students who are home-schooled vary between 0.5 million and 1.2 million.[47] Despite the fact that at least one study suggests that home-schoolers are learning more than schooled students,[48] the recent growth in home-schooling has generated a good deal of controversy. When a charter school in California offered its services to home-schooled students by means of the Internet, the state legislature passed a law limiting the practice to students within the county and adjacent counties.[49] Nonetheless, as the Internet's educational potential is more fully exploited, it is likely to give further impetus to the home-schooling movement.

*Voucher Programs*

Residential selection, magnet school, interdistrict enrollment, private schools, and charter schools are mechanisms that provide options to a wide range of groups, but, on balance, these options, when taken together, tend to give more choice to middle- than low-income families. Public and privately funded vouchers, as currently designed and operated, serve almost exclusively a low-income population. In this respect, they provide in a few places an

46. Christopher J. Klicka and Gregg Harris, *The Right Choice* (Gresham, Oreg.: Noble Publishing Associates, 1992), pp. 356–57, as cited in Coulson, *Market Education*, pp. 120–21.

47. Patricia Lines, "Home Schools: Estimating Numbers and Growth." U.S. Department of Education technical paper, 1998; Current Population Reports. Population Characteristics: School Enrollment—Social and Economic Characteristics of Students: October 1995. Paul Hill, University of Washington, has provided me with this information.

48. The study is based on a group of families who agreed to participate, making it difficult to generalize to all home-schooled students. Lawrence M. Rudner, "Scholastic Achievement and Demographic Characteristics of Home School Students in 1998," *Education Policy Analysis Archives* 7, no. 13 (April 1999). For a commentary on this article, see Kariane Mari Welner and Kevin G. Welner, "Contextualizing Home-schooling Data: A Response to Rudner," *Education Policy Analysis Archives* 7, no. 13 (April 1999).

49. Jessica L. Sandham, "Calif. Rules Hitting Home for Charter Schools," *Education Week*, September 8, 1999.

egalitarian complement to other choice programs by offering choice opportunities to those that otherwise have none.

School voucher programs have, with public and private funds, established themselves in many cities and states. In just ten years, the number of students involved has climbed from zero to more than sixty thousand. During the 1999–2000 school year, nearly fifty thousand students were participating in sixty-eight privately funded voucher programs, and another twelve thousand or more in three publicly funded ones.[50]

*Publicly funded voucher programs.* The three publicly funded voucher programs are to be found in Cleveland, Milwaukee, and the state of Florida. In Cleveland, students began matriculation in private schools in the fall of 1996; in the fall of 1999 the number of participating students was nearly four thousand. In 1999 students received a scholarship of up to $2,250, substantially less than the amount spent per student by Cleveland public schools or the amount provided to students at community schools.

The Milwaukee program, initially established in 1990, originally allowed students to attend schools without a religious affiliation. Only a few hundred students participated in the program in its first year. In the 1998–99 school year, the program, after overcoming constitutional objections, was expanded to include religious schools, and the number of participating students in 2000 increased to approximately twelve thousand. In that year participating students received a scholarship or voucher of up to nearly $5,000.[51] A fairly small number of students became eligible for participation in the Florida program for the first time in the fall of 1999 when the legislature said that students attending "failing" schools could apply for vouchers. In 1999 participating students could receive a scholarship or voucher of up to $3,389.[52] Initially,

50. Children First America, "68 Private Programs and Counting," *School Reform News*, October 1999, insert, p. B.

51. Paul E. Peterson and Jay P. Greene, "Vouchers and Central-City Schools," in Christopher H. Foreman Jr., ed., *The African American Predicament* (Washington, D.C.: Brookings, 1999), p. 85.

52. "Florida Begins Voucher Plan for Education," *New York Times*, August 17, 1999, p. A15.

only two schools met the legislative definition of failing, but many more were expected to fall within this category in subsequent years. But no additional students became eligible in 2000 because the concept of failing was redefined and the performances on state-wide tests of students attending potentially failing schools improved. All three of the publicly funded programs are designed in such a way that students are to be selected by means of a lottery, if the number of applicants exceeds the number of school spaces available.

*Privately funded voucher programs.* Privately funded voucher programs are operating in many cities. In 1999, the Children's Scholarship Fund greatly expanded the size and range of these programs by providing forty thousand vouchers to students from low-income families nationwide.

In the United States, the private sector often plays a major role in social experimentation. Ideas that are initially too untried and controversial for governments to attempt will often be explored by private or nonprofit entities, with the sponsorship of tax-exempt private foundations. The Ford Foundation sponsored the "gray areas" program that became the model for the community action program of the war on poverty established in 1965.[53] Results from evaluations of privately funded preschool programs provided the impetus for Head Start. Privately funded services for disabled students antedated and facilitated the design of the federally funded special education program enacted in 1975.[54] In all cases, privately funded programs provided important information to policymakers about the potential value of a social innovation.

Learning about school vouchers is taking place in much the same way. Several privately funded voucher programs are currently providing valuable information about the way in which voucher programs operate in practice. These privately funded voucher programs differ from traditional scholarship programs in

53. J. David Greenstone and Paul E. Peterson, *Race and Authority in Urban Politics: Community Participation and the War on Poverty* (New York: Russell Sage, 1973).

54. Paul E. Peterson, *Making the Grade* (New York: Twentieth Century Fund, 1983), chaps. 4–5.

two important ways. First, the offer of the voucher to students is not conditioned on student performance. If more applications are received than can be funded by resources available to the private foundation sponsoring the program, the vouchers are distributed either by means of a lottery or on a first-come, first-served basis. Second, the scholarship is not tied to a particular school or religious denomination. Instead, the family may choose from among a wide variety of participating secular or parochial schools with any one of a multiplicity of religious affiliations. In these ways, the private programs are approximations of what is developing in the public sector.

The privately funded voucher programs that have been studied by independent research teams are located in Dayton, the Edgewood school district in San Antonio, Indianapolis, New York City, and Washington, D.C. For the major characteristics of these programs as well as other voucher programs, see table 1.[55]

## RELATIONSHIPS AMONG SCHOOL CHOICE PROGRAMS

One cannot understand the full range of school choices available to families apart from an appreciation of the relationships among the wide variety of programs and policies that have been outlined. In every state, families have some choice of school, even if it is limited to paying for a private education or choosing to live in a neighborhood served by a school the family thinks desirable. In many metropolitan areas, including Cleveland, families have a choice among magnet schools, charter schools (designated as community schools in Ohio), and a voucher program—as well as selecting a neighborhood of choice or paying for a private school.

When several programs are located in the same place, they can affect one another in important ways. Schools that once participated in a voucher program may establish themselves as charter schools, perhaps because charter school funding generally exceeds state funding under voucher programs.[56] Parents with students in

55. This table is taken from Peterson and Greene, "Vouchers and Central City-Schools," p. 85.

56. Jeff Archer, "Two Cleveland Schools Plan Rebirth With Charter Status," *Education Week*, July 14, 1999.

## TABLE 1. CHARACTERISTICS OF SCHOOL CHOICE PROGRAMS FOR LOW-INCOME FAMILIES

| City or State | Sponsor | Religious Schools Included | Grades | First School Year | Initial Enrollment | 1999–2000 Enrollment | Number of Schools 1999–2000 | Maximum Payment 1999–2000 (in dollars) | Selection Method |
|---|---|---|---|---|---|---|---|---|---|
| Milwaukee | State of Wisconsin | No | preK–12 | 1990–91 | 341 | 7,913 | 93 | $5,106 | Lottery |
| Indianapolis | ECCT[a] | Yes | K–8 | 1991–92 | 746 | 2,600 | 85 | 800 | First come[b] |
| Milwaukee | PAVE[c] | Yes | K–12 | 1992–93 | 2,089 | 781 | 114 | 1,000/elem. 1,500/high | First come |
| San Antonio | CEO[d] | Yes | 1–8 | 1992–93 | 930 | 1,137[e] | 55[e] | 4,000[e] | First come |
| Washington, D.C. | WSF[f] | Yes | K–12[g] | 1993–94 | 30 | 1,300 | 120 | 1,700/elem. 2,200/high | Lottery |
| Cleveland | State of Ohio | Yes | K–8 | 1996–97 | 1,996 | 3,500 | 59[h] | 2,250[h] | Lottery |
| New York City | SCSF[i] | Yes | 1–5 | 1997–98 | 1,200 | 1,790 | 240 | 1,400 | Lottery |
| Dayton | PACE[j] | Yes | K–12 | 1998–99 | 542 | 680 | 46 | 1,785/elem. 2,300/high | Lottery |
| Florida | State of Florida | Yes | K–12 | 1999–2000 | 146 | 146 | 5 | 3,500 | Lottery |

a. Educational Choice Charitable Trust
b. Program enrollment in Indianapolis is supplemented with periodic lotteries.
c. Partners Advancing Values in Education
d. Children's Educational Opportunity
e. San Antonio data is for the 2000–2001 school year.
f. Washington Scholarship Fund, Inc.
g. Students must be in grades K–8 to begin the Washington program.
h. Cleveland data is for the 1999–99 school year.
i. School Choice Scholarships Foundation
j. Parents Advancing Choice in Education

private schools may decide to save money by enrolling their children in charter schools instead.

All these choice programs provide traditional public schools an incentive to modify their practices in such a way as to maintain their enrollments—and the per-pupil state aid that they have previously received. Already there is some evidence that the availability of school vouchers is affecting public school policies and practices. In the Edgewood school district in San Antonio, Texas, for example, the local school board accepted the resignation of its superintendent and, in a reversal of an earlier decision, established a school-uniform policy.[57] In Florida, the first two schools judged to be failing by the state—and therefore placed immediately in the voucher program—made significant policy changes after receiving their ignominious designation. One school introduced uniforms, a new phonics reading program, and class-size reduction in kindergarten; the other introduced Saturday and after-school tutoring sessions and had school staff visit parents at home to discourage truancy. Both schools have begun to focus on the basics of reading, writing, and math, in part by hiring more full-time reading and writing specialists.[58]

Within a year of the enlargement of the voucher program in Milwaukee, a new school board, elected in a hotly contested race, accepted the resignation of the school superintendent and announced its determination to respond to the challenges provided by the new choice arrangements. In Albany, New York, all the students at a particular elementary school (deemed to have the lowest scores in the city) were offered a voucher by a private individual; the school board responded by changing the principal, the teaching staff, and the curriculum.

More systematic evidence is available from ongoing research on other choice experiments. According to a study of the impact of

57. Anastasia Cisneros-Lunsford, "Munoz Leaving District, Edgewood Chief Gains New Position," *San Antonio Express-News*, September 10, 1999; Anastasia Cisneros-Lunsford, "Edgewood Oks Uniforms for Youngsters," *San Antonio Express-News*, April 28, 1999.

58. Jessica L. Sandham, "Schools Hit by Vouchers Fight Back," *Education Week*, September 15, 1999.

charter schools on traditional public schools in Arizona, "districts that have lost large numbers of children to charter schools make efforts to win those children back. Sometimes those efforts pay off."[59] Similarly, in Massachusetts, districts losing students to interdistrict programs are making efforts to retain their student body, with some apparent success.[60]

These are only preliminary pieces of information. It is not yet possible to know how this ferment in American education, which is undoubtedly giving families greater choice than previously available, will affect education policy and governance in the long run. Nor do we know for certain how school choice will affect students and families in the long run. It is important to continue to try out the full range of school options in a variety of contexts in order to determine which, if any, may benefit students and their families in the long term.

## WHEN VOUCHER PROGRAMS ARE INTRODUCED

Fortunately, a substantial amount of information has recently become available on the way in which the most controversial of all choice programs, school vouchers, works in practice. A series of studies provides us with valuable information about the kinds of students and families who participate in voucher programs; the reasons families select a particular school, when offered a voucher; the effects of vouchers on student learning; the school climate at voucher schools; and the impact of vouchers on homework, school-home communications, and parental satisfaction. Also, there is limited information available on the effects of school vouchers on civil society. In the remainder of this chapter, I shall identify some of the issues that have arisen around these topics and report results from recent evaluations.

59. Robert Maranto, Scott Milliman, Frederick Hess, and April Gresham, "Lessons from a Contested Frontier," in Robert Maranto, Scott Milliman, Frederick Hess, and April Gresham, eds., *School Choice in the Real World: Lessons from Arizona Charter Schools* (Boulder, Colo.: Westview, 1999), p. 237.

60. Susan L. Aud, *Competition in Education: 1999 Update of School Choice in Massachusetts* (Boston: Pioneer Institute for Public Policy Research, September 1999), p. 36.

## Voucher Recipients

Critics say that voucher programs will "skim" or "cherry-pick" the public schools, attracting the participation of the most talented students and the higher-income, better-educated families. As a consequence, public schools will be left with an increasingly difficult population to educate and without the support of informed, engaged parents. Defenders of vouchers have replied that families have little incentive to move their child from one school to another if the child is already doing well in school.

Considerable information is now available on the types of students and families who participate in means-tested voucher programs. In general, there is little evidence that voucher programs either skim the best and brightest students from public schools or attract only the lowest-performing students. On the contrary, voucher recipients resemble a cross-section of public school students, though in some cases they may come from somewhat more educated families.

In the Edgewood school district in San Antonio, Texas, vouchers were offered to all low-income residents. Those who accepted the vouchers had math scores that, on beginning their new private school, were similar to those of students in public schools and reading scores that were only modestly higher. Voucher students were no more likely to have been in programs for gifted students, though they were less likely to have been in special education. Household income was similar, as was the percentage of families with two parents in the household. Mothers of voucher recipients had, on average, an additional year of education.[61]

In Cleveland, the parents of students with vouchers were found to be of lower income and the mothers more likely to be African American than a random sample of public school parents. Mothers had less than a year's worth of additional education beyond

61. Paul E. Peterson, David Myers, and William Howell, "An Evaluation of the Horizon Scholarship Program in the Edgewood Independent School District, San Antonio, Texas: The First Year." Paper prepared under the auspices of the Program on Education Policy and Governance, Harvard University, 1999, tables 2, 3, pp. 41–42.

that of the public school mothers, and they were not significantly more likely to be employed full time.[62] Nor were the students themselves the "best and the brightest." On the contrary, students with vouchers were less likely to have been in a program for gifted or talented students than were children remaining in public schools. However, students with vouchers were less likely to have a learning disability.[63]

## Reasons for Accepting a Voucher and Attending Private School

Questions have been raised about the bases for the choices made by voucher participants. In the words of one group of critics, "when parents do select another school, academic concerns are not central to the decision."[64] To determine what was paramount in the minds of voucher participants, parents in the Edgewood school district in San Antonio were asked to give the *single* most important reason for their choice of private school. Nearly 60 percent of parents accepting vouchers said "academic quality," "teacher quality," or "what was taught in class" was the single most important reason. Only 15 percent listed the religious affiliation of the school as the single most important reason.[65] In New York City, parents who received vouchers were asked which considerations were very important for their choice of school. The six reasons most frequently mentioned were teacher quality, what is taught in class, safety, school discipline, school quality, and class size. Religious instruction was seventh on the list, convenient location was ninth, and the sports program and a school where a child's friend was attending were tied at the bottom of the list.[66]

62. Peterson, Howell, and Jay Greene, 1999, "An Evaluation of the Cleveland Scholarship Program," table 1, pp. 16–17.

63. Ibid., table 2, p. 18.

64. Carnegie Foundation for the Advancement of Teaching, p. 13.

65. Peterson, Myers, and Howell, "Horizon Scholarship," table 1.5, p. 44.

66. Paul Peterson, David Myers, and William Howell, "An Evaluation of the New York City School Choice Scholarships Program: The First Year." Paper prepared under the auspices of the Program on Education Policy and Governance, Harvard University, 1999, table 2, p. 35.

*Reasons for Not Using a Voucher*

When parents are asked about their reasons for not making use of a voucher, they provide a wide range of explanations for their decision. Most parents said that they had found a school they wanted their child to attend. Only a tiny percentage of those who do not find the school of their choice said that it was because they were not a member of the religious group with which the school is affiliated.

In New York City, for example, 72 percent of the families who were offered a voucher said they were able to attend a school the family preferred. Families could give multiple reasons for not finding the school of their choice. The reason parents most frequently offered (by 15 percent of the parents) was the cost of the school— the privately funded voucher in New York was only $1,400, which was significantly less than the tuition charged by most private schools.[67]

*School Quality and Student Learning*

Proponents of school vouchers expect that schools will perform better—and students will learn more—if families can choose their children's schools. There will be a better match between the students' needs and the schools' characteristics. A stronger identification between family and school will be realized. Preliminary information on some of these questions is now available.

*Test scores.*   The debate over student achievement is likely to continue for some years to come, not only because it is very difficult to measure how much children are learning in school but also because different groups and individuals have different views as to what in fact *should* be learned in school. According to test score results, African American students from low-income families who switch from public to a private school do considerably better after two years than students who do not receive a voucher opportunity. However, students from other ethnic backgrounds seem to learn

67. Ibid., table 5, p. 38.

after two years as much but no more in private schools than their public school counterparts.[68]

## High School Completion and College Attendance

It is too early to know what impact vouchers will have on high school completion rates and college attendance. However, information on the effects of attendance at a Catholic high school are contained in a recent University of Chicago analysis of the National Longitudinal Survey of Youth, conducted by the Department of Education, a survey of more than twelve thousand young people. Students from all racial and ethnic groups are more likely to go to college if they attended a Catholic school, but the effects are the greatest for urban minorities. The probability of graduating from college rises from 11 to 27 percent if such a student attends a Catholic high school.[69]

The University of Chicago study confirms results from two other analyses that show positive effects for low-income and minority students of attendance at Catholic schools on high school completion and college enrollment.[70] University of Wisconsin Professor John Witte points out that studies of private schools "indicate a substantial private school advantage in terms of completing high school and enrolling in college, both very important events in predicting future income and well-being. Moreover, . . . the effects

68. William G. Howell, Patrick J. Wolf, Paul E. Peterson, and David E. Campbell, "Test-Score Effects of School Vouchers in Dayton, Ohio, New York City, and Washington, D.C.: Evidence from Randomized Field Trials," paper presented before the annual meetings of the American Political Science Association, 2000. Available from Program on Education Policy and Governance, Kennedy School of Government, Harvard University, 2000, and at *http://data.fas.harvard.edu/pepg/.*

69. Derek Neal, "The Effects of Catholic Secondary Schooling on Educational Achievement," Harris School of Public Policy, University of Chicago, and National Bureau for Economic Research, 1996, p. 26.

70. William N. Evans and Robert M. Shwab, "Who Benefits from Private Education? Evidence from Quantile Regressions," Department of Economics, University of Maryland, 1993; David Siglio and Joe Stone, "School Choice and Student Performance: Are Private Schools Really Better?" University of Wisconsin Institute for Research on Poverty, 1977.

were most pronounced for students with achievement test scores in the bottom half of the distribution."[71]

*School discipline.*   School discipline seems to be more effective in the private schools voucher students attend than in the inner-city public schools their peers are attending. Parents and students who have received vouchers report less fighting, cheating, property destruction, and other forms of disruption than do the parents and students who are in public schools.

In Washington, D.C., students in grades five through eight were asked whether or not they felt safe at school. Twenty percent of the public school students said they did not feel safe, as compared to 5 percent of the private school students.[72]

Nationwide information on public and private schools yields similar information. A survey undertaken by Educational Testing Service found that eighth-grade students encounter more such problems in public than in private schools. Fourteen percent of public school students, but only 2 to 3 percent of private school students, say physical conflicts are a serious or moderate problem. Four percent of public school students report racial or cultural conflicts are a serious or moderate problem and 5 per cent say drug use is, while less than 1 percent of private school students indicate they are. Nine percent of public school students say they feel unsafe in school, but only 4 percent of private school students give the same response.[73]

---

71. John F. Witte, "School Choice and Student Performance," in Helen F. Ladd, ed., *Holding Schools Accountable: Performance-Based Reform in Education* (Washington, D.C.: Brookings, 1996), p. 167.

72. Paul E. Peterson, Jay Greene, William Howell, and William McCready, "Initial Findings from an Evaluation of School Choice Programs in Dayton, Ohio and Washington, D.C.," Paper prepared under the auspices of the Program on Education Policy and Governance, Harvard University, table 9A, p. 53. This finding remains statistically significant after adjustments are made for family background characteristics.

73. Information in the preceding two paragraphs contained in Paul E. Barton, Richard J. Coley, and Harold Wenglinsky, *Order in the Classroom: Violence, Discipline and Student Achievement* (Princeton, N.J.: Policy Information Center, Research Division, Educational Testing Service, 1998), pp. 21, 23, 25, 27, and 29.

*Homework.*   Parents of students in voucher programs report
that their children have more homework than do the parents of
students in public schools. This finding was consistent across a
range of studies. In Cleveland, parents of students in the voucher
program were significantly less likely than a cross-section of Cleveland public school parents to report that "teachers do not assign
enough homework."[74] In New York City, 55 per cent of the parents with students in private schools reported that their child had
more than one hour of homework a day, while only 34 percent of
a comparable group of students remaining in public schools reported this much homework.[75] Similarly, in the Edgewood school
district in San Antonio, 50 percent of the parents of students receiving vouchers reported more than one hour of homework,
while only 16 percent of parents of students in public schools reported this much homework.[76]

*Parental–school communications.*   Parents of students in
voucher programs report more extensive communications with
their school than do parents with children in public schools. In
Cleveland, "parents of scholarship students reported participating
in significantly more activities than did parents of public school
students." Results from a teacher survey further "support this
finding."[77] Similarly, in New York City, parents of students in private schools reported that they were more likely to receive grade
information from the school, participate in instruction, attend
parent nights, and attend regular parent-teacher conferences.[78] In
the Edgewood school district in San Antonio, parents of students
with vouchers were more likely to report that they had attended a

74. Peterson, Howell, and Greene, "Cleveland Evaluation," table 5, p. 23.

75. Paul E. Peterson, David Myers, William Howell, and Daniel Mayer, "An
Evaluation of School Vouchers in New York City," in Mayer and Peterson, 1999,
table 12-2, p. 328.

76. "An Evaluation of School Choice Scholarships," table 1.13, p. 52. Similar
results were obtained when school effects were estimated controlling for family
background characteristics. See table 2.4, p. 63.

77. Kim K. Metcalf et al., 1998, pp. 18–19.

78. Peterson, Myers, Howell, and Mayer, "School Vouchers," table 12–3,
p. 329.

school activity at least once in the past month than were parents of students in public schools. They were also more likely to report that they had attended a parent-teacher conference.[79]

### Suspensions, Expulsions, Absenteeism, and School Changes

Most educators think that, all things being equal, it is better that students stay in the same school, especially during a given school year; students usually learn more when not subjected to the disruption that comes from changing schools. Of course, parents should be allowed to move their child from one school to another if family circumstances require or if a school is not suitable. But forced changes in the middle of an elementary education—either by government fiat or by an individual school—should not be undertaken, unless the reasons for doing so are compelling.

Most studies indicate that students in voucher programs do not move from one school to another any more frequently than do students in public schools. Also, suspension rates were essentially the same for students with vouchers and for students in public schools. However, in Washington, D.C., suspension rates were higher for voucher students in grades six through eight the first year they entered private school.

These findings are not peculiar to Cleveland. In the Edgewood school district in San Antonio, voucher parents were no more likely to report their child had been suspended than were public school parents. And the parents of students in the voucher program were more likely than public school parents to say their child had remained in the same school all year long. Plans for attending the school during the coming year were similar for the two groups of families. Less than 1 percent of parents of students with vouchers reported that their child had been asked not to return.[80]

## PARENTAL SATISFACTION

Many economists think that consumer satisfaction is the best measure of school quality, just as it is the best measure of any product.

79. Peterson, Myers, and Howell, "An Evaluation of School Choice Scholarships," table 1.14, p. 53.
80. Ibid., tables 1.18, 1.19, pp. 58–59.

According to this criterion, vouchers are a clear success. All evaluations of vouchers have found higher levels of parental satisfaction among parents receiving vouchers than among comparison groups of parents with students in public schools. In Cleveland, voucher parents were much more satisfied with their school than parents who had applied for but did not use the voucher offered to them. For example, 63 percent of the parents with vouchers said they were very satisfied with the academic quality of the school, as compared to 29 percent of those who had not used them. Similar differences in satisfaction levels were observed for school safety, school discipline, class size, and parental involvement.[81]

Some interpreted these findings as showing only that those who had applied for but not received a voucher were particularly unhappy with their public school, not that private school families were particularly satisfied. Those not receiving the voucher or scholarship might simply be called a bunch of "sour grapes" uncharacteristic of public school parents in general. To ascertain whether the "sour grape" hypothesis was correct, the satisfaction levels of voucher parents were compared with the satisfaction levels of a random sample of all of Cleveland's low-income, public school parents. Very little support for the "sour grape" hypothesis could be detected. Voucher parents were considerably more satisfied with the academic program, school safety, school discipline, and other characteristics of the school their child was attending if the child had a voucher.[82]

The findings from other cities parallel those in Cleveland. In Milwaukee, the evaluation team found that "in all three years, choice parents were more satisfied with choice schools than they had been with their prior public schools and more satisfied than [Milwaukee public school] parents with their schools. . . . Attitudes were more positive on every item, with 'discipline in the school' showing the greatest increase in satisfaction."[83] Studies of the Indianapolis program and an early voucher program in San

81. Greene, Howell, and Peterson, table 1.8, p. 56.
82. Peterson, Howell, and Greene, table 3c, p. 21.
83. Witte, "Who Benefits from the Milwaukee Choice Program?" p. 132.

Antonio (predating the one in the Edgewood school district) also found higher levels of parental satisfaction, when families with vouchers were compared to families with students in public schools.[84] A comparison of similar groups of students from low-income families attending public and private schools in Washington, D.C., and Dayton, Ohio, also found much higher levels of parental satisfaction with the private schools.[85]

## IMPACT OF VOUCHER PROGRAMS ON CIVIL SOCIETY

A major concern of critics of school vouchers involves their potential impact on civil society. Even if students learn to read, write, and calculate more by means of a voucher program, these gains will be more than offset, it is argued, by the polarization and balkanization of our society that necessarily accompany greater parental choice in education. In the words of commentator Michael Kelley, "public money is shared money, and it is to be used for the furtherance of shared values, in the interests of *e pluribus unum*. Charter schools and their like . . . take from the *pluribus* to destroy the *unum*."[86] Amy Gutmann, the Princeton political theorist, makes much the same argument, if in less colorful prose: "Public, not private, schooling is . . . the primary means by which citizens can morally educate future citizens."[87]

Some information about the impact of vouchers on civil society is now available. Despite the concerns many have expressed, vouchers typically have positive effects on racial and ethnic integration, racial and ethnic conflict, political participation, civic participation, and political tolerance.

84. David J. Weinschrott and Sally B. Kilgore, "Evidence from the Indianapolis Voucher Program," in Peterson and Hassel, *Learning from School Choice,* pp. 307–34; R. Kenneth Godwin, Frank R. Kemerer, and Valerie J. Martinez, "Comparing Public Choice and Private Voucher Programs in San Antonio," in Peterson and Hassel, *Learning from School Choice,* pp. 275–306.

85. Peterson, Greene, Howell, and McCready, tables 7A, 7B, pp. 49–50.

86. Michael Kelly, "Dangerous Minds," *New Republic,* December 20, 1996.

87. Amy Gutmann, *Democratic Education* (Princeton, N.J.: Princeton University Press, 1987), p. 70.

## Racial and Ethnic Integration

Private schools are more likely than public schools—or at least no less likely—to be racially and ethnically integrated, perhaps because private schools can draw students from a more extensive catchment area, and religious schools may provide a common tie that cuts across racial lines.

Nationally, private school classrooms are estimated to be 7 percentage points more integrated than public schools.[88] Consistent with the national picture, voucher recipients in New York City moved from a less racially integrated to a more racially integrated setting when they left public schools for private ones.[89] However, no differences between public and private schools were observed in the Edgewood school district.[90]

In Edgewood, students were asked with whom they ate lunch, because interracial conversations at lunch time suggests that students enjoy eating together, a particularly meaningful finding. Students with vouchers were just as likely as public school students to say that they ate lunch with people of other ethnic backgrounds. Another study of public and private schools in San Antonio that directly observed students at lunch found that students in private schools were in fact more likely to sit with someone of another racial group at lunch time than students attending public schools.[91]

## Racial Conflict in School

Students in private schools are often less likely to be engaged in or witness racial conflicts. Nationally, more interracial friendships are reported by students in private schools than in public schools. Students also report less interracial fighting in private schools than

88. Jay P. Greene, "Civic Values in Public and Private Schools," in Peterson and Hassel, *Learning from School Choice*, p. 97.

89. Peterson, Myers, and Howell, table 6, p. 39.

90. Peterson, Myers, and Howell, table 8, p. 47.

91. Jay P. Greene and Nicole Mellow, "Integration Where It Counts: A Study of Racial Integration in Public and Private School Lunchrooms," report number 98–13, Program on Education Policy and Governance, Kennedy School of Government, Harvard University, 1998.

public ones, as also do administrators and teachers.[92] Consistent with these national findings, parents of students with vouchers in Cleveland reported less racial conflict than students in public schools.[93] Similar differences between public and private schools were reported by parents in New York City, Washington, D.C., and Dayton, Ohio.[94] However, in the Edgewood school district students in public and private schools were equally likely to report racial conflict at their school.[95]

### Civic Participation and Political Tolerance

Private school students are also more community-spirited than those enrolled in public schools. Nationwide, students at private schools are more likely to think that it is important to help others and volunteer for community causes. They also are more likely than public school students to report that they in fact did volunteer in the past two years. Finally, private school students were more likely to say their school expected them to volunteer.[96]

Public school administrators themselves (in a confidential survey) are less likely to say their school does an outstanding job of promoting citizenship than private school administrators do. Similar differences appear when administrators are asked to rate their school's performance in teaching values and morals or promoting awareness of contemporary and social issues.[97] Students educated in private schools are also more likely to be tolerant of unpopular groups.[98]

92. Greene, "Civic Values," p. 99.

93. Paul E. Peterson, William Howell, and Jay Greene, "An Evaluation of the Cleveland Voucher Program After Two Years," Paper prepared under the auspices of the Program on Education Policy and Governance, Harvard University, table 6, p. 24.

94. Peterson, Myers, and Howell, "An Evaluation of School Choice Scholarships," table 8, p. 41; Peterson, Greene, Howell, and McCready, "Washington, D.C., and Dayton Evaluation," tables 9A, 9B, pp. 53–54.

95. Peterson, Myers, and Howell, table 1.8, p. 47.

96. Greene, "Civic Values," p. 101.

97. Ibid., pp. 102–3.

98. Jay Greene, Joseph Giammo, and Nicole Mellow, "The Effect of Private Education on Political Participation, Social Capital, and Tolerance: An Examina-

## CONCLUSIONS

Choice in American education is now widespread and has taken many forms—charters, magnet schools, tax-deduction programs, interdistrict enrollment programs, private schools, choice by residential selection, and school vouchers. Many of these programs give greater choice to middle- and upper-income families than to poor families. In this context, school vouchers, as currently designed, provide an egalitarian supplement to existing choice arrangements. They do so without restricting choices to parents with specific religious affiliation or any religious affiliation at all. Given the widespread public interest in finding better ways of educating disadvantaged children, it is particularly important that pilot voucher programs be continued so as to permit an assessment of the effectiveness of school vouchers as tools for achieving greater equity in American education, especially since early evaluations of their effectiveness have yielded promising results. If vouchers don't work, they will be discarded. If vouchers do work, their adoption will gradually spread. But if their exploration is prematurely ended, the country will be denied a valuable tool that could help it consider the best ways of improving its educational system.

---

tion of the Latino National Political Survey," working paper, Program on Education Policy Governance, Kennedy School of Government, Harvard University, 1998.

# CHAPTER 11

# What Is Public about Public Education?

*Paul T. Hill*

Some say that public education is threatened and beleaguered. In big cities, where many parents have lost confidence in their neighborhood schools and want out, public education might cease to exist. The threat comes from initiatives like vouchers, charter schools, schools provided by for-profit firms, and private scholarship programs that let disadvantaged children attend private schools. These concerns are familiar to any moderately attentive reader of newspaper editorial pages.

How can this be so in a nation that has long been committed to universal education? What has come of America's belief that an educated population is the bulwark of democracy? Have we given up on the idea that free people must be able to inform themselves, understand arguments in light of their own interests, and support themselves economically so they can avoid economic coercion? If public education is threatened, does this mean we have abandoned these commitments?

I argue that America's commitment to public education is stronger than ever and that the initiatives claimed to threaten it do nothing of the sort. Our commitment to universal education is sustained, not threatened, by initiatives that try to create new schooling options for children in low-performing schools. Willingness to disrupt existing institutions shows that we as a people can tell the difference between an unchanging commitment and a changeable instrument. Existing schools—and alternatives like voucher programs and charter schools—are neither good nor bad in themselves. Their value, or lack of it, comes from the purpose they serve. Schooling institutions that educate children effectively and prepare them for full participation in a democratic society have great value. Institutions that do not fulfill that purpose have little or no value.

In everyday language we identify a public school as a building that provides instruction for children in a particular neighborhood. But no one would seriously contend that a building is what makes a school public. Buildings can be abandoned, and they can even be sold or leased to businesses and to schools run by religious groups. So, what makes a school public? Being overseen by a an elected school board? Being supported by tax dollars and offering instruction at no cost to parents? Serving absolutely any child who lives in a defined attendance zone? Accepting any form of behavior or degree of effort that any child cares to exhibit? Being subject to laws and regulations promulgated by the state legislature? Being free to employ only those teachers who belong to a particular union? Being perfectly racially integrated, so that the student body and teaching force exactly reflect the ethnic composition of the local community? Having a fixed curriculum so that all teachers cover exactly the same material on the same schedule?

In fact, none of those attributes identify a public school. Not all local school boards are elected. School districts can and do assign some students (usually those with special needs) to attend schools run by churches or other private organizations. Some schools run by local school boards charge tuition and fees. Some occupy privately owned buildings. Some have admissions priorities and can turn down students who lack prerequisite training or to enhance racial balance. Some have strict attendance and behavior codes, and all can require unruly children to go elsewhere. All schools, including those run by churches and for-profit organizations, are governed by state laws and regulations protecting children. Some states forbid teacher collective bargaining and closed union shops. Few schools run by local school boards exactly mirror the ethnic composition of the surrounding community, and many diverge far from it. Some school boards authorize magnet and experimental schools that use distinctive methods of instruction and follow their own schedules.

Public education cannot be defined in concrete terms as an activity that is done by specific people in a particular place or via a particular method. Public education is a goal, ensuring that every American knows enough, and has all the required skills, to take a full part in our country's social, economic, and political life. Public education is not a fixed institution but a standard against which institutions are measured. Thus, a school does not accomplish the goal of public education just because it is provided by government.

The current condition of our inner-city schools proves that government is capable of providing schools that do not give children what they need to become full participants in modern society. Nor does faithfully implementing the decisions of a majority ensure that schools will produce graduates who have all the knowledge and skills necessary for full participation in our country's social, economic, and political life. Majorities can decide to run all schools in ways that fit their members' values and serve members' children effectively but that do not meet the needs of families in the minority. Majorities can also mandate that all teaching will be done in a particular way even if other feasible methods would be better for some children. These outcomes can be called democratic but they do not achieve public education's goal, to help every child gain the knowledge and skills he or she needs to be a fully functioning member of an open, diverse, economically prosperous and fair society.

However obvious these points may be, there are those who would not agree with them. Amy Gutmann and Dennis Thompson write approvingly of a communitywide deliberation in which parents from the religious right were rebuffed in their objection to certain instructional modules in social studies.[1] They endorse the

---

1. Amy Gutmann and Dennis Thompson, *Democracy and Disagreement; Why Moral Conflict Cannot Be Avoided in Politics, and What Should Be Done About It* (Cambridge, Mass.: The Belknap Press of Harvard University Press, 1996), pp. 63–66.

conclusion reached via deliberation: the majority offered these parents an ultimatum—accept these materials for your children or leave the publicly supported schools and pay for your own. However Gutmann and Thompson offer no evidence (because none exists) that the instructional materials in question would have had the desired effects on children's attitudes or that students who did not encounter these materials would somehow become less desirable citizens.

Defining public education as a result of deliberation whose results are binding on everyone eliminates the possibility of differentiated solution—where parents who object to a particular sequence of instruction would not have to subject their children to it. Gutmann and Thompson are right that the dissident minority could not legitimately prevent the majority from using social studies materials that they believed good for the community and for children. However, a differentiated solution, possibly including a new school with an approach to instruction acceptable to the dissident parents, or simply an option in social studies, might lead to more effective educational experiences for all the community's children. The solution would have taken extra work, but it would not have been as costly as a protracted conflict where dissident parents disrupt the school and where those families' children attend school under a cloud.

There is, in short, no reason why "public" must mean "uniform" or coercive. Of course, politics and government matter in education. Government uses its authority to compel children to attend school, and all citizens are taxed so that all children can be taught. But that does not mean that schools *are* government or that politics should determine everything schools do. Like the human body, which needs certain chemicals such as salt but can be destroyed by too much, public education needs government and politics but can be destroyed by them. Some attributes of government—inflexibility, caution, and focus on procedure—work against the flexibility and individualization required by effective education. Some attributes of politics—turbulence, self-seeking by interest groups, and the expectations that winners take all—are in tension with the idea that public education must prepare everyone, not just those on the winning side.

My objective in this chapter is to convince readers that everything "public" in public education is not captured by the term "government run"—that public education is not defined by school boards that act as little legislatures, by categorical funding, by civil service employment of teachers, or by a government monopoly. Public education rests on something deeper, a permanent American commitment to educating children by whatever means work.[2]

In areas of endeavor where there is great uncertainty about what is needed and what will work, constant creation and testing of options is not merely permissible but necessary. In light of these facts—that different children need different things and that the links between a particular approach to instruction and results are uncertain—the cause of public education is served, not harmed, by allowing parents to seek what their children need and encouraging multiple competing organizations to provide options.

That is why I argue that current efforts to experiment and create options for children, going under many names from vouchers to charters and school contracting, are signs of the health of our national commitment to public education, not threats to it.

Defining public education as a broad national commitment rather than a specific set of institutions raises as many questions as it settles. Children have finite amounts of time, so they must attend particular schools, not all possible schools. Similarly, communities have finite amounts of money available to pay for schooling, so some choices must be made. For any particular group of children or community, there must be some process of choice among all the possibilities. Public education is enhanced if community choice processes are open to differentiated solutions, amenable to evidence, and constantly revisited. Public education is diminished if community choice processes are arbitrarily limited to serve the economic interests of particular providers or consumer groups or to privilege certain political or ideological interests.

2. For a review of the many possible meanings of the "public" in public education, see Frederick M. Hess, "Making Sense of 'Public' in Public Education, University of Virginia (draft available from the author), 2000.

After years of stagnation, Americans' ideas about what public education should be and what it should accomplish are very much in flux. The question to be answered is clear: How can we as a society best use tax revenues, the regulatory power of the state, and the scarce time of children to create a more democratic, just, and economically secure society? Nobody has the answer, but people of goodwill, many of whom do not agree with one another, are searching for it.

This chapter explores these arguments more deeply in light of a particular case, as described below.

## WHAT CAN BE DONE ABOUT SARIE'S EDUCATION?

Patricia has a daughter, Sarie, who attends second grade in a local district-run school. Patricia is worried about how well Sarie is learning to read. From early in the first grade, Patricia has known that Sarie was not reading as well as her sister's son who is the same age but goes to school in a different district. Patricia has gone to the school to see about what can be done about Sarie, and she has been worried about what she has seen. Teachers and the principal seem harassed, and though they are willing to talk with her, she gets the feeling that they don't see anything unusual about Sarie's reading level. She has observed classes and is never quite sure when the children are supposed to learn reading. She has talked to other parents, some of whom share her concerns, and she and three other parents have talked with the principal, who listened respectfully but said, "there is nothing I can do about this; your children have experienced teachers."

Patricia visits a religious school in the neighborhood, and sees a big difference. The place is peaceful and studious and it is obvious that children are reading. At the New Year's break, Patricia takes advantage of a publicly funded voucher program targeted on low-income minority children in low-performing schools, and enrolls Sarie in the religious school.

I address three questions that arise from the scenario:[3]

First, in pulling Sarie out of her first school and placing her in one run by a private organization, did Patricia weaken public education?

3. If the scenario were changed so that Patricia placed Sarie in an independently run charter school, these questions would be the same. The ensuing discussion emphasizes vouchers and private schools, but a focus on charter schools would not alter the analysis.

Second, was the voucher program harming public education by reducing by one the number of children for whom her former school
could claim public funds?

Third, in providing an alternative to the school provided by the
city school system, were the religious organization and its financial
supporters working against the cause of public education?

Some readers might bridle at the implication that a mother who
chooses a better school for her daughter is failing a civic duty; or
that the teachers and administrators who toil for low pay in inner-
city religious and independent schools are harming poor children
who remain in the district-run schools; or that individuals and institutions that put money into such schools are enemies of public
education. However, these points are definitely in dispute.

In one day, three letters to the editor of the *New York Times*
defined the range of ways people think about these questions.[4]
Commenting on an April 15, 2000, op-ed piece in which Samuel
G. Freedman argued that New York Schools Chancellor Harold
O. Levy should be required to transfer his children from the private schools they now attend to schools run by the city school
system, one writer says that Levy "should give his children the
opportunity he had as a boy to experience the racial, cultural, and
economic diversity that is available in the New York City public
schools. . . . Imagine a world in which the governing elite enrolled
their children in public schools: just think how conditions would
improve for the children and their teachers!" A second writer
pointed out a parent's responsibility to do the best possible for his
or her own child: "If he [Mr. Freedman] were appointed administrator of public hospitals would he similarly rely on public hospitals if he or his family members were seriously ill? If he became the
top Housing Authority administrator would he move his family to
the projects?" A third writer, a New York City high school teacher,
agreed that Mr. Levy's obligation depends on the quality of the
schools. "He should want the best for his children, and the New
York City system should provide it. The problems are many, and

4. "The Schools Chief, and a Parent," editorials/letters, *New York Times*,
April 19, 2000, p. A22.

he should immediately make every effort to enlist talented people of character, sensitivity, and leadership into the system. Perhaps when there is improvement in the public domain of education, Mr. Levy will then enroll his own children."

I will try to eliminate the confusion evident in the argument about parents' choices by showing that Patricia, Mr. Levy, and other parents who leave failing schools in favor of schools that they conscientiously believe will be more effective with their children are acting in the public interest; that the voucher program that paid for Sarie's schooling in a parochial school is not harming but advancing the cause of public education; and that schools providing these options are advancing the cause of public education. The common premise from which all these conclusions follow is that whatever educates the public's children is public education.

### PARENTS CHOOSING EFFECTIVE SCHOOLS ARE ACTING IN THE PUBLIC INTEREST

Does Sarie's mother have an obligation to keep her child in a school in which she is not learning? Some would say yes, that she has an obligation to serve the public interest, which is promoted by ensuring that all children are educated together, whether or not an individual child learns. They recognize that parents worry about their own children. "As parents we want [our children] to do well in school—both academically and socially—so they will find a satisfying job and get ahead in life. This is a *private* purpose of schooling."[5]

These authors exhibit confusion about a distinction that economists and political scientists draw between private and public

---

5. Bruce Fuller, Elizabeth Burr, Lisa Huerta, Susan Puryear, and Edward Wexler, *School Choice: Abundant Hopes, Scarce Evidence of Results* (Berkeley: Policy Analysis for California Education, 1999), p. 9. See also Valerie E. Lee, Robert B. Croninger, and Julia B. Smith, "Equity and Choice in Detroit," in Bruce Fuller and Richard F. Elmore, eds., *Who Chooses? Who Loses: Culture, Institutions, and the Unequal Effects of School Choice* (New York: Teachers College Press, 1996), p. 88.

goods.[6] In this distinction a private good has two attributes: it can be enjoyed by some individuals and not by others, and its supply is limited so that consumption by one person reduces the opportunities of others. A public good, on the other hand, is one whose use and benefits cannot be limited to just a few individuals, but which affect everyone. Thus, national security is considered a public good; a candy bar eaten by one person is a private good.

Is children's learning to read, work, analyze, and advance themselves a private or a public good? It is both: an individual and his or her family benefit from learning these things but so does the broader society.[7]

The position that an individual child's learning to read is a purely private good is easy to articulate, but it does not hold water. Consider the possibility that all the parents in a city chose to keep their children in district-run schools, despite such severely dwindling quality that eventually none of the school graduates could read and debate well enough to take part in community life or perform a productive job.[8] In that case, the whole city would be harmed, by a whole generation of people not prepared for democratic citizenship and unable to sustain a modern economy. Any one individual's skills (or ignorance) has a small but real impact on the community as a whole.

What is a parent's obligation? Should Sarie's mother (or for that matter New York City Schools Chancellor Levy) sacrifice her own

6. See, for example, Paul A. Samuelson, "The Pure Theory of Public Expenditures," *Review of Economics and Statistics* 36:387–89, 1997; James S. Coleman, *Foundations of Social Theory* (Cambridge, Mass.: The Belknap Press of Harvard University Press, 1990), p. 34; and Dennis W. Carlton, and Jeffrey W. Perloff, *Modern Industrial Organization* (New York: Harper Collins, 1994), p. 116.

7. Charles Wolf has called education a "quasi-public good—quasi because although the whole community benefits from having individuals who are smart and capable, those individuals also benefit personally." See Charles Wolf Jr., *Markets or Governments: Choosing between Imperfect Alternatives* (Cambridge, Mass.: MIT Press, 1988), p. 38.

8. Tragically, exactly this result has occurred in some areas of our greatest cities, where only half the children complete high school and many graduates are marginally literate.

child's learning? Again some would claim that individual children must be sacrificed to the public interest. In discussing a case very like Sarie's, education researcher Valerie Lee and others comment that the removal of more than a few such children (and their parents) "from inner-city schools would have a noticeably negative effect on schools that enroll large proportions of disadvantaged children." The same authors "urge policymakers, educators, and families to consider the potential effects of such social policies [i.e., in the authors' earlier words, valuing the free will of individuals to seek a better life] on all poor and minority families, even if those policies seem to offer some benefit to individuals and families."[9]

These authors would argue that Sarie should not have left her neighborhood district-run school for two reasons: first, because her departure could hurt the school and, second, because Patricia's efforts on Sarie's behalf might have led the whole school to improve.

Do the departures of individuals hurt schools? There is rhetoric about this topic but no firm evidence. For every anecdote about teachers being discouraged by the departure of the child of a caring parent, there is a counteranecdote about children who, on the departure of a child who was the apple of the teacher's eye, benefited by receiving more attention.[10] Arrayed against stories about how a particular school has been weakened by declining enrollment are studies showing that competition strengthens all the schools in a community.[11] For every story about a heroic parent's effort to turn

9. Lee, Croninger, and Smith, *Equity and Choice in Detroit*, p. 89.

10. The literature on tracking (assigning children to different instructional programs based on proxies [or race] taken to indicate academic ability) shows that minority children who attend school outside their neighborhoods are *more* likely to be assigned to less challenging tracks than similar children in predominantly minority schools. See Jeannie Oakes, *Multiplying Inequalities: The Effects of Race, Social Class, and Tracking on Opportunities to Learn Mathematics and Science* (Santa Monica, Calif., RAND, 1990).

11. Caroline M. Hoxby, "Does Competition among Public Schools Benefit Students and Taxpayers?" *American Economic Review*, 2000. See also Mark Schneider and Paul Teske, "School Choice Builds Community," *The Public-Interest*, fall 1997. See also Schneider and Teske, "Institutional Arrangements and Social Capital: Public School Choice," pp. 86–90. *American Political Science Review*, 1997.

around a low-performing school, there are stories of parents who have tried for years to improve a bad school and failed, to the detriment of their own children and to the benefit of no one.

Some parents may choose altruistically to stay in weak schools despite possible risks to their own children. But when parents subject their children to unnecessary risks, altruism can look more like abdication of responsibility. Consider a parent who can afford to move out of a violence-ridden neighborhood but decides to stay, hoping to minister to the fallen and possibly to provide, in the person of his orderly and nonviolent child, an example to others. If that child were maimed or killed by neighborhood gunfire, wouldn't many people of goodwill think she had sacrificed her own child to a dubious principle? Of course, clear evidence that the children of such pioneers were never injured, and that their presence always helped others, might change the argument.

The idea that a parent like Patricia has an obligation to fight for others' children has some moral appeal. We are right to admire parents who do this, up to a point. They are justified in standing and fighting if they have a practical chance of making a difference quickly enough to prevent harm to their own child's education.

Debate about parents' rights and obligations toward choosing schools often hinge on ideas proposed by A. O. Hirschman. He identified three ways that customers (including school parents) can influence the quality of goods and services offered by business firms and government agencies: *exit* (when dissatisfied, finding another provider), *voice* (demanding improvements), and *loyalty* (staying with a provider and working to improve its performance). In general he argues that the three modes of influence go together; in particular, the effectiveness of voice and loyalty is enhanced by the ever-present possibility of exit. However, he makes a special argument for schools, saying that middle-class parents should use voice rather than exit because their demands for school quality can lead to improvements that benefit all students.

Hirschman assumed that the quality of a school's services is indivisible, so that an improvement made to satisfy a vocal parent benefits all. That turns out to be wrong, at least most of the time.

Schools have limited supplies of things parents want—access to the best teachers, the most prestigious programs, competent instruction in science and mathematics—and these assets are frequently rationed on the basis of parental assertiveness.[12] Thus, demanding parents who stay in a troubled school might not raise its overall quality. They can corner the best it has to offer, possibly leaving the remaining students with below-average classes and teachers.

Some things about schools can be indivisible and enjoyed by all. Examples include safety and the attractiveness of building and grounds. These do seem to benefit from the efforts of vocal parents. But the things that matter most about schools often do not improve across the board.

Clearly, a commitment to voice without exit does not eliminate competition and self-seeking. Aggressive and sophisticated parents use voice to get what their children need. And they can feel justified in doing so. But they should not deceive themselves that their presence helps other students who might in fact get less of what the schools have to offer. Sophisticated parents' activism can even weaken the position of less sophisticated parents who might, if the more aggressive parents exercised exit, be taken more seriously by teachers and principals.

But what if many other parents imitate Patricia: Wouldn't the school Sarie left then have so little money that it could not continue to run all the programs it offered before families started leaving? This can and does happen. Schools of all sorts, including schools run by churches and private organizations, have suffered declines in enrollment due to loss of family support. Some have adapted their programs to provide effective instruction to the children remaining, and others have continued to decline until all families left them. In the former cases, the children left behind are frequently better off in schools that have faced their weaknesses and rethought their programs. In cases where troubled schools have ultimately closed, children served by the abandoned schools have then enrolled in other schools.

12. See, for example, Alfie Kohn, "Only for My Kid: How Privileged Parents Undermine School Reform," *Phi Delta Kappan*, April 1998, pp. 569–77.

Whether enrollment decline in a school harms or benefits children depends more on the actions of teachers and administrators—both in the schools left behind and in other schools in which the children might enroll—than on the actions of families who left in search of a better option. Similarly, whether the ultimate collapse and abandonment of a school harms or advances the goals of public education depends on what happens to the children. An individual school is not public education but an instrument that is either effective or ineffective in promoting the goal of ensuring that all children learn enough to be able to take a full part in our country's social, economic, and political life.

Thus we reach a negative answer to the question "Do the parents of children who are not well served by their neighborhood schools have an obligation as citizens to stand and fight?" The answer is surely no. Individuals should not have to sacrifice their own children's futures for a vague possibility of helping others and are certainly not compelled to engage in a fruitless effort. No public purpose would have been served by Sarie's staying in a school that was not teaching her to read. The principle of democratic theory that one accepts an adverse decision in the hope of prevailing later does not apply here: a mother who sacrifices her daughter's one opportunity to learn as a child can never regain what has been lost.

In a situation where a parent has no assurance that her actions can improve schooling for other children, her private interest and the goals of public education point in the same direction. Patricia should do anything she can to make sure her child learns the skills and habits necessary for full membership in adult society.

## People Giving Children Choices Are Acting in the Public Interest

Are private individuals who put their own money into vouchers (or put their time and money into creating new charter schools) harming public education? What about state legislators who enact state-funded voucher or charter school programs that send public funds to independently run schools? Some would say that such

people are doing mischief, drawing students away from existing
district-run schools and also, by reducing district-run school enrollments, affecting the amount of state funds public schools receive. On that basis, critics claim that voucher sponsors are
working against the public interest in education. On the other
hand, groups promoting choice claim that competition can inspire
greater effort and effectiveness on the part of all schools, both
those in the conventional public system and the charter and private
schools that offer families alternatives.

Studies of the effects of competition on district-run schools in
general show that it has positive effects. As Hoxby has shown,
schools in localities with many private schools, and many options
provided by nearby district-run school systems, have higher test
scores and other indicators of quality.[13] Newspaper reports of the
improvement processes in schools facing competition show how
improvement happens.[14]

Competition can make all schools better, or it can send some
into decline. Much depends on whether all competitors are free to
improve. If district-run schools are able to take advantage of reduced enrollment by cutting administrative expenses, intensifying
teacher collaboration, and limiting the range of instructional offerings, they might become better, not worse. After all, charter and
parochial schools typically operate with far less money per pupil
than does the conventional public school system, and most can
maintain a reasonable instructional program and adapt, albeit
painfully, to changes in student enrollment.

Research on schools' response to competition shows that everything depends on the actions of teachers and principals in the
schools experiencing loss of pupils. Those schools whose staff have
habits of collaboration and joint problem solving adapt readily to
marginal changes in enrollment and funding. Schools with nonco-

13. Carolyn Minter Hoxby, "Do Private Schools Provide Competition for
Public Schools?" National Bureau of Economic Research Working Paper 4978,
December 1994.
14. See James Dao, "How to Make a Poor School Change: A Well-Financed
Exodus of Students Is Countered by a Flurry of Fixing," *New York Times*, Sep-
tember 29, 1997, p. B1.

operative cultures (weak leadership, poor labor relations, little collaboration among teachers) adapt poorly.[15]

Ultimately, the argument about whether vouchers or charters harm district-run schools turns on the question of whether all the rules that limit district-run schools' adaptability are necessary. Is it the essence of public education that every school has a fixed administrative overhead or that a school must not be free to change its teaching staff or instructional program as funding and student needs change? An affirmative answer to this question implies that these rules, which many public educators agree are barriers to school quality, are necessary elements of public education. If these rules are not necessary—if instead they are the accidental result of politics and bargains made over time, as different groups gained leverage in the courts or state legislature—then it is not inevitable that competition will harm district-run schools.

Schools whose reputation for "goodness" is based on their vast and diverse course catalogs may be forced to reduce the numbers of exotic language and arts courses they offer. Schools that cannot marshal community support or whose teachers cannot learn to collaborate in the face of external competition will probably get worse. So will schools that lose so many students that they can no longer afford to occupy their buildings. These results, however, put the finger on very weak schools whose "success" depends on the coerced patronage of families that would have preferred to send their children elsewhere.

Most of the children eligible for private or public vouchers cluster in particular low-income neighborhoods. School districts affected by competition have offered no evidence on the effects of children's departures for these schools—possibly because there are no visible effects due to the fact that the affected neighborhoods

15. Frederick Hess, Robert Maranto, Scott Millman, "How School Leaders Respond to Competition: The Mitigating Effects of School Culture," paper prepared for presentation at the Conference on School Vouchers, Charters, and Public Education, John F. Kennedy School of Government, Harvard University, March 9–10, 2000. See also Paul Teske, Paul Schneider, Sara Clark, and Jack Buckley, "Does Competition from Charter Schools Leverage Change in Traditional Public School Systems? A Tale of Five Cities," from the same conference.

might also be the first settlement areas for new in-migrants. The best evidence about the financial effects of children's departures comes from the experience of small school districts that have become home to several charter schools. Marblehead and other small cities in Massachusetts lost as many as 20 percent of their pupils and had to eliminate part-time art teachers and nurses. Other neighborhood schools losing enrollment have also increased class size (sometimes only temporarily until the school gained enough students to justify allocation of an additional teacher).

Evidence of adverse effects on children is hard to find. To date, the numbers of children lost to any district-run school system, including those with large voucher programs like Cleveland and Milwaukee, have been far smaller than the numbers of children who leave district-run schools because of family moves and individual dropout decisions. During school year 1998–99, for example, six thousand Milwaukee children used vouchers to enroll in private schools while more than twenty-five thousand dropped out. Most cities have growing student populations, so that the current financial effects of students leaving to accept vouchers are essentially nil. Charter schools have similarly modest effects, except in a few cities (Mesa, Ariz., Marblehead, Mass., where more than 10 percent of students have left district-run schools).

Other evidence about the effects of lost enrollment comes from New Zealand, where, according to Fiske and Ladd, schools that lost enrollment quickly declined due to parent and teacher flight.[16] Whether these findings apply directly to the U.S. context is unclear since New Zealand made it virtually impossible for declining schools to adapt their policies or programs. Declining schools were not allowed to reconfigure their administrative structures, recruit or choose teachers, or combine with other schools to share resources or programs.

What the New Zealand findings do demonstrate is that schools that are not free to change the ways they use staff, time, and

16. Edward B. Fiske and Helen Ladd, *When Schools Compete* (Washington, D.C.: Brookings Institution, 2000).

money are in no position to improve or to cope with changes in financing or student needs. That is nothing new: it has long been the basis of dispute within the public school system, between people running successful magnet schools (which typically enjoy considerable freedom to reconfigure their staff and schedules and can pick among large numbers of teacher applicants) and more highly regulated neighborhood schools.

To return to the case of Sarie and Patricia: in the short run, whether the voucher with which Patricia paid private school tuition harms the broad cause of public education depends on the actions of the public school system itself. If the system allows Sarie's former school to adapt to change, the consequences are likely to be positive, not negative.

To the degree students like Sarie who use vouchers (or enroll in charter schools) benefit at all—whether by learning more advanced material, scoring higher on standard tests, being motivated to attend school more faithfully or stay in school longer,[17] or by gaining a label (e.g., graduate of a highly regarded school) that helps them get admitted to college or hired by employers—there is some addition to society's stock of people prepared to live successful adult lives. Although the jury is out on whether voucher users gain all these benefits, there is evidence for all of them. Most large voucher programs are too new to demonstrate long-term effects on students' life prospects, but there is some evidence that children participating in the older private voucher program have greatly enhanced long-term outcomes, including higher-level employment and completion of college degrees.[18]

17. Rigorously controlled studies of the links between vouchers and student achievement are ongoing. At present, the results are mildly positive in virtually every case. Although any results on vouchers, pro or con, will inevitably be controversial, the weight of evidence is definitely toward positive effects, with one exception—middle-school boys in the District of Columbia. See Jay P. Greene, "A Survey of Results from Voucher Experiments: Where We Are and What We Know," paper prepared for presentation at the Conference on School Vouchers, Charters, and Public Education, John F. Kennedy School of Government, Harvard University, March 9–10, 2000.

18. Paul T. Hill, "The Educational Consequences of Choice," in Terry Moe, ed., *Private Vouchers* (Stanford, Hoover Institution Press, 1995).

There is no reason why a given school district cannot run a smaller group of schools that are at least as good individually as the existing district-run schools. (Many school systems were forced to do exactly that in the 1970s, when enrollments declined by more than 50 percent, largely due to middle-class flight from school busing.)[19]

The real question might be whether the private or charter school system can supply enough quality schools to serve all the children whose parents might wish to enroll. A great excess of demand over supply might allow many charter or voucher-redeeming schools of dubious quality to prosper; it would certainly create competition for slots in well-established private schools that could favor the most aggressive and sophisticated parents.[20]

However, a concerted supply response, by private entrepreneurs, charter school sponsors, religious schools, or philanthropies (or, preferably, a combination of all of them) could mean that the quality of educational offerings available in the locality would rise, not fall. Major private investment in new schools would not be anything new: today, both private and district-run schools rely heavily on philanthropic donations for everything from new program development to teacher training. Due to constant pressures to maintain current service quality and pay teachers, public school districts have great difficulty sustaining expenditures on even such basic investment functions as teacher training and hiring, performance evaluation, school improvement, and building upgrades.[21] Some districts rely heavily on philanthropy. Private investment in new schools is therefore not a new breach of the bright line be-

19. See Laura Kohn, *Priority Shift: The Fate of Mandatory Busing for School Desegregation in Seattle and the Nation* (Seattle: Center on Reinventing Public Education, University of Washington, March 1996).

20. For a more complete discussion of this problem, see Paul T. Hill, "The Supply Side of Choice," in Stephen Sugarman and Frank Kemerer, eds., *School Choice and Social Controversy* (Washington, D.C.: Brookings Institution, 2000).

21. For an expanded discussion of roles for private investment in public education, see Paul T. Hill, Christine Campbell, and James Harvey, *It Takes a City: Getting Serious about Urban School Reform* (Washington, D.C.: Brookings Institution, 2000), chaps. 5–7.

tween private investment and public education. The only thing new is that new charter or voucher-redeeming schools will be controlled by entities other than the local school board.

A major supply-side effort associated with charters or vouchers would produce what some public educators fear: parents pursuing "the private purposes of education through a decentralized archipelago of independent schools."[22] The point, however, is that everything depends on the quality of the schools produced and chosen.

### PRIVATELY RUN SCHOOLS THAT WORK ARE ACTING IN THE PUBLIC INTEREST

Do people who operate private or charter schools threaten the public interest in education? Aside from vindicating the principle of freedom of speech, is there any public purpose served by religious and independent schools? Are some private schools, as Bryk and Lee suggested of Catholic schools, the best exemplar of the common school that Dewey and others extolled?[23] Or are private schools, as James B. Conant suggested of Catholic schools, ultimately divisive?

No question in the field of education is the subject of as much confused discussion as this one. Some theorists hold for the district-run school as an integrating institution, one that assembles people from many different backgrounds and gives them a common experience. For some, such integration is good in itself and needs no justification. For others, however, the common school experience is instrumental: it is assumed to create tolerance and common understanding, which eliminate prejudice and lay groundwork for civil settlement of disputes among people who, in adulthood, might find themselves on different sides of partisan, neighborhood, or labor-management disputes. Unlike those who

22. Fuller, Burr, Huerta, Puryear, and Wexler, *School Choice: Abundant Hope*, p. 9.
23. Anthony S. Bryk, Valerie E. Lee, et al., *Catholic Schools and the Common Good* (Cambridge, Mass.: Harvard University Press, 1993).

think diverse associations are good in themselves, and those that consider them instrumental would not approve of schools that educated individuals from many backgrounds, but bred distrust or conflict.

Still others are skeptical about the necessity, or even the value, of exposing students to people from a vast array of backgrounds. Although agreeing that schools serve as bridges between nuclear families and the broader society, these people think that, intelligently run, almost any school, including one made up of people of the same sex, race, and religion, can serve this purpose.

How diverse is diverse enough? No school, much less a child's group of frequent associates, can represent every dimension of diversity present in this country. Is it necessary for a white child to attend a school in which he can get to know children of both sexes from every major ethnic and racial group, political party, and religion? Is a school where a child does not get to know, say, a Mormon or a Cambodian worse in this respect than one in which these groups are represented? What about a school where no students are homosexual? What about personality types: Is it more or less important for a child to learn to deal with a person with tendencies toward passive-aggressiveness, obsessive-compulsion, or bipolar disorder than for her to encounter members of an ethnic group whom her parents have always despised? Do white Catholics need to encounter black Muslims, or is going to school with black Catholics good enough?

In this area the rhetoric is heavy and the definitions are light. Nobody can say when a school is diverse enough or too diverse. Moreover, nobody can say for sure in what ways diversity of contacts in school leads to desired adult attributes. There is reason to fear that isolation of poor and minority children will limit their ability to adapt to the broader society. But isolation in itself is not always bad: yeshiva graduates, who experience extremely distinctive schooling and have time for few friendships outside their schools, have extremely good track records of economic success, political participation, commitment to the disadvantaged, and so on.

Despite these grave ambiguities, diversity of contacts in school and their assumed effects on student attitudes are the core objections that many educators raise against vouchers and other programs creating options outside the district-run school system. If these objections are so important, an objective observer might expect there to be evidence that district-run schools are better than other schools at creating these contacts and encouraging these attitudes. There is, however, little such evidence. To the contrary, most of the evidence points to the superiority of schools run by organizations other than public school systems.

*Diverse Contacts*

With respect to contacts, there is a growing literature about racial tensions in district-run schools, often leading students to limit even casual contacts to persons of the same race as themselves. The isolation of African American high school students—imposed by the students' own tastes as well as the actions of others—is particularly marked. Students active in sports and student organizations report more diverse friendships, but in large district-run schools these are relatively rare.

Studies of students in private, especially Catholic, high schools show much broader contacts between students of different races and social origins.[24] Private schools are, on average, relatively well integrated, in part because many deliberately seek diversity and dedicate scholarship funds so that low-income and minority children can attend. Few private schools have exactly the same racial mix as their surrounding school districts—but almost no district-run schools perfectly reflect their districts. Because housing is highly segregated, districts in which, say, one-third of the children are white and two-thirds African American have few schools that even approximate that mixture. In many such localities a majority of schools are overwhelmingly either white or black. Thus, as

24. Much of the evidence for this analysis comes from Jay P. Greene and Nicole Mellow, "Integration Where It Counts: A Study of Racial Integration in Public and Private School Lunchrooms, 1998," available at *www.la.utexas.edu/ research/ppc/lunch.html*. See also Jay P. Greene, "Civic Values in Public and Private Schools," in Paul Peterson, ed., *Learning from School Choice* (Washington D.C.: Brookings Institution, 1999).

Greene has shown, most private school students experience a more
racially and class-integrated school than do most public school
students.

In addition to the gross demographic facts, there is reason to
think that, on average, private school students associate across
race and class lines more than district-run school students. Private
schools' small size and higher rates of participation in extracurricular activities probably explain some of the difference.[25] But, as
Greene and others have shown, the facts that these schools were
chosen by students and their parents and that the schools are free
to state in advance what levels of decorum and effort are required
for success in the school, build a basis for mutual trust among
people from disparate backgrounds.[26] There is no question that
the school's ability to expel uncooperative students creates strong
incentives for compliance. Private schools rarely expel students because the boundaries are so clear that few students breach them.
In contrast, district-run schools that have ambiguous boundaries
experience more misbehavior and ultimately suspend or "involuntarily transfer" greater numbers of students.[27] But the fact that
students and their families must make commitments before enrolling in a school is an important reason private school students and
their parents trust one another.[28]

All these results are based on small studies. No one has a nation-

25. In the author's own unpublished research, students who have moved
from large public high schools to smaller private ones often remark on how much
easier it is for students to "stick with their own kind" in large schools. As one
tenth-grade male said, "At MI High there were many different groups of kids.
People were all jocks or drudges or rich preppies or intellectuals or something
else. Things were tense with African Americans, so we mostly avoided one another. I had some African American friends from drama, but that was about
it. . . . Here the class is so small that you have to deal with everybody, there's no
hiding. If you are in a bad mood everybody notices. If you don't like somebody
you have to find a way to get along. If somebody is obnoxious the whole class
has to let them know."

26. See Jacqueline Jordan Irvine, *Growing Up African-American in Catholic
Schools* (New York: Teachers College Press, 1997).

27. See Paul T. Hill, Gail E. Foster, and Tamar Gendler, *High Schools with
Character* (Santa Monica, Calif.: RAND, 1990).

28. See Paul T. Hill, "The Educational Consequences of Choice," in Terry
Moe, ed., *Private Vouchers* (Stanford: Hoover Institution Press, 1995).

ally representative account of students' experiences in all kinds of schools. Perhaps a nationally representative study would show less difference between students' social experiences in district-run and private schools than these studies indicate. However, given how consistent current findings are, it is extremely unlikely that a national study would show that district-run schools are markedly better than private schools in creating opportunities for interracial and interclass friendships. Thus there is no factual basis for the argument in favor of public education, and against private schools, on the grounds of promoting such contacts.

## Prosocial Attitudes

For many, the one goal that district-run schools can attain, and that private schools supposedly cannot, is to advance common knowledge and values.[29] These values are described in many different ways, but the common core include openness, willingness to negotiate differences, and tolerance of others' views. Some writers, as discussed above, consider these the distinctly public goals of education, as compared to the self-seeking and therefore private goals of learning skills necessary for economic success.[30]

These are certainly important values for citizens of a diverse and democratic society. But the facts do not support the contention that district-run schools are the only, or even the best, means of imparting those values. Nor, as we shall see, is it so easy to distinguish a school's effectiveness in teaching basic skills and complex reasoning abilities from their ability to impart desirable values.

Studies of Catholic and Jewish schools have shown repeatedly that graduates have a better understanding of U.S. constitutional processes and rights guarantees, express greater commitment to freedom of speech, espouse more tolerant attitudes toward minor-

29. Fuller, Burr, Huerta, Puryear, and Wexler, *School Choice: Abundant Hope.*

30. Fuller and others take different positions at different times on this distinction between the public and private outcomes of education. At times Fuller labels "boosting the stock of skills necessary for sustaining economic growth" as a public purpose of education.

ity groups, vote more often, and participate more in community affairs than do similar graduates of district-run schools.[31] This is no surprise; both sets of schools expressly teach American values, the sanctity of the individual, respect for the poor, and the unity of mankind under God. The author's own research on Catholic schools has turned up Catholic school readers from the 1940s that taught the value of neighborhood integration, cross-racial friendships, and preached against the evils of invidious comparisons between rich and poor.[32] A yeshiva student's statement tells the story of Jewish education: "We are taught that Jews require a tolerant society, and that the only way to have such a society is to practice tolerance yourself."

New research on much larger samples of schools and students sheds further light on different kinds of schools' effectiveness in teaching prosocial attitudes. Wolf and others studied political tolerance among students at four Texas colleges, three public and one private.[33] They found that students educated in private high schools exhibit more tolerant attitudes about minorities and greater commitment to freedom of speech and open political processes than do students from district-run high schools, controlling for race, income, and other demographic factors. This leads them to conclude, at least for the relatively academically advanced population they studied, that the "assumption of a public school advantage in this area is undeserved. . . . While we should expect more from our public schools we should also fear our private schools less when it comes to instilling civic values in the next generation of Americans."[34]

Campbell provides more telling evidence, from a study of stu-

31. See Andrew M. Greeley and Peter Rossi, *The Education of Catholic Americans* (Chicago: Aldine, 1966).

32. See the second-grade reader by Sister M. Marguerine, *These Are Our Neighbors* (Boston: Ginn and Company, 1942). See in particular the story "Pretty Patches," pp. 189–94.

33. Patrick Wolf, Jay P. Greene, Brett Kleitz, and Kristin Thalhammer, "Private Schooling and Political Tolerance: Evidence from College Students in Texas," paper prepared for presentation at the Conference on School Vouchers, Charters, and Public Education, John F. Kennedy School of Government, Harvard University, March 9–10, 2000, p. 21.

34. Ibid.

dents still in high school.[35] Based on an analysis of the 1996 National Household Education Survey, a large, nationally representative sample of students and their parents, Campbell studied the connection between the type of high school a student attends and several measures of prosocial attitudes and behavior. To isolate the effects of the school, Campbell's analysis controls for differences in family income and education, as well as for parents' attitudes about civic engagement, community service, participation in politics, confidence that their participation makes a difference, tolerance, and respect for civil liberties. In comparing students from several types of schools—public schools where students are assigned by neighborhood, magnet public schools, Catholic schools, non-Catholic religious schools, and secular private schools, Campbell does not find any set of prosocial attitudes on which public school students score higher than the other groups of students.[36] To the contrary, he finds that

> Students in Catholic schools score consistently higher than students in all other schools even when differences in family income, parents' education, and social attitudes are controlled for.
>
> Neighborhood-assigned public schools score lower than the other types of schools on participation in voluntary service, civic speaking and participation skills, confidence that participation makes a difference, and knowledge of facts about politics. Magnet public schools score lower than all private schools on every measure but tolerance and civic skills.
>
> On only one measure—political tolerance—do students in neighborhood-assigned public schools score higher than students in any private school. Non-Catholic religious schools (a broad category covering the range between Christian fundamentalists to Quakers to Muslims) score lowest on this measure.[37]

35. David Campbell, "Making Democratic Education Work: Schools, Social Capital, and Civic Education," paper prepared for presentation at the Conference on School Vouchers, Charters, and Public Education, John F. Kennedy School of Government, Harvard University, March 9–10, 2000.

36. These findings closely resemble those of a smaller study reported by Christian Smith and David Sikkink, "Is Private School Privatizing?" *First Things*, April 1999, pp. 16–20.

37. This finding, though the only one that reflects poorly on non-Catholic religious schools' teaching prosocial attitudes, is nonetheless a matter for concern. Many educators specifically fear religious right schools for this reason. (See David C. Berliner, "Educational Psychology Meets the Christian Right: Differing

Perhaps Campbell's most important finding is that students' overall learning is not independent of their attitudes. In general, student attributes like having higher grades, expecting to attend
college, spending more time watching or reading news are all
highly correlated with the prosocial attitudes and behaviors he
measured. Students in Catholic schools display these attributes far
more often than one would expect given their family backgrounds;
moreover, Catholic schools often place less emphasis on student
government, current events classes, and other overt efforts to influence student attitudes. With respect to Catholic schools in particular, Campbell concludes:

> This finding about the cognitive dimension of political engagement is
> perhaps expected, given the literature on the academic effects of at-
> tending a Catholic school. It is likely that if a school teaches math and
> reading well, it also teaches civics well. . . . The fact that the acquisi-
> tion of political knowledge is a function of the same mechanism as the
> acquisition of knowledge about chemistry, math, and literature does
> not detract from its consequences for civic activity.[38]

Campbell refers to the oft-reproduced finding that Catholic
schools are especially effective in teaching academic skills and preparing students for college. Though Catholic schools' results for
students of privileged homes are seldom better than those of secu-

---

Views of Children, Schooling, Teaching, and Learning," *Teachers College Press*
vol. 98, no. 3 (spring 1997): 381–416. Although other research shows that graduates of such schools display tolerance and respect for rights (see Wolf et al.
*Private Schooling and Political Tolerance*), there is very little research on what
religious right schools teach and how the experience affects student attitudes.
Such research is clearly desirable. In the meantime, concern about the negative
effects of schools that might teach "fringe" ideologies has led the authors of
every recent proposal for vouchers, charters, or school contracting to include a
provision for government licensing and oversight, specifically to ensure that
schools do not teach hatred, violence, or racial superiority. Thus, the safeguards
against these evils would be the same under charter, voucher, or contracting proposals as under the present district-run model of public education. See, for example, John Chubb and Terry E. Moe, *Politics, Markets, and America's Schools*
(Washington, D.C.: Brookings Institution, 1990). See also Paul T. Hill, Lawrence
Pierce, and James W. Guthrie, *Reinventing Public Education: How Contracting
Can Transform America's Schools* (Chicago: University of Chicago Press, 1997).
See also Finn, Manno, and Vanourek on charter schools, 1999.
    38. Campbell, op. cit., p. 32.

lar private schools or public schools in suburban areas, they are markedly better for low-income and minority students, including non-Catholics. These results have been reproduced by researchers from many different disciplines using many different methods and data sets and are about as well established as anything in social science.[39] Moreover, explanations for the effectiveness of Catholic schools are strongly consistent with Campbell's conclusions. The key attributes of Catholic schools cited in virtually all studies include focus on core academic skills; shared expectations that even the most disadvantaged can master complex material; a centripetal curriculum that draws all students toward mastery of core skills and disciplines; emphasis on reading, writing, analysis, and debate; community and climate of caring; and emphasis on development of a sense of responsibility for oneself and others.

Catholic schools are certainly not the only ones with these attributes. Other schools, including some district-run schools, also have them—what sets the Catholic schools apart is that they do so consistently. Moreover, it is hard to see how these schools fall short of the aspirations of people like Fuller and Hochschild who think prosocial attitudes are a primary purpose of public education. As Campbell comments, "Strong evidence has accumulated that private—particularly Catholic—schools are a private means to the very public end of facilitating civic engagement."[40]

However, for the purposes of this chapter it is not necessary to prove that Catholic schools or private schools in general are always better at inducing prosocial attitudes than are district-run

39. See, for example, Bryk, Lee, et al., op. cit.; James S. Coleman, Thomas Hoffer, and Sally Kilgore, *Public and Private High Schools* (Washington, D.C.: National Center for Education Statistics, 1981); James S. Coleman, *High School Achievement* (New York: Basic Books 1982); James S. Coleman and Thomas Hoffer, *Public and Private High Schools: The Impact of Communities* (New York: Basic Books, 1987); Paul T. Hill, Gail E. Foster, and Tamar Gendler, *High Schools with Character* (Santa Monica, Calif.: RAND, 1990); Hill, *Educational Consequences of Choice*; Jacqueline Jordan Irvine and Michele Foster, eds., *Growing Up African American in Catholic Schools* (New York: Teachers College Press, 1997); and Derek Neal, "The Effects of Catholic Secondary Schooling on Academic Achievement," *Journal of Labor Economics* 15, no. 1 (1997): 98–123.
40. Campbell, *Making Democratic Education Work*, p. 40.

public schools. It is enough to show that district-run schools are definitely not better.

School-based research by the present author and others reveals the great differences among high schools in the opportunities they offer for reading, discussion, reflection, and debate, especially about broad social issues and historical events.[41] These activities do not happen in schools unless they are designed in to the curriculum, instructional methods, use of time, and incentives for teachers and students. These activities are also driven out by conflict, disorder, lack of teacher collaboration, requirements to cover large amounts of unrelated facts in a limited time, and pressures on teachers to avoid controversial topics. Unfortunately, too many district-run public schools—especially for seventh grade and above—have all these attributes. Large size, rapid student and teacher turnover, labor-management conflict, and weak home-school links make rich instruction difficult. Pressures to celebrate all points of view and to steer away from topics that might cause conflict further impoverish discussion. Regrettably, schools that profess to celebrate all groups and to accept all ideas are often forced to skate on the surface, treasuring differences but never exploring issues in any depth.

The conclusion that district-run public schools are probably not better at preparing children to be democratic citizens—and might even be worse than private alternatives—throws a new light on the debate about the goals and meaning of public education. Critics have long argued that mechanisms of government oversight hamstring district-run schools and make many, especially in big cities, unable to concentrate on effective teaching and learning. This analysis has been the basis of reform proposals for public vouchers, charter schools, and school contracting, all of which intend to free government-sponsored schools from the burdens of

41. See, for example, Hill, Foster, and Gendler, op. cit. See also Ted Sizer, *Horace's Compromise*; Richard G. Niemi, and Jane Junn, *Civic Education: What Makes Students Learn* (New Haven: Yale University Press, 1998). Also see Paul T. Hill, Lawrence Pierce, Paul Schneider, and Sara Taggart, *Schools' Integrative Capital* (Seattle: University of Washington Center on Reinventing Public Education, 1998).

regulation in return for accountability for student learning. The present author, in particular, has argued for reinventing public education, so that elected officials would set goals and standards and hold schools accountable for performance; but school boards would not hire teachers, and bureaucracies would not operate any schools. Every public school would be an independent organization, operating under a performance contract. Schools would receive a set dollar amount for every child they enroll, and be free to use money to hire teachers and administrators, and buy instructional materials and services. A public school would thus be any school that operated under a performance contract with a state or local education authority, accepted public funds as full tuition for its pupils, and was open to all students.

The strongest arguments against these proposals have focused on their supposed effects on racial and class integration and students' ability to learn prosocial attitudes.[42] Some critics have also claimed that such reforms would do little to make schools more effective, but none have found a basis for claiming they would be worse.

Now it appears that academic learning is not separable from the other purposes of public education: schools that teach effectively can be—and normally are—better at providing diversity of contacts and imparting prosocial attitudes. There is, moreover, no evidence that schools that emphasize attitudes and social experiences are at all effective either in imparting skills and knowledge or in forming students' attitudes.[43]

Thus we return to the question at the beginning of this section: Do groups that provide alternatives to district-run public schools threaten the goal of public education? The answer must be in the negative. To the contrary, many such groups appear to serve the end of education very well indeed, at least as well and often far better than government-run schools and districts.

42. See, for example, Carol Ascher, Norm Fruchter, and Robert Berne, *Hard Lessons: Public Schools and Privatization* (New York: Twentieth Century Fund Press, 1996).
43. Hill, Pierce, Schneider, and Taggart, *Schools' Integrative Capital.*

## CONCLUSION: WHAT IS PUBLIC?

The foregoing sections answer the questions posed at the beginning:

- First, a parent who transfers her child from a district-run school in which she is not learning to a privately run school where the child has a better chance to learn is not harming public education but advancing it.

- Second, a private group that makes such a transfer possible by paying tuition in an independently run school is also not harming public education. Whether the benefits it creates accrue only to the individual children who transfer or benefit all other students by raising the average quality of education in a locality depends on supply-side responses by district-run and private schools, not on the people who pay for vouchers.

- Third, private entities that offer instruction are not harming public education. In many cases, given the deficiencies of district oversight and school operation, privately run schools may be serving the goals of public education far better than government-run schools.

The reason government is justified in paying for education and requiring school attendance is that all Americans share an interest in children's learning to read, compute, think for themselves, and live as productive and tolerant adults. A school that does not teach children all these things effectively does not serve the public interest, whether it is run by government or by some other entity. A school that teaches children effectively does serve the public interest, whether it is run by government or by some other entity. Similarly, parents who take the initiative to find a school where their children will learn are acting in the public interest, and parents who needlessly let their children remain in a school where they are not learning are sacrificing their own children to no particular end.

The problem with defining public education as a specific set of institutions or processes is that doing so confounds means and ends. In the case of the school Sarie left, it would be public because it was controlled by an elected school board and government bureaucracy. But did government control mean that Sarie's school advanced the cause of public education? Or for that matter did any legitimate community representative consciously want it to operate as it did? No public deliberative process overtly decided that Sarie's school would become a sick organization and a dumping ground for incompetent individuals. Those outcomes were accidental results of rules and processes created for other reasons: to facilitate politicians' control of public funds, to allow powerful individuals to find jobs for and protect individuals loyal to themselves, to allow senior teachers to teach in the best places, and so on. In the case of Sarie's school these processes created a school that was not public in any real sense, one in which Patricia and other parents could do nothing to get a decent education for their sons and daughters.

The fact that a given school's condition can be traced back to the actions of an elected board or legislature does not mean that it is public. As Terry Moe has argued,[44] policy and legislation reflect the temporary ascendancy of one coalition of pressure groups after another. Each successful coalition leaves behind rules and procedures that favor its members, so that in the long run the actions of government agencies are constrained in ways that current majorities would never choose. Over time, ironically, past majorities can become more influential than current ones.

There is, moreover, little reason to think that bureaucratic routines and rule-driven practices are compatible with goals of public education. There is a need for some form of public oversight of schools to protect children from schools that do not teach effectively and to make sure taxpayer funds are not stolen or used to advocate violent solutions to social problems. Public oversight need not result in coercion or uniformity. The key is to redefine the powers of local school boards so that they can authorize but not run schools, and oversee schools solely on the basis of whether students learn, not on the basis of rule compliance.[45] A school

44. See Terry E. Moe, "The Politics of Bureaucratic Structure," in John E. Chubb and Paul E. Peterson, *Can the Government Govern?* (Washington, D.C.: Brookings Institution, 1989).
45. See Paul T. Hill, Lawrence Pierce, and James W. Guthrie, *Reinventing Public Education: How Contracting Can Transform America's Schools* (Chicago: University of Chicago Press, 1997).

board so empowered could tend a diverse portfolio of schools, creating new alternatives as needs arose and reassigning public funds from ineffective providers to effective ones.

Defining public education as a commitment to a goal of universal competency rather than as a fixed set of institutions requires a continual search for the best way to educate children and is open to the possibility that any locality might pursue many different approaches. It makes public education a constant topic of discussion and experimentation, not a set of permanent arrangements. It is consistent with a democratic society that can innovate, trying new structures and methods and discarding old ones.

Public education is a set of goals: universal education, focused on learning, economic, social, and political opportunity for all, community, citizenship, and tolerance. Americans rightly celebrate public education as a bulwark of democracy. But when we confuse the goals of public education with the means by which we provide it, we can give undeserved protection to unproductive institutions that are nothing more than accidents of politics and history.

# Index